THE CLASSICS OF GOLF

Edition of

GOLF BETWEEN TWO WARS

by
Bernard Darwin

Foreword by Herbert Warren Wind
Afterword by Ben Crenshaw

Foreword

Before Bernard Darwin decided in 1908 to give up his career in the law and turned to writing about golf as his primary occupation, other men had written about the game, and quite a few had written about it very well. To name just three of the superior early golf writers, there was Sir Walter Simpson, who, in 1887, wrote "The Art of Golf," a knowledgeable and witty dissertation that dealt with how the game should be played and a number of other things, such as the remarkable hold golf comes to have on those who play it; Horace G. Hutchinson, the British Amateur champion in 1886 and 1887, who knew the game backwards and forwards, and who served as the editor of the volume on golf in the renowned 1890 edition of the Badminton Library *of sports; and Willie Park, Jr., an outstanding golfer and golf-course designer, who, in 1896, became the first golf professional to write a golf instruction book, "The Game of Golf." There were other early golf writers of considerable merit—James Balfour and Andrew Lang are two who come quickly to mind—and yet today we think of Bernard Darwin, a twentieth-century figure, as the man who invented golf writing. I suppose this is because, once Darwin dipped his toe into golf writing, the reports he produced regularly for the* Times *of London over a forty-five year period and his ruminative essays for the weekly* Country Life *possessed a quality that no one else has ever approached. Darwin wrote on many subjects besides golf. He brought out, among other things, an appreciation of the English public school, a guide to the historic landmarks of London, two children's books, two books on Charles Dickens, biographies of W. G. Grace,* the great cricketer, and of John Gully, a bare-knuckles boxing champion who became a member of Parliament, and, when he was seventy-eight, his autobiography, "The World That Fred Made." (Fred was the name of his grandfather's groom. Darwin, as a very young boy, felt that Fred could do anything or make anything.) Especially gifted as an essayist who wrote on a wide range of subjects, Darwin may well have been one of the very best in that field in the long interval between William Hazlitt, his personal idol, and E.B. White. We are simply very lucky that a man of his high talent was so smitten by golf that he wrote endlessly about it.

Bernard Richard Meirion Darwin was born in 1876 in Downe, Kent. He came from a family that had high social position, intellectual prestige, and all the money it needed. His grandfather was Charles Darwin, the great naturalist, who propounded the theory of evolution. His father, Francis Darwin, was a doctor who did not practice medicine but became an eminent botanist. Bernard's mother died when her son was born. After his grandfather's death in 1881, Bernard and his father moved from Downe to Cambridge, where he grew up amidst a large cluster of aunts and uncles who were extremely brainy and somewhat eccentric. Golf entered Bernard's life when he was eight. At that time the game was just beginning to catch on in England, but his father was very enthusiastic about it, and each summer he took himself and his son off to a seaside resort that had a good course. After a few years at Felixstowe, in Suffolk, Mr. Darwin shifted to Cromer, in Norfolk, and later to Eastbourne, in Sussex, on the Channel. Mr. Darwin had caught the golf bug from his brother-in-law Arthur Ruck. Arthur and his brother Richard, needing some place close at hand to play and practice, laid out a nine-hole course in the Aberdovey area of Wales, where the Ruck family lived. Later on, Richard Ruck designed a full eighteen-hole course, the Aberdovey Golf Club, for which Bernard formed an ardent affection as a young man—an affection that, if anything, deepened as he grew older. Of all the people who have written about golf, there is no doubt whatsoever that Darwin was the best golfer. He was a semi-finalist in the British Amateur in 1921. The following year, when the first Walker Cup match was played at the National Golf Links of America, Darwin, the captain of the British team, lost his foursome but won his singles. He won such coveted amateur events in Britain as the Golf Illustrated Gold Vase, the President's Putter, and the Worplesdon Mixed Foursomes (partnered with Joyce Wethered). Incidentally, Darwin was captain of the Royal & Ancient Golf Club of St. Andrews in 1934–35.

To go back a bit. After Francis Darwin had moved his family to Cambridge, Bernard attended the Perse day school for two years. In those days, as it still is to a lesser degree, it was the practice of well-to-do British families to send their sons to boarding school at a very young age, like nine or ten. Bernard was eleven when he was enrolled in Summer Field, a school near Oxford. He adjusted nicely to life there, starring as a Latin scholar and as a cricketer. He went on from Summer Field to his public school, Eton, which he also enjoyed. (In Britain a public school is the equivalent of a prep school in this country.) He moved on from Eton to Cambridge University, where his college was Trinity. During his third term he changed his field of concentration from Classics to Law, and worked fairly hard preparing himself for the Tripos examinations which would earn for him an honors degree at the end of his third and final year. At Cambridge he played on the university golf team, which he captained his last year, but aside from this his years at Cambridge were sort of a let-down. The trouble, he recognized, was that one should not attend a university in his family's home town—it muffles the whole experience.

Darwin then went down to London and the Temple, and, with the help of some private coaching over a couple of years, he passed the examinations and became a solicitor. He found that the work of a solicitor was extremely boring. He thought that the cure might lie in becoming a barrister in-

stead. After three years of study, he was duly called to the bar in 1903. He found the life of a barrister very disappointing; few of the cases he worked on truly interested him. The avenue to his escape appeared in 1907. A friend of his, who had been conducting a golf column called "Tee Shots" for the Evening Standard, *was leaving to go with the* Morning Post, *and he had recommended Darwin as the man best qualified to succeed him. Darwin's golf pieces found a most responsive audience. The following year he was lured away from the* Post *by the* Times, *and soon after that he was asked to contribute golf articles on a regular basis by* Country Life. *Writing about golf meant being around golf, a milieu he loved, and now, fairly confident that his new career would enable him to support his wife and their children, he therewith at the age of thirty-two "sold his wig" and, bidding farewell to the law for good, walked happily into his new world. The articles that most people write for newspapers and magazines, superb as they may be, are very perishable items. Fortunately, Darwin's work was an exception. His lengthy, thoughtful Saturday pieces for the* Times *and his lively essays for* Country Life *were from time to time collected and published as books: "Second Shots," "Out of the Rough," "Rubs of the Green," and many others. They still possess Darwin's special flavor and relaxed vitality.*

What made Darwin such a superlative golf writer? To begin with, there was nothing he liked better than being out on a testing course watching skillful golfers competing in a tournament. He never stayed in the press tent or lolled around the clubhouse. He was out on the course walking tirelessly and watching keenly. As an able golfer himself, he could appreciate the technique of the various stars, and this, coupled with an intuitive knowledge of golf-course architecture, gave him the ability to sense the shot values of the holes that the top amateurs and professionals were asked to play under tournament pressure. In both his dispatches and his reflective essays, he carried the reader right out onto the course with him. A natural writer, he expressed himself vividly, and since he also possessed a pawky sense of humor and an inexhaustible zest for the game, he made his reports and his reflections almost compulsory reading for any individual who seriously cared about golf.

Darwin had his own heroes. He spent many hours in the company of Harry Vardon, J. H. Taylor, and James Braid who made up what was known as The Triumvirate. Among them, they won sixteen British Opens between 1894 and 1914. These three professionals happened to be men of exceptional character and honest charm, and it is not going too far to say that they played a very large part in the great rise in golf's popularity in England and also in the continued growth of golf's stature in Scotland. Darwin made his first trip to the United States in 1913, and, as fortune would have it, he was the scorer for Francis Ouimet in the epochal playoff in the 1913 United States Open in which Ouimet, an almost unknown young American amateur, defeated Vardon and another British Open champion, Ted Ray. Understandably, Darwin had hoped that one of his countrymen would win the playoff, but by the seventeenth hole, after Ouimet had clearly outplayed the two invaders, Darwin found that he had to root for a victory by Ouimet—he had deserved it by the superior quality of his play. Darwin always paid a good deal of attention to amateur golf. This was easy in the 1920s when British golf included such amateur stars as Cyril Tolley, Roger Wethered, and Ernest Holderness, and when Bobby Jones appeared on the international scene. With his perceptive mind, Darwin appreciated not only the shotmaking ability but also the attractive personalities of the American professionals—Walter Hagen, Gene Sarazen, Leo Diegel, et al—who, after the First World War, started to cross the Atlantic annually to play in the British Open, and generally to win it. His portraits of them as golfers and as personalities in "Golf Between Two Wars" are memorable—Darwin at his best.

Darwin may have been the only man present at Ouimet's historic triumph in the 1913 U.S. Open at The Country Club in Brookline, who was also on hand in 1953 when Ben

Hogan won the British Open at Carnoustie. Darwin and Hogan, so utterly different in many ways, got along famously. Darwin was captivated by Hogan's concentration, his intelligent course management, the accuracy of his shots, and his ability to repeat his swing perfectly on shot after shot during the three days of the tournament. They had a good chat together, which both of them thoroughly enjoyed. After Hogan had won the championship by four strokes with a total of 284—he had improved his scoring on each round: 73, 71, 70, and 68—Darwin made the consummate comment: "If he had needed a 64 on his last round, you were quite certain he could have played a 64. Hogan gave you the distinct impression he was capable of getting whatever score was needed to win."

It was in 1953, by the way, that Darwin, at seventy-seven, left the Times. *However, he kept on writing until a short time before his death at eighty-five in 1961, putting out new books, continuing his essays on golf for* Country Life, *and contributing articles to the American magazine,* Sports Illustrated. *In these last years, he suffered from the gout, the remedy for which had not then been discovered. However, he continued to attend certain tournaments whenever he could. The last tournament I saw him at was the 1955 British Amateur, at Lytham St. Annes. It was there that the American amateur, Don Bisplinghoff, from Florida, made a strong showing and reached the fifth round. One morning during the championship, Darwin, who had his troubles getting the name right, said to a group of friends, "Bisplinghoff. Bisplinghoff. Bisplinghoff. It's like putting. Some days you have it, and some days you don't."*

Herbert Warren Wind

GOLF BETWEEN TWO WARS

by

Bernard Darwin

1944

CHATTO & WINDUS

LONDON

PUBLISHED BY
Chatto & Windus
LONDON

1944
PRINTED IN GREAT BRITAIN

CONTENTS

*

ILLUSTRATIONS

*

ILLUSTRATIONS

FOREWORD

NOBODY can watch all the golf of any consideration played in this country during twenty-two years, and it would certainly kill him if he did. I have watched at least a certain amount of it, but there are obvious gaps in my experience; I have for example seen very few of the professional tournaments on inland courses which have become more and more numerous in recent times. As one is more likely to be interesting about what one has seen with one's own eyes, or perhaps I should say, less likely to be tiresome, I have written chiefly of the occasions on which I was present, and passed over the others with very slight mention. This must make for some lack of proportion but it is my fervent hope that it may also make for some lack of dullness.

I have meandered hither and thither, not sticking strictly to any chronological order, and I have tried to look up as little as possible, not purely from laziness but because the memory retains most clearly the striking things, and those which fade from it are generally not so well worth recalling. This is doubtless a rule having many exceptions since the most trifling little scenes and most casual conversations have a trick of sticking in the mind to the exclusion sometimes of the more solid and important. Nevertheless it has seemed to me that the sketch of a period drawn largely from one personal memory, however fallible and partial, is likely to have less of monotony than any more regular history book. At any rate it is on that principle that I have found it most amusing to myself to write, and he who does not amuse himself cannot hope to amuse other people. If my recollections can do no more perhaps they may help to refresh those of the reader, so much more vivid and better worth recalling, so that he loses himself for a little while in a pleasant reverie of the links.

B. D.

Chapter 1

TWENTY YEARS

War-time, in which there is so little golf and none of it serious, is well adapted to looking back at peace-time, when there was so much and so desperately solemn: when short putts missed were really tragic and life's chief ambition was the mastering of the swing 'from inside out'. It is easier to see the wood for the trees. At the same time let me say at once that though I begin flippantly I shall soon recover an older mood and be as serious about golf as anyone can desire. The flippancy is but a pose, for though one may forget about golf for a while memory wants but little stirring.

When it was first suggested that I should write this book it seemed to me that there would be nothing to say since nothing particular had happened. But when under ingeniously persuasive treatment I began to think, it seemed to me that on the contrary almost everything had happened between 1919 to 1939. Let me take the merest preliminary glance at the events of these twenty years. There was nothing perhaps so fraught with fundamental change to the game as the sudden bursting on the world of the Haskell ball, at Hoylake in 1902. But the coming of steel shafts and with it of the numbered and graduated irons was a major event, if not an upheaval in the playing of golf. Then in the field of politics, there was the foundation of the English and Scottish Unions. Ireland and Wales had Unions far older, but it is no disrespect to them to say that it was the spread of Unionism, if I may so term it, to the other two countries, which had by far the more profound effect. It is one hard to define perhaps save in the matter of that system of scratch scores, which more nearly approximated men to women and is still something of a puzzle to those whose philosophy is comprised in the words "Why can't you let it alone?" But it has led to the good organising of many things which I have no doubt, though naturally a little lazy and sceptical in these matters, are all the better for it, and have thus tended to the greatest happiness of the greatest number.

Neither must I forget the taking-over of the Championships

by the Royal and Ancient in the place of a heterogeneous body of clubs and the extension of the Championship 'rota', which is in fact a rota no longer, to include a number of famous and deserving courses. "But come," as Mr. Smangle remarked, "this is dry work." The fact is I dislike politics and prefer to turn to the enormous increase, much of it due of course to the politicians, in the number of golfing events. In the larger international field we have had the institution of the Ryder Cup and the Walker Cup matches, the one professional, the other amateur, between Britain and the United States. Then in the more domestic but still international sphere, there is the annual meeting in which all the four countries play one another. For myself I had an old affection for the England *v.* Scotland match, which was merely an appetiser before the Amateur Championship. So I was at first sorry to see it go and a little suspicious of its successor; but having duly watched the international tournament for a number of years I admit its superiority. Horse, foot and artillery its supporters have marched over me and I willingly and wholeheartedly admit that they were right.

The English Championship and the Scottish Championship have likewise been instituted and supplied a felt want. So have the Boys' Championship (as to which perhaps from lack of knowledge I feel less enthusiastic) and the Girls' Championship, an admirable competition but never quite so engaging since the competitors seemed to grow older and more sophisticated and there were fewer pig-tails whirling through the air with the vigour of youthful swings, fewer bare legs and short socks. And then to descend from the rarefied atmosphere of championships these twenty years have seen the birth of other competitions, which have possibly brought more undiluted pleasure to the players than any others, since they have been solemn enough and yet of an extraordinary friendliness. Nobody who has ever played in the Mixed Foursomes or the Halford Hewitt Cup will ever cease to be grateful to those who founded and promoted them. Nothing can keenlier arouse in their bosoms a pleasure that is akin to pain than the thought of the dark fir trees of Worplesdon or the windswept sand-hills of Deal, yes even at half-past seven in the morning, at which untimely hour Group Captain John Morrison has been known to play his approach to the second hole. Perhaps too, though this is a rather private and esoteric festival, even if productive of much fine golf, I may include the President's Putter of the Oxford and Cambridge Golfing Society at Rye. If at the thought of it I instinctively clutch my coat closer round me against the January blast, so also I expand in the warmth of the Dormy House fire and stretch out my hands to the blaze. We still cannot tell when the next meeting will be, nor how many more names may have to be sadly remembered in the toast of "Absent Friends"; but this I know, that there is scarcely anything to which every member looks forward to with a greater and more unspeakable thrill "if he is spared". And so no known number of wild horses—four, eight, sixteen, thirty-two—can keep it out of my list or out of my book.

There is one phenomenon inseparable from the gliding of any period of years, though it is more marked when there comes the interruption of a war, and that is the passing of an elder generation of players and the coming of a new one. In the last Open Championship before the war at Prestwick in 1914, Vardon and Taylor had been drawn together on the second day's play and after a desperate duel before a seething and unruly mob, Vardon had won the Championship with Taylor as runner-up. These two were then about 43 years old and when the five years of war were over their long supremacy was over. They had been so great that it was hard to believe that they were not immortal. I remember making a bet in 1919 that no one of the great four, Vardon, Braid, Taylor and Herd, would ever again win the Open Championship. The bet was never in fact paid and I often wished that I might have to pay it, but I had been ruthlessly right. I was nearly wrong, as witness Herd's noble effort when he was second at Deal in 1920, witness also his winning of the 'News of the World' tournament as late as 1926 and Taylor's wonderful golf in the Hoylake Championship of 1924, when, if the qualifying rounds had been reckoned (I am not saying that they ought to be reckoned), he would have been head of the list. No, their sceptre had not departed by any manner of means, but no man can go on for ever, and the first few years after the war must necessarily be for them something in the nature of a sundown, however gorgeous its colours. It was not, however, a wholly new generation of players unknown before the war that was at once to succeed to the throne. It

3

was at first the time of the younger pre-war golfers, of Duncan and Abe Mitchell in particular with the Whitcombes and Havers coming up behind them.

It was in the amateur ranks that the brand new generation, the young warriors who had been boys or almost boys before the war, more immediately made themselves felt. As I remember it, the first amateur competition after the war was the Active Service tournament at Sandy Lodge in 1919. There was a number of players who had been more or less well known before the war and who now, having gratefully thrown off their uniforms, coyly reappeared as Majors and Captains and what-not for that occasion only. Most of us did not play very well, but the one man who unquestionably did play very well was Mr. Lister-Kaye who had been known before the war as a cricketer, but not as a golfer. Harry Vardon, who was a fine and uncompromising judge of golfers, roundly declared that he was the best player in the field and Mr. Lister-Kaye looked like it and played like it. In the final against Lord Charles Hope he remained worthy of Vardon's eulogy till he was five up with five to play and then came a sudden and a sad collapse; all those five holes melted away one after the other and the nineteenth went the same way. So the pre-war golfers pulled through after all and Mr. Lister-Kaye never, as far as I know, came back to give his proofs anew. That he was good was patent to anyone with eyes to see, but "the meteor drops and in a flash expires", and exactly how good will never be known now. It was in my experience a unique case.

The next members of the war generation to appear were by no means so evanescent. If they swam suddenly into our ken they remained there for years as bright and familiar constellations. The 'Golf Illustrated' Gold Vase at Mid Surrey in 1919 produced a considerable gathering of the pre-war clans, some of them from far away; Mr. Lassen, I remember, came from Yorkshire and Mr. Michael Scott from France. Insurgent youth did not win, for in fact by some singular chance I won myself, but it became apparent that it soon would. There were two young golfers in whom the spectators soon became interested; one was called Wethered and the other Tolley. I don't think I saw Mr. Wethered play that day, though I met him to speak to, but in Mr. Tolley I took an acute personal

4

interest since after eighteen holes his was, equal with one or two others (including my own), the leading score. I had gone out very early, so early that after lunch I lost my caddie and was pleasantly depicted by Mr. Tom Webster looking for him inside my bag of clubs. When I had finished, with a score which could only win if at all by the veriest inch, I had plenty of agonising time to wait and went out to watch Mr. Tolley. I was greatly relieved to find him hitting his tee shots with a cleek, since disaster had overtaken him, but it was clear from the first glance at that swing, so full of grace and power, that there would be many other days when the disaster would be other people's. Those two names, afterwards almost inseparable, became much better known in the autumn when their owners went up to Oxford, but that day at Mid Surrey began the making of them. The owner of another famous name to be often bracketed with theirs was also in the list and, if I remember rightly, very near the top of it. Mr. Holderness, as he then was, strictly speaking of a pre-war vintage, since he had played for Oxford from 1910 to 1912, but all his more conspicuous achievements were still to come and before the war few had realised all the golf there was in him. Those three were not wholly to obliterate the pre-warriors. Mr. Harris had a championship coming to him for which he had to wait some time; so had Mr. Scott, when he was on the verge of qualifying for the Senior Golfers' Society. But already in 1919 youth had staked out a predominant claim.

It was naturally enough the younger generation that was to provide the chief figures of our twenty years. Many distinguished ones were to arise, including two men who were not only great golfers but men of outstanding, forceful and remarkable character, Walter Hagen and Henry Cotton. Nevertheless, with all respect to the others, I venture to think that the golfing historian of the future will call this particular epoch that of Bobby Jones and Joyce Wethered. Those who know their *Trilby* will remember a little scene in which the great singer, Glorioli, confides to Little Billee that in each century two human nightingales are born, that he, Glorioli, is the male *rossignol* and the female La Svengali. I translate that scene to myself in terms of golf and the two names I have mentioned seem the only and the inevitable ones to fill the gaps. A century is, to be sure, a long time, but each of the two, Bobby and Miss Wethered, are in the class of game-playing geniuses that only arise once in a very long while. In the nineteenth century there was young Tommy Morris I suppose—it can only be a matter of hearsay—and, I am quite sure, Harry Vardon. In the twentieth as far as it has gone their successors seem to me clear. There will be more to say about them later on but I may as well make my profession of faith at once.

Finally, in this preliminary survey, there comes what seems to me the most striking event of all. This is the rise of the great American golfing empire, its supremacy and complete subjugation of Britain for a number of years. Then at the end of our period comes an honourable recovery on our part, its two most cheering pieces of evidence being the defeat of the embattled professionals of the United States in Cotton's championship at Carnoustie in 1937, and in 1938 our victory awaited through sixteen heart-sickening years in the Walker Cup.

It is true enough that long before the war we "had been warned", in the now familiar phrase, about American golf. In 1903 an Oxford and Cambridge Society side had toured the United States. They had done very well; they had lost but a single match, and that against a team representing all America and, should 'ifs' ever be permissible, they would not have lost that one if Mr. J. A. T. Bramston had not been already a sick man and so unable to last the course. Here was nothing unduly to alarm us at home. Nevertheless Mr. John Low on his return had spoken of the young Americans who would some day invade us. "Already," he had cried like a prophet on a mountain top, "I hear the hooting of their steamers in the Mersey." And in the very next year there came an event to confirm his words, for an American golfer, not young indeed but middle-aged, Mr. W. J. Travis, came over, a lone invader, and won our Amateur Championship. He too, when he got home, said something; he said that many of our golfing idols had feet of clay.

That win of his had been a wounding blow, but for a number of years nothing happened to rub it in, so that the sting of it faded and was nearly forgotten. Mr. Jerome Travers came here in 1909 but was not himself and so was not a menace. Two years later came Mr. Chick Evans and he was clearly a beautiful golfer, but he was beaten comparatively early.

6

McDermott, the first of the really good 'home-bred' professionals, invaded us, but at the first attempt he sealed his fate
by hooking numberless balls into Archerfield Wood and at a
subsequent one he played well but not quite well enough to
threaten the triumvirate. Complacency reigned again and
then in 1913 it received a severe and memorable shock when
Mr. Francis Ouimet, scarcely emerged from the schoolboy,
first tied with Vardon and Ray for the American Open
Championship and then beat them roundly on playing off.

Yet even after that unpleasant awakening we were in a
measure lulled to sleep again. In the summer of 1914 there
came here the astonishing Mr. Ouimet, together with the
other two best amateurs in America, Mr. Jerome Travers,
now hard, fit and well, and Mr. Chick Evans, and another
very good player Mr. Fred Herreshoff. We were duly
frightened this time, but all the great men went down swiftly
like so many ninepins, Mr. Travers, the most feared of all,
before Mr. C. A. Palmer, something over fifty and partially
crippled with lumbago.

After all, Britons thought to themselves, perhaps they are
not so dreadfully good after all. Then came war and for five
years and more there was no temptation to think any more
about the subject. Nevertheless, the storm was brewing. "It
does not take a long time," said Madame Defarge, "for an
earthquake to swallow a town. Eh well! Tell me how long
it takes to prepare the earthquake?" It was in 1920 that the
earthquake shook us to our foundations, when there came over
a team of young American amateurs to play in the Championship at Hoylake and to play a match against Great Britain
before the Championship. People realised how good some
of the visitors such as Mr. Ouimet and Mr. Evans were, and
there were many stories of the infant phenomenon Bobby,
but it was not generally realised how good they all were. Mr.
John Low renewed his old prophecy. After the Committee
had sat long in choosing the British side, someone said that we
had chosen a good one. "They're a' graund players in our
club," quoted Mr. Low to me *sotto voce*. "I wonder what we
shall say tomorrow night." By luncheon-time on the morrow
all was in effect over for the Americans had won every one of
the four foursomes and by nightfall our side was destroyed by
nine matches to three.

In the Championship which followed those conquering invaders fell unexpectedly. It was an odd Championship played on an odd, sun-dried, waterless course and only one of them survived into the last eight, but that made little difference; we had seen how good they were, how smooth and rhythmic their swings, how accurate their putting, and so when in the following year our first Walker Cup side sailed for New York we knew what was to be expected. When the team returned beaten by 8 matches to .4—incidentally a far better result than that achieved by several of their successors—there was nothing to be surprised at.

For the moment I may leave the sad story of the Walker Cup, which was at last to have a happy ending, and turn to the professionals. Their awakening did not come quite so soon as did that of the amateurs, for in the championships of 1920 Walter Hagen toiled bravely round Deal with scarcely anyone watching him to finish very low indeed on the list. Jim Barnes was sixth, but after all he was a Cornishman and not an American. A year later, however, it was the professionals' turn to be shaken, when an American Scot, Jock Hutchison, won the Open Championship after a tie with Mr. Wethered. Walter Hagen came over to win next year. In 1922 Havers gallantly, but momentarily, stemmed the flood and after that for ten years running our Championship Cup was politely brought home only to return instantly across the Atlantic. In 1926 when Mr. Jones won at St. Anne's, seven out of the first nine had U.S.A. after their names, and in the tenth year, at St. Andrews of all places, two Americans tied for it.

That long lean time had been the more depressing because in matches our professionals had more than held their own. Not indeed when they visited the United States but certainly at home. In the first international at Wentworth, which was the forerunner of the Ryder Cup matches, they nearly swept the board against adversaries who did not perhaps take the match very seriously and had their eyes fixed on the championship. Then when the Ryder Cup had been instituted there came two victories, one at Moortown and another at Southport, as to which no such excuses could be made and the Americans clearly meant to win if they could. Yet as soon as the championship came round there was the same sorry, monotonous story to be told, and so when finally those two invaders tied for our championship it seemed that universal darkness had buried all.

The longest lane has proverbially a turning, and since that year when Shute and Craig Wood tied at St. Andrews, no one from over the sea has won our Open Championship. It is true that save in one year, 1937, the invasions were perceptibly less formidable. Perhaps the prize, having been so often won, appeared less worth winning. In 1926 at St. Anne's Bobby Jones and Al Watrous were playing together, and with two holes to go it was almost certain that one of them must win. That one seemed to be Watrous. Appearances were deceptive and every schoolboy knows of Bobby's shot to the seventeenth green from the sandy wilderness on the left which transformed the situation, but at the moment when Watrous was about to play his second Mr. Fownes was justified in saying to me as he did: "He's got his shot for 100,000 dollars."

Perhaps by 1933 our championship was not worth so much or perhaps money for the trip here was less easy to come by. At any rate there was a perceptible slackening of the yearly invasion. But having admitted so much, it is right to add that our own men did much to turn the tide by their own efforts. Cotton showed that the cup could be kept at home and Perry, Padgham, R. A. Whitcombe, Burton and he himself profited by that revelation and followed that bright example. Confidence came back and though for a brief while during the qualifying rounds at Carnoustie the old American terror stalked once more across the links, it was quickly and gloriously dispelled. Whatever may happen after the war when everybody has to begin again there will be no 'inferiority complex' on the part of our professionals. They will recognise in the Americans magnificent and formidable golfers but not invincible ones.

The same is true, I hope and believe, of our amateurs. I have told before in print, but I like to tell again, how when the Walker Cup had been won at last my old friend Sam McKinlay advanced to me in the club-house at St. Andrews, transfigured with a solemn joy and with hand extended, saying: "Well, Bernard, we have lived to see this day." The spell had been broken, and though we may be beaten and beaten again we shall never approach the match with the same cynical, defeatist and hang-dog air. I shall beyond doubt have much to say later about that victory and all the hard preliminary work that went to gain it. Meanwhile it makes a good ending to this first chapter. The word 'impossible' had been expunged from the dictionary and the British amateur, like Mr. Micawber, had recovered his moral dignity and could once more walk erect before his fellow man.

Chapter 2

DUNCAN AND MITCHELL

THE first professional tournament of any account after the war was held over the Old Course at St. Andrews when the first place was tied for by George Duncan and Abe Mitchell. There, could have been no result more appropriate, for in the early years of the 1920's these two were unquestionably among our own players the leading figures. Both were very fine and interesting golfers, and if I add that despite all they won, neither did the fullest possible justice to his great powers, that is in a way the highest compliment I can pay them.

Neither of them were products of the post-war period. When the war ended Duncan was some 36 years old and Mitchell four years younger. As long before as 1906 Duncan had been chosen to play for Scotland, and it was in that year that he and Mayo had thrown down their gallant, almost impudent, gauntlet to Vardon and Braid and received reasonable chastisement for their temerity. He had won the 'News of the World' and the French Championship and had at least flattered to deceive a little at the last in the Open. Notably in 1911 at Sandwich he had been one of the half-dozen or more who seemed likely to win before Vardon and Massy ultimately tied. Mitchell had burst upon the world later and more suddenly. Before 1910 only a few people knew that there was at Forest Row an artisan, one of a great golfing clan, who was a brilliant player and in particular a prodigious hitter. Then came the Amateur Championship at Hoylake. The unknown gardener was chosen to play for England against Scotland, distinguished himself in the match and subsequently reached the semi-final of the Championship. Two years later at Westward Ho! he reached the final, seemed at one time to have victory in his grasp and was ultimately beaten at the thirty-eighth hole by Mr. John Ball in one of the matches truly to be called historic. In 1913 he became a professional and in the last Open Championship before the war he finished fourth at Prestwick. Assuming that the immortals of the pre-war era must now at length put on mortality, these were the two men who seemed destined to succeed them, and their tying for that first prize was but a confirmation of everyone's prophecies. That they did not wholly fulfil those prophecies was due partly no doubt to the new and fierce opposition from America, partly, I think also, to their both lacking something of that indomitable stone-wall quality and love of fighting which had distinguished the Triumvirate.

Whether in point of pure golfing genius or of an artist's rejoicing in a beautiful art, it would .be difficult to conceive a finer golfer than George Duncan. He had something of the artist's incalculable temperament. He could be incalculably brilliant; no one could play such "mad stuff", as I think Sandy Herd called it. He could also be suddenly and incalculably bored, and even perhaps a little peevish. It was part of his artist's nature that he was something of a dreamer of dreams and a player of parts before himself as the solitary audience. To keep his eye on the ball, trust to his fine swing and play "bread and butter shots" could never satisfy him. He liked to have a fresh system for every day and imagine himself playing his strokes after the manner of some other golfer who had caught his fancy. The best golf I ever saw him play was when he won the 'Daily Mail' tournament at Westward Ho! in 1920. When I talked about it to him several years later he told me who had been his models for the various shots during those two days, recalling them all perfectly clearly and perfectly seriously.

If ever there was a natural golfer here was one, but he fully lived up to a doctrine I have heard laid down by Mr. Robert Harris, that the way to be a good golfer is to learn golf first and think about it afterwards. Duncan came from Aberdeen to England (I take his word for it for I never saw him at this stage) a flat swinger with an open stance and a modified palm grip. Then he fell prostrate before the genius of Harry Vardon, and entirely remodelled his swing on upright lines, with an overlapping grip, so that he looked like a moving picture of Vardon thrown with something of swiftness added to it on to the screen. This was artifice, but grown into a second nature, with all the gracefulness and ease that belongs to an unstudied and natural movement. Just as there are some authors who are "writers' writers", who are specially studied and admired by their fellow craftsmen for their technical skill, so Duncan was the "pros' pro", whom his fellows were never tired of watching. And up to the green there could be no player that better repaid it. The dash, confidence and power of his driving were fascinating, and in no shot was he seen to greater advantage than in a wooden club shot up to the hole, whether with a brassey or with the spoon which was his particular love. One of the features of Vardon's game that had early impressed him was his getting to the hole whenever he could by the "all air route", and all Duncan's shots with whatever club, were played, whenever possible, well in the air and bang up to the hole. Moreover when he was in one of his 'mad' moods all clubs seemed the same. He could put his mashie shots very close, but his brassey shots were just as likely to finish dead. In such a mood he was I think more entirely dazzling than anyone I ever saw—up to the green.

Some people found his putting as attractive as the rest of his game and there was about it the charm of swift decision. He acted on the advice attributed to Alec Smith, the old Carnoustie player, once champion of the U.S.A.—"Miss them quick". But Duncan's putting lacked, or at any rate seemed to me to lack, the smoothness of striking which marks the best putters; he did not roll the ball up to the hole and was inclined on his bad days rather to jab it there. He did not wholly deserve Mr. Tom Webster's remark, "George, you're our best googly putter," but he did now and then put odd spins on his ball. When a man can lay his approaches as near the hole as Duncan often did, people are apt to criticise his putting unfairly, if he does not hole, as nobody could hole, all the ensuing putts. Duncan could unquestionably hole plenty of putts at times; but whereas in the rest of his game he had his art to fall back upon in his less inspired moments, on the green he relied too largely on inspiration. The extreme rapidity which suited him so well up to the green was less satisfying when he got there. It is possible to miss them too quick.

Abe Mitchell was, I think, almost if not quite as impressive as Duncan in point of natural genius, but he was impressive in a different way. His play was marked above everything else by immense power. The tautness of his body at the moment

13

of hitting and the rather clipped follow-through—possibly a deceitful appearance—suggested strength, strength particularly of hands and wrists. When I first played with him once or twice on Ashdown Forest in his amateur days, an experience as pleasant as it was alarming, it was rather rugged strength; but when he had had experience of other courses and especially after he had become a professional, his game, and in particular his iron play, became far more polished. I doubt if he ever hit the ball quite so far again as he did at Ashdown, where he constantly drove across the whole stretch of fairway and into the little strip of heather beyond: but if he lost anything in power it was a loss voluntarily incurred and he gained immensely in control. Most of the holes at Ashdown had been only a drive and a pitch for him and he was already a skilful pitcher, but he acquired a new range of longer iron shots played noticeably "within himself" of which he had previously known no need. It is difficult exactly to appraise his putting, the more so as one is always inclined to be too critical of professionals' putting because they make so few mistakes in other parts of the game. Moreover the professionals, as they sometimes say with some little bitterness, have to hole putts for their living. I must compromise by saying that he was not a bad putter but, judged by American standards which were soon to raise our whole conception of that art, not an especially good one.

These two men, though they did not actually finish first and second, were the two outstanding figures in the first Open Championship after the war and on the subsequent career of one of them it had, I fancy, a lasting effect. On the first day at Deal there was as between the two only one in it; indeed there seemed to be only one man in it in the whole field and that Abe Mitchell. Deal is a tremendous course, as anyone can testify who has had to endure that long beat home against the wind, with never a "let-up", nothing but hard grim work and one or two shots towards the end, notably at the fifteenth and seventeenth, when a foot or two in the pitching of the approach shot may make all the difference—a putt for three or "what worlds away". When Mitchell had holed the first two rounds in 74 and 73 and his nearest pursuer was the noble veteran, Sandy Herd, six strokes behind him; when moreover Duncan had taken two 80's and was thirteen strokes behind, it seemed that Abe was going to follow Taylor's dictum that the way to win a championship is to win it easily. He was playing magnificently and who could stop him?

It has been constantly pointed out that the man to back on the last day of a championship is he who "gets his blow in fust", and this last day at Deal was as good an illustration as need be. Duncan was out early and Mitchell started comparatively late. From the very start Duncan, with an apparently impossible leeway to make up, was evidently in the mood, going out for everything and bringing everything off. In his younger and more temperamental days he had often begun brilliantly; he had "gone up like a rocket and come down like the stick". Now his was to be the converse lot of coming up from behind by a splendid and long sustained spurt. He finished in 71, a wonderful round, which humanly speaking, however Mitchell had played, must have diminished to some extent the gap between them. But the gap was so big, and Mitchell had been so full of confidence that even a 71 did not seem greatly to matter.

Now I must enter for a moment the unsatisfactory but alluring region of 'ifs'. It was a cold morning and Mitchell, having hours to wait, made the mistake of coming up early to the course and hanging about to look at other people. That is never a wise thing to do; he could hardly help feeling anxious but he need not have been chilled. What would have happened if he had stayed warm and comfortable in his rooms to the last moment? That is one 'if', and here is another. What would have happened if almost exactly at the moment when Mitchell was starting Duncan had not finished in his 71 amid much cheering? Five minutes earlier Mitchell might have set out without getting that nasty jolt. Whatever might have happened, what did happen is history. Mitchell reached the first green in two, though his approach, as I recall it, was not a particularly good one. Still all seemed well enough—till he took three putts. Much the same thing happened at the second and the third and at the Sandy Parlour; he made no gross mistakes but at each hole a stroke was frittered away, and then as a culminating horror he topped his tee shot into a bunker almost in front of his nose, tried for too much, took two to get out and took seven to the hole. If anything could make things worse it was the fact that there is

15

always a long hold-up on the sixth tee at Deal, and Mitchell had to wait through what must have seemed an eternity of remorse before going on again. He pulled himself together as well as he could and he finished in 84, but the whole thirteen strokes of his lead had vanished like a puff of smoke. By the time he had finished Duncan was on his way round for a second time with the chance of victory miraculously restored to him and playing as Andrew Kirkaldy might have said, like a roaring lion. Duncan never looked back; he added a 72 to his 71, and though Mitchell stuck dourly to his guns with a 76 it was all over as far as he was concerned, and it was the indomitable Sandy, now 52 years old, who came within two shots of Duncan and might have won but for a cruel disaster at the sixteenth hole. Herd was second with 305, Ray third and Mitchell fourth.

I have written at some length about that championship because I cannot help feeling that it had a profound effect on Mitchell's career. He remained for years a grand golfer and was, I think, the best match player in the country, but he never again really looked like winning the Championship. Yet—and this is the biggest and most speculative 'if' of all—I can never get it out of my head that had he won at Deal he might have won several more times. As it was, the shadow of that Deal disaster lay heavy upon him. It strikes me—I may be wrong but I will say it nevertheless—that Abe is very fond of golf but not fond of big golf. By nature a gentle and peaceful creature, he never really enjoyed, as some more fortunate people do, the trampling and the hum of the crowd and the clash of battle. He has fought hard and well because it was his business to do so, but he did not like the fight for its own sake. In that respect he reminds me of another great player who was always happier in playing with his friends and disliked the 'fuss' of championships, Mr. Robert Maxwell. He never took the field again after the war and so does not come into my period, but I cannot refrain from saying what a tremendous golfer he was. Tremendous—that is the epithet for Abe Mitchell. To see him at his best, serene and un-worried, was to find it impossible to believe that anyone could beat him and I still find it surprising that anyone ever did.

George Duncan

John Ball

Chapter 3

THE AMERICAN INVASION

IN 1920 there first appeared in this country at the age of 28 Walter Hagen, not only a very fine player but an extra-ordinarily picturesque figure, a godsend to those who like to write "colourful" descriptions and retail anecdotes. He was a man as to whom it was hardly possible to take a neutral view; you might like or dislike him but he compelled your attention; his character and flavour were such that they could not be neglected. The sum of his golfing achievements is so large that it is only possible to set down a few of them, and in any case the man himself was to most people more interesting than his feats; he had such a way with him that crowds were ready to watch him when he had not the remotest chance of winning. In fact apart from numberless big tournaments in his native country—and he had the happy knack of winning when there was the largest number of dollars at stake—he won two American championships and four British ones. Yet I am inclined to cite as his most remarkable feat the winning for four consecutive years of the American P.G.A. tournament. That correspond to our 'News of the World' tournament and is played for by matches and, con-sidering the strength of the opposition, to win it four years running (he won it in another year as well) was truly astonish-ing. It showed more than anything else that power of dominating, almost of cowing his rivals which was one of his strongest assets.

There have been, I think, more skilful and certainly more mechanical and faultless players than Hagen, but none with greater sticking power or a temperament more ideally suited to the game. He was a strange mixture of two usually contrasted elements, on the one hand the casual and the happy-go-lucky, on the other the shrewd, long-headed, observant and intensely determined. His manner while playing was a reflection of his nature, for he could "let up" between strokes and converse in a carefree manner with a spectator and then switch off this mood and switch on one of single-minded attention to the next stroke to be played. No doubt while he was talking with such apparent *insouciance* his mind was busy looking ahead, but he had an almost unique power of relaxing and never presented that aspect of stern and solemn pugnacity without which the less happily gifted cannot concentrate their minds.

Much, too much, has been written of Hagen's gifts as a "showman" and no doubt he fully understood that his casual manner, with a touch of flamboyant swagger about it, went down well with the crowd. No doubt also he could and did turn it on as some people can turn on, sometimes too palpably, their charm. But the casualness was natural to him and not forced. It helped him to take a strenuous life easily and unexhaustingly. It likewise enabled him to run things fine in point of time and even to be late in a way which might exasperate other people but did not cause Hagen himself to turn a hair. Others might wish to lie in bed or to stay in their baths, but they could not do so because of some malignant sprite whispering in their ears that they might have to hurry to the tee or even be disqualified. Hagen stayed in his bath as long as he pleased and trusted to the chapter of accidents. Possibly he was rather a spoilt child in this matter in that promoters of tournaments knew his value and were always ready to make allowances for what was "pretty Fanny's way". There were occasions, notably in a certain match here against Abe Mitchell, when Hagen did considerably ruffle everyone by this inconsiderate lateness. There were not wanting those who said that it was part of a deep-laid scheme to disturb his adversary, much as in older and less scrupulous days men would deliberately fret a nervous adversary by breaking away at the start of a hundred yards' race. Personally I think such accusations were utterly unfounded. I do not for a moment believe that he had any such design; this would not have accorded with his code; he was just irretrievably casual and had the bump of punctuality, if there be such a thing, very imperfectly developed.

That Hagen had an overpowering effect on some of his opponents was clear enough. His demeanour towards them, though entirely correct, had yet a certain suppressed truculence; he exhibited so supreme a confidence that they could not get it out of their minds and could not live against it.

They felt him to be a killer and could not resist being killed. He had a very shrewd eye for their weaknesses and, strictly within the limits of what was honest and permissible, he would now and then exploit them to his own advantage. I heard a story the other day of Hagen's tactics which seems to me eminently characteristic, and I believe it to be true. He was playing in one of those four consecutive finals of the American P.G.A. tournaments which he won, and with one hole to play the match was all square. Hagen having the honour sliced his drive and the ball sailed away into a wood on the right while his adversary went rigidly down the middle. Hagen carefully examined his ball and emerged from the wood for a minute to have the crowd moved back, as if he were going to make the best of a bad job and play out sideways. He went back into the wood, had another look and then, as if suddenly spying a loop-hole of escape, played a magnificent iron shot through a gap in the trees right on to the green. The flabbergasted enemy put his ball tamely into a bunker and the match was over. Now it would be a poor compliment to Hagen's intelligence to imagine that he had only just seen this loop-hole. He had seen it at once; he had reckoned that his second shot would be a disappointment to the enemy and that the disappointment would be heightened by the little preliminary drama. That was legitimate whether according to the law or to Hagen's code of ethics. You may approve or disapprove but you cannot but be struck by the cold, clear brain that can thus think things out at such a moment.

Hagen's dominating personality and his extreme astuteness have given rise to many stories, some of which at least are apocryphal, and to his being endowed by the public imagination with all manner of mysterious and almost sinister powers. This is to my mind largely nonsense. For instance, whenever the Ryder Cup Match was about to be played and Hagen was the American captain, it was said that he would out-manœuvre our captain, whoever he might be, and twist him round his finger. That Hagen was an excellent captain no one can doubt, as good a one as a team could desire; but when all is said what can the captain of a golf side do besides putting his men in the best possible order and encouraging them in every possible way? He is not like the captain of a cricket eleven who may turn the whole fortunes of the day by understanding an enemy's weakness and making an inspired change in the bowling; he does not even know beforehand in what order the enemy will be arrayed. He can be the best possible leader but he can be no more, and to attribute to him machiavellian designs or mesmeric powers is absurd. People like to believe these things because they enjoy having their flesh made to creep, but such stories must not be taken too seriously.

Let me say something of the more technical and perhaps less interesting side of Hagen's game. He was, I should say, a strong rather than a conspicuously accurate driver with a tendency to make one or two really crooked shots in the course of a round, and a preference for a strong shot with an iron to a wooden club through the green. On the whole his wooden club play was the least impressive part of his game, though it became both sounder and more stylish on his later visits to this country. When he first appeared here there was a touch of something that the hypercritical might call "straggling" about his swing, and this disappeared. Duncan has pointed out about certain players (Ray was one of them) that they came gradually to keep their bodies throughout the swing in the same space which it occupied in addressing the ball. Perhaps, if it be not fanciful to say so, something of this change came to Hagen. He looked less forceful and more compact. His long iron play was always very fine but it was in pitching, in all sorts of bunker shots, especially the more delicate ones, and in putting that he excelled. He had a fine stance on the green, comfortable and yet rock-like, and a velvety touch. It would hardly be possible to name a better putter day in and day out, but that which more than anything else at once fascinated the crowd and made him so formidable was his power of recovery.

If it could be said of anyone that he was not afraid of bunkers it could be said of Walter Hagen. He wasted no time on vain regrets; he assumed that he would make a wild shot or two in a round and accepted the results not merely with philosophy but, as it almost seemed, with a lifting of the spirits. "There she lies," he was supposed to say of a ball in trouble and that was the one important fact; how it had got there was part of the irrevocable past and did not matter; the point was how to get it out again as well as possible, and no man had a greater repertory of recovering shots nor used a greater variety of clubs for them from a putter upwards. Especially was he skilled in taking the ball out cleanly from a bunker, a shot needing immense confidence, since a grain or two of sand may ruin it. I shall never forget one such shot he played at the fifteenth hole at Sandwich, I think in the second championship he won there. It was in the last round and he was apparently well set to win though he had nothing much to spare, for Sarazen was behind him with a good chance. That bunker is a fairly deep one with a fairly steep bank, and many a stout-hearted player, however good the lie, would in his situation have played an 'explosion' shot and made as sure as might be of his five. Hagen took one good look at the ball, then flicked it out with exquisite precision close to the hole, and that as if it were the easiest shot in the world, played in the least important of half-crown games. The beholder of such strokes, and he played many of them, was divided between a desire to damn his eyes for his impudence and fall on his neck for his dauntless skill.

I had first seen Hagen at the Country Club at Brookline in 1913, but he was then only beginning to come into prominence in his own country and he had not, I am afraid, made any particular impression on me. I have a much clearer recollection of Jim Barnes, then of Tacoma. Barnes, although the sturdiest of Englishmen and Cornishmen, had then an aspect which to the stranger suggested the Wild West. His mop of fair hair, his tall and lanky frame, his looseness of build—everything about him brought to mind some of the San Francisco figures in *The Wrecker*. Both he and Hagen were well in the hunt almost to the end in that championship, for when both Vardon and Ray faltered in the last round they gave several people a good chance of catching them, though only Francis Ouimet succeeded in taking it. I was, however, so much occupied first in watching our own two champions and then in chasing Francis with a frantic crowd over his last nine holes, that Barnes and Hagen had to be left to the imagination. By a good fortune that does not always attend the reporter, both faded out a little and finished three and two strokes respectively behind the winners. It was in any case a different Hagen who came here in 1920, seven years older and with the prestige of two American championships at his back. He was obviously good and he and Barnes accomplished at least one considerable victory in a four-ball match, but I do not think we were very much afraid of him; our faith in our own men was as yet unshaken and as it turned out there was nothing to fear. Barnes finished sixth but Hagen failed rather dismally, though everyone admired the good-humoured way in which he ploughed round on the last day with never a soul to watch him. He might have said with Disraeli, "The time will come when you will hear me," but the time had not quite come yet.

He played far better at St. Andrews in 1921 than at Deal in 1920 and America's time had come, but through another agency. The winner was Jock Hutchison, a St. Andrews golfer born and bred, who had emigrated to the United States some time before and was about 37 years old. I said just now that the reporter was not always fortunate and I look back on the Championship of 1921 as one of my unlucky ones, in that I seemed constantly to be watching the wrong man. As all the world knows Mr. Wethered tied with Hutchison and I should be ashamed to tell how few strokes I saw him play. Kerrigan, another American invader, was third, and in the course of a particularly hectic last round there came to me a rumour that Kerrigan had certainly won, whereupon I reflected gloomily that I had not seen him play one single stroke. I saw plenty of Hutchison for he was one of the favourites from the start and led the field on the first day; whatever else happened he represented the post of duty. He did not strike me then as by any means the typical St. Andrews player. If he had breathed the St. Andrews swing "into his growing frame with the sharp salt breezes of the East Neuk of Fife" it had been considerably modified and Americanised since. In any case I think it must always have possessed characteristics markedly its own, for it gave an odd impression of a man swinging by numbers. It was all very rhythmically done, but there was that suggestion of a "three-piece" swing, with the three pieces perfectly and smoothly dovetailed.

That which above everything else won Hutchison his championship was his pitching. I do not know if he was the first man to carry the punching of the faces of irons to an extreme point but he was the first to show us here the value of it. His iron faces were rough and bristling with punches and he had thoroughly mastered the art of playing with them, so that he could almost bring the ball back from the pitch, and playing his strokes as he did with confidence and boldness he could largely set at naught many of the characteristic difficulties of his native greens. There was nothing about this that was not perfectly legitimate, but there was, I think, a fairly general· feeling that it came too much under the head of "buying a shot in the shop". So when this practice of roughening faces was later made illegal there were no dissentient voices. It had incidentally been otherwise when in 1904 Mr. Walter Travis had won the Amateur Championship putting with a Schenectady putter and this club was subsequently barred here but not in the United States. Then there was a feeling that the club had been barred because a stranger had beaten us with it. That certainly was not the reason, but the barring was perhaps from the point of view of international politics a maladroit gesture, the more so because Mr. Travis had not made himself very popular here—I think we were partly to blame—and had said some unfriendly things about us when he got home again.

However, I am wandering from the point and must come back to St. Andrews. From the start Hutchison set a fierce pace for he began with a 72, a fine round helped by at least one stroke of luck when he holed his tee shot at the eighth hole, and very nearly by another when he was within an inch or so of holing out again at the ninth, which is 300 yards or so in length. It is said that a spectator rushed forward and took the flag out and that had he stood still the ball would probably have gone in. Well, that is one of the many 'ifs' of history and at any rate Hutchison had little to complain of with two consecutive holes in three strokes. He led the field by two strokes from Duncan, the holder, Massy, Kerrigan, Barnes and Hagen, so that already the foreign legions were massing at the top of the list and Britain's position was clearly threatened. Mr. Wethered, who was to come near to being its saviour, had begun with a 78 and attracted no attention. In the second round Hutchison played very well again for a 75 and kept the lead; Barnes with another 74 was second now only a stroke behind; then came Duncan and Herd, with all St. Andrews praying for him. Mr. Wethered improved with a 75, but he was still six strokes behind Hutchison.

The third round is always said to be *the* critical one in an

Open Championship and it certainly had this time a kaleidoscopic effect on the field. When it was finished Herd, having again improved by one stroke, sent everybody into the seventh heaven by leading with 222. Equal with him was Barnes with a third 74. Mr. Wethered had made a great stride with a 71 and was 225 and Hagen with a 72 joined him. Kerrigan had come back again after a bad second round and was 226. Hutchison had had his bad round of 79 and was also 226. It seemed as if almost anything might happen.

I have already confessed that I scarcely saw Mr. Wethered play a stroke that day, but apart from the magnificence of his golf, and it was truly magnificent, there are two things perhaps worth saying about it. On the last day he had a late starting time and he wanted to go south that night to play in a cricket match next day, whereupon a place was made in the list for him and his partner to start earlier. This seems an entirely natural and simple thing to do, but in looking back I think it was a mistake. The professionals did not like it for they argued that if one of them had asked for this favour it would not have been granted, and I daresay they were right. The time of starting can make a great deal of difference one way or the other, as all experience shows, and it is therefore better on these occasions to stick quite rigidly to the draw.

So much for the first thing; the second is that unlucky kick which Mr. Wethered gave to his ball in the third round. It is always assumed as an incontestable and logical proposition that if he had not incurred this penalty stroke he would have beaten Hutchison by one stroke. This seems to me an unjustifiable assumption. If he had not incurred the penalty Mr. Wethered might have beaten Hutchison by one stroke or by more than one stroke or he might not have tied with him. To assume otherwise is to neglect one obvious fact, that every happening in a round of golf has some effect on the player's mind and the state of his mind has some effect on his stroke. It is such an assumption as we all make about our own rounds, but it is founded on unsound premisses. All we can say about this penalty stroke is that Mr. Wethered did very unluckily lose a shot at a particular hole. What would have happened if he had not, no human being can tell.

Again I am wandering and again I must get back to strict business. Mr. Wethered was out early and improved on his

24

72 with a 71. There was only one sad thing about this great last round, and here is, I admit, another of those prohibited 'ifs' though of a different kind. He needed a four for 70, he had hit a fine drive and he pitched very short and took a five. There are some who have an almost fanatical regard for running up at St. Andrews and would say this was in the nature of a judgment. I would not say so, for there is no finer pitcher than Mr. Wethered and none with greater power of back-spin and he was right to play his own game. One can only grieve because a five at that last hole is not merely a loss of a stroke, it is a waste of a stroke.

While Mr. Wethered was doing these superb things the situation was gradually getting clearer. Herd and Barnes fell right away with 80 apiece. Havers and Duncan came well up but not quite well enough. That terrifying and by me unseen Kerrigan had a 72—good enough, heaven knows, but not quite the incredible score which rumour had given him, and was two behind the leader. It was now only Hutchison who could do it and he had a 70 to tie. It was a desperate deal to ask and yet, as I remember, many people thought he would do it and he looked like it all the time. I remember that he hit a prodigious hook off the last tee when he wanted a four to tie and thus he duly got his four. There were those who complained that such a drive ought to have been trapped. Such remarks showed a sad lack of golfing sense. There is, humanly speaking, no trouble at the home hole at St. Andrews and a man can drive as far to the left as he pleases. If there had been trouble it is in highest degree the improbable that Hutchison would have hit that hook.

The excitement that night at St. Andrews was tremendous, for there were present all the ideal elements—America versus Britain, and yet Scotland against England, for Scotland does not lightly give up its claim to its citizens; professional against amateur and that amateur engagingly young, and, another point not to be forgotten at St. Andrews, a member of the Royal and Ancient. Next morning before the play began there was the sensation of a lull before the storm and of half-painful, half-agreeable shivers down the spine, which is sometimes the almost unbearable prelude of a great foot race. I can still see Hutchison, adding a little touch of preliminary drama, "warming up" in true American fashion by hitting

ball after ball away from the edge of the turf on to the beach.
I never remember a more intense thrill before a game, but it
was a thrill in which high hopes did not figure. All hearts,
save some local ones perhaps, might be with the amateur, but,
grandly as Mr. Wethered had played, there was a feeling not
to be fought down, that if play goes on long enough the
professional is almost bound to win. For four rounds the
amateur had held him but these were the fifth and sixth
rounds. In fact Hutchison always looked likely to win.
Mr. Wethered hung on well in the morning with 77 against 74
but faded just a little in the afternoon and took 82 against 76.
The United States had won its first Open Championship,
though it was imperfect consolation that Hutchison was a
Scot in disguise. The cup had to make its first voyage across
the water since Massy had won at Hoylake.

In the next year, 1922, came Hagen's turn. The American
professionals have a habit of saying of a tournament that it
was So-and-so's tournament, meaning, I take it, that So-and-so
was from the start playing winning golf, that the run of the
green was with him, that his victory was all the time predestined. I have always had it in my mind that this 1922
Championship was Hagen's, that he looked all the time a
winner. I am still inclined to think that there was such a
feeling in the air at Sandwich, but a glance at the scores show
me that such an intuition came very near to being wrong and
that I had forgotten a good deal. Duncan's wonderful last
round spurt (there is something of tragic bitterness still in
remembering how it just failed) had wiped everything else
from the mind. In fact it looked very like an American
championship from the start and still more so with one round
to go, but it was not at all sure that the agent of victory was to
be Hagen.

What happened was very briefly this. Hagen got briskly
off the mark and after the first two rounds he was at the head
of the field with a 76 and a 73, with Barnes one stroke behind
him. Hutchison, defending his title, had had his bad round
to begin with: his scores were 79 and 74. Incidentally if he
had the luck with him at St. Andrews he did not have it at
Sandwich. A just too strong approach at the fourth hole
went through the fence by a few inches while other more
fortunate balls rebounded from it, and I believe he hit the

rail of a bridge over the Suez Canal at the fourteenth. No doubt he ought to have taken care *not* to hit that rail and bad luck is a thing hard to define, but at least that other indefinable thing, the run of the green, was hardly with him. Once again the third round appeared to alter the whole complexion of affairs, and here a curious parallel may be drawn between Hutchison and Hagen. At St. Andrews Hutchison had slipped back with a 79 in the third round and now it was Hagen's turn to suffer in exactly the same degree. Hutchison bounded forward with a 73. So with one round to go it was Hutchison who led with 226 and behind him came in a triple tie, Hagen, Barnes and Charles Whitcombe, who had made a sudden and splendid thrust with a 72. It still looked like an American win for, fine player as we knew Charles Whitcombe to be, this 'was the first time he had been prominent in a championship and he was hardly to be regarded as of the same stature as those three invaders. As to Duncan he seemed to have put himself out of court with an 81 and was six shots behind the leader.

There was no fading-away by any of the leading four in the last round. Barnes 73, Whitcombe 75, Hutchison 76 all wrought manfully but Hagen played irresistibly well for his 72, and when he led by a stroke all was apparently over. He himself, and I have a clear vision of him, was smoking a cigar in evident relief and in complete solitude near the first teeing ground. Duncan remained far out in the distance and I resolved, rather against the grain at the end of a tiring day, to go and look for him. Partly a sense of duty urged me on and partly a wild hope. I knew that in Jack White's year both Taylor and Braid had broken 70 in heroic attempts to catch him in the last round and what had happened once might happen again. But the Sandwich of 1922 was a different course from the Sandwich of 1904. Duncan was to be sure incalculable, but the hope was a faint one.

Trudging across the course, cursing my own conscience, I picked up Duncan and his partner by the twelfth green and then I had my reward in six holes of delicious agony. He had but a handful of spectators with him and these were divided between joy and despair. They were full of joy over Duncan's astonishing play up to the flag and of despair because he could not crown these inspired approach shots by holing the putts.

27

As I have said elsewhere, Duncan in a 'crazy' mood does produce those feelings, for the putts look so holeable for those who have not got to hole them. I cannot believe that he had been putting downright badly, but his approaching had given him chances of doing wholly marvellous things and he had not quite clinched them. Still he had good hope and he continued to play superbly and to get no help from Providence on the greens. One shot I seem to remember particularly, a lovely second lashed right up to the fifteenth pin, and a three at that hole would have been worth much fine gold—but the putt never looked in "off the club". Still on he went till he had a four for a 68 and a 68 would tie with Hagen. We thought he would do it; the tee shot was perfect and out came his spoon. Clearly he played to let the ball drift in a little from the left, his natural shot with the club. It started away to the left but alas! it never quite came in. In the case of a minor player I should say that here was bad luck, that he hit the ball just too well and truly. That is what most of us would say about a shot of our own, but that will not serve in the case of such a player as Duncan. There is nothing to say but that he did not quite play the shot he intended. His pitch or pitch-and-run was hit hurriedly and ended very short. It was all over; the man who had first set up a mark to be shot at had won again and the spurt had failed. But it remains one of the great spurts of golfing history.

The next year saw a temporary, not as we fondly hoped a permanent turning-back of the tide of American victories, for Havers won at Troon, with Hagen hot on his heels. It was the first time the Championship had been played at Troon, which came well out of the ordeal. It is a good and testing course if it lacks the charm of its neighbour Prestwick. It is well suited to the spectator, who having gone straight ahead for a certain number of holes can rest and be thankful near the little short hole which is called "The Postage Stamp", while the players struggle with the hillier circuit at the far end. Then he can pick them up again, having seen a good many amusing odds and ends from his eyrie, and so plod steadily home. Havers's win was a gallant and thoroughly well-deserved one for he was the most consistent golfer in all the field. In the last year before the war when barely 16 he had achieved the remarkable feat for a boy of qualifying for the

Championship; he had been fourth at St. Andrews in 1922 and now, having just had his 26th birthday, he came right to the front. He had a splendid physique, a fine notably up-standing and controlled style; he was not perhaps a very good putter by those American standards by which people had now to be judged, but he seemed good enough ; he had a good temperament with apparently just a valuable touch and no more of lethargy. When once he had won he raised high patriotic hopes and everyone looked on him as a future rock of strength against invasion; and yet in fact he never won again and never but once looked likely to. He remained as he is still, a very fine hitter of the ball, but the appetite for championships did not come to him in the eating. There are some players in whom ambition once satisfied is never quite so keen again and perhaps—I do not profess to know—he was one of them.

At any rate at Troon Havers played with a calm power hard to over-praise. For three consecutive rounds he had a 73 and then had to face the horrid ordeal of the fourth with just two strokes in hand from Hagen, three from Macdonald Smith and only one from Kirkwood. There was a time in the middle of the round when he frittered away a putt or two but the rest of the game remained steadfast enough. I remember, when it was clear that he could afford to drop no more shots, the joy of seeing him hit a straight and magni-ficent stroke right on to the plateau green, of the one-shot seventeenth hole. He finished in 76 and it was just good enough. Hagen was supposed to like and I believe genuinely did like a chase in which he knew exactly what he had to do. Even so I have a notion that he was human enough to play better as a rule when he had not that horribly precise know-ledge. Now he had 74 to tie and he took 75. So did Mac-Donald Smith and there was a general disposition, soon to be shaken, towards believing that the lean years were over for good.

Two invading players figured in that story about whom I must say something before I end this chapter: Macdonald Smith and Kirkwood. The latter indeed we had seen two years before but this was Macdonald Smith's first appearance, to be frequently renewed later. Kirkwood, an Australian who afterward settled in the United States, was certainly a remarkable player and since he was at different times 3rd, 4th and 6th in the Championship it must be conceded that he was a very good one, but somehow he did not look quite good enough. His style was a little lacking in rhythm and power as compared with that of the great masters: there was not the conspicuous firmness of foot and balance which marks them. Yet his mastery over club and ball was astonishing and his exhibition of trick shots, accompanied by very entertaining patter, was highly popular. It used to be said of him rather unkindly that he could do anything with a ball except hit a perfectly plain-sailing straight shot, and it may well be that what Mr. George Glennie would have indignantly called his "monkey tricks" were not very good for his straightforward golf. However that may be, he was always a threat but never a threat quite fulfilled.

Macdonald Smith was a golfer of a very different and a higher class, one who deserves serious consideration for the depressing honour of being the best player who never won a championship. Like Jock Hutchison he was a born Scot and had learnt his golf at Carnoustie where he was a member of a great golfing family. Before he was 20 he had gone to the United States and in 1910 had tied for the Open Championship there and lost on the play-off. It was the nearest he was ever destined to get to it. For some little time afterwards he rather mysteriously vanished from golf and I believe worked in a shipyard. At any rate when he came back to golf he soon made his presence felt and in the course of a long career won many big tournaments and doubtless many dollars, won almost everything except his heart's desire. I am always a little frightened of Scottish adjectives, being unable to distinguish clearly between "snell" and "caller", but I should be inclined to call Macdonald Smith a douce man, pleasant, quiet, shrewd, careful, knowing his business thoroughly and sticking to it. Perhaps he was not quite so unmoved as he looked, for somehow or other when the end drew near the prize always eluded his grasp.

Heaven knows he was a good enough player to win, and this was obvious to those who saw him for the first time at Troon. He had a fine, round, slow, smooth swing which seemed, perhaps because one knew he came from Carnoustie, to have in it something of the swing which Bobby Jones had learnt as a child from Stewart Maiden, another product of the Forfarshire school.

He was a supremely elegant player. He seemed, as it were, to do it all by kindness; everything he did suggested ease rather than strength, and his putting, with a notably long pause at the end of the take-back of the club, was wonderfully smooth. One might without reflection have fancied him playing with rather light clubs and it was a shock to handle them and find them in the nature of "barge poles", very stiff and thick in the shaft and decidedly heavy. He must have had plenty of strength at once to use them and to stop them from running away with him. Mac Smith was very careful in everything he did, in coming over early to get well acclimatised and learn the course, in taking a preliminary swing before the shot, in planting his feet with the greatest nicety. Even though the heart grew sick at the cup going steadily back across the Atlantic, he was one of the invaders that one would have liked to see win. He had his chances, and especially one great chance to which I shall come presently. There is only one Championship every year and Fortune does not like having her favours flouted.

Chapter 4

AN AMATEUR TRIUMVIRATE

THUS far I have followed where the records of the Open Championship have led me and so naturally among the professionals. It is good to have a variety and so now let me turn for a space to the amateurs. The professionals will get another innings presently and the amateur champions a good long one after that.

When golf began again after the war there were not among the professionals, as I have said before, any immediately new discoveries. If what might irreverently be called the old gang in the form of the Triumvirate had lost its prominence through the inevitable years, there was an almost middle-aged gang to succeed it, and all the leading names were already well-known ones. It was otherwise with the amateurs. Here three new players arrived with a bang. Ernest Holderness (now Sir Ernest) was not indeed quite new for he had been known as a good golfer on the Oxford side just before the war, and by 1920 he was 30 thirty years old; but he was new in the higher circles. Cyril Tolley and Roger Wethered, born respectively in 1896 and 1899, were brand new. Another post-war player, W. I. Hunter, won the second Championship after the war and might well have disputed their pre-eminence if he had not gone to America and turned a professional; but, as it was, it is hardly too much to say that these three, all Oxford golfers, to a great extent dominated amateur golf for the first four or five years after the war and remained outstanding figures in it for a long time afterwards. It was not that all the pre-war players were decrepit and done for. Very far from it, for Robert Harris was presently to win the Championship and so was Michael Scott, at the mature age of 54. There were plenty of others who could still play well, but the new school of amateurs had emphatically arrived and taken first place.

Holderness was, as has been said, of a pre-war vintage, and one can best compare him in the quality of his game with the great pre-war amateurs. He was not enormously long or

C. J. H. Tolley

R. Burton

Walter Hagen

gifted with any vast power, but he was long enough to keep going with anybody and he was extremely straight and accurate. One never expected to see him hit a huge shot, but neither did one ever expect to see him hit a crooked one. He might have been a product of the Hoylake school, I do not mean in style, but in the power of consistently accurate play such as marked the three great Hoylake amateurs. He might almost be called an old-fashionèd golfer in contrast to the young post-war players who had immense power and hit the ball the most astonishing distances, but now and again for no ascertainable reason hit it astonishingly crooked.

Am I fanciful in thinking that there was one unaccountable difference between the older and the newer amateurs? If the older players hit a particularly long shot it was as a rule also a particularly straight one: they had hit the ball particularly well and clean, they had timed it perfectly and so it went both far and sure. On the other hand some players who arose after the war could hit the ball apparently quite clean and quite true and make it travel the most unconscionable distance, just as far as their straightest but this time in a direction very far from that intended. I can find no explanation of this phenomenon that entirely satisfies me. It is true that the further men hit the ball the more glaring will seem their occasional errors and the further will the ball go into the rough. It is conversely true that through advancing age and shortness a player may get a fallacious reputation for accuracy, because he can scarcely hit far enough to reach the rough. Again it may be truly said that the best players hit harder at the ball than their predecessors. There has, I take it, been an increasing scale of hard hitting at golf ever since the days of Allan Robertson whom we should doubtless think today, if he could be revived for our benefit, a very gentle player. There is a well-known story of the late Ted Ray being asked by an aspiring pupil how he could learn to hit the ball further. "Hit it a —— sight harder, mate," was Ray's answer. This advice has been followed by a younger generation, and the harder a player hits the more prone he is, I suppose, to occasional aberration. Yet when all is said there remains for me a little mystery unexplained. Have the younger players discovered some new method of hitting that was unknown to all but a very few of their predecessors? Is it simply that they hit harder? Is it the devil that lurks within the jerkin of the modern ball and only responds to blows of uncompromising vigour, so that the gap between the long and the ordinarily respectable driver becomes, as it unquestionably does, much greater than of old? I cannot answer any of these questions as I should like. All that remains clear is that, allowing for the despairing exaggeration of age, youth does nowadays hit the ball a prodigious distance.

This may seem an irrelevant disquisition but it is not wholly so, for Tolley and Wethered were the first and most conspicuous champions of the new generation and they conspicuously possessed its quality of hitting the ball very hard and very far and on occasions not very straight. Why Cyril Tolley should ever hit a ball anything but straight has puzzled many who have gazed with envy on that apparently perfect swing, so smooth, so round, so, if I may thus express it, well-oiled and having so admirable a rhythm. "Majestic" has long been the stock epithet, now grown somewhat hackneyed, to apply to his demeanour and his general game. It has always been appropriate to his full swing. In fact year in and year out he has been a very fine driver, and if so much power must lead to occasional wanderings, probably too much importance has been attributed to them.

Roger Wethered's case has been rather different. He has equally great power and a full wooden club shot of his possesses a reverberating crack such as I almost fancy I could tell among those of a hundred players; but during much of his eminently successful career he has had to struggle hard against errors of direction in his driving. When he first appeared on the Oxford side these errors were scarcely noticeable and I believe Arthur Croome, a very acute observer, deserves the credit of first scenting their possibilities. Someone asked him his opinion of the new player; he answered in terms of the highest praise and then added, "He'll always be apt to have trouble with his wooden clubs." He was a true prophet. Wethered has done all manner of fine things to which his magnificent iron play, his admirable temperament and his—to the other man—heart-breaking power of recovery have all contributed, but it has always been the wooden clubs that have made these miracles of retrieving necessary and there are limits even to recovery. Why the driver has been so

fickle (the brassey has been a more faithful ally) is a problem
that has puzzled the best golfing brains most anxious to help.
If I, having no such pretensions, had to make a guess, I should
say that being so great an iron player he fell into a habit of
playing his wooden clubs too much as if they were irons.   It
used to be a maxim of Mr. Laidlay's that "Once you begin to
swing an iron you go wrong ".   Whether or not it was sound
I am not prepared to say, but is not its exact converse true of
wooden clubs?   However, these are too deep waters.   Enough
that he did sometimes drive crooked, and if he had not—well,
what would have happened to all the other golfers?

It is almost inevitable to compare these two fine players
because they were at first so constantly bracketed together in
any golfing discussion.   They went up to Oxford and played
two years together for the Oxford side; and they were great
friends and so were constantly seen in one another's company.
It was natural to compare them, and their supporters were apt
to indulge in long and rotatory arguments as to their respective
merits, even as in another walk of life men used to argue, so
we are told, about Dickens and Thackeray.   These arguments
as to which was the better on his best day lacked valuable
data because they were seldom opposed to one another on
any public occasion, and when they were it seemed fated that
one or other should be emphatically not at his best.   The
goddess who presides over the draw seemed to keep them
asunder.   I think I have only seen them meet twice; on the
first occasion one of them won by about 7 and 6 and on the
next the other won by 6 and 5.   Together one might see them
play as a successful foursome combination in Walker Cup
matches, but the single combat so often looming in the distance
scarcely ever materialised.

If I am to venture on any detailed comparison I should
say that Tolley was always and unquestionably the finer
driver alike in method and result.   Wethered equally beyond
question, was the better iron player; he was both very powerful
and very accurate and he had what in another game would
be called great power of cue; he had a wonderful capacity for
stopping the ball on the green, and a natural liking for playing
any kind of shot with the maximum of back-spin.   Among
those legendary figures who are supposed to be able to make
the ball screw back from the pitch he would take a high place,

35

and to play with him on a garden course, consisting of the maximum of hazard and the minimum of green, was something of a revelation. In point of putting the popular vote would at first have been certainly in Tolley's favour and that rightly. His was always a smooth and caressing stroke and yet a bold one; he had a capacity for holing long putts which was made the more impressive by a habit of walking after the still moving ball with a view to picking it out. Occasionally the ball disobeyed this imperious behest but very often it submitted. In time, however, Wethered caught him up in the putting owing, I believe, to a lesson from Francis Ouimet on the value of the stiff or at any rate the firm left wrist. He became day in and day out a very good putter indeed, not perhaps of the "sensational" order but, what was more important, one very unlikely to have a bad day.

Temperament is always a delicate subject specially if it is that of one's friends. I will only say this much in contrasting these two. Tolley's confident and "majestic" air has disguised from many people the fact that he is a highly-strung player who can suffer agonies; further that these agonies most often beset him against an adversary whom he ought comfortably enough to beat. He had the power to rise to the great occasion against a foeman really worthy of his steel and that was the time to see him at his best, whereas he was apt to allow too many loop-holes to opponents who were by comparison pygmies. Wethered was more phlegmatic in this matter, regarding each opponent simply as one to be beaten if possible without regard to that opponent's reputation one way or the other. So at least I read the riddle.

Holderness's game differed from that of these two, who are inevitably named together, in various ways, some very difficult to define and some easy. Among the latter is the fact that he had much less time in which to play, being a busy Civil Servant, by contrast with care-free undergraduates. Yet whereas they sometimes played as if they were out of practice he seldom if ever did, nor do I think that in his keenest years he ever was materially out of practice in the sense that he always made time to keep in familiar touch with his clubs, and to play a few shots, if it was only with a soft ball indoors. Another difference perhaps more apparent than real was that Holderness lacked the physique of the other two.

He certainly was not so big and strong but I can think of hardly any player who gave a greater impression of being wiry. His very waggle, without being flamboyant, was essentially athletic. When I watched him I often thought of Abraham Gray in beloved *Treasure Island*, who, as he tested it, made his cutlass sing through the air. He was, I am sure, a very great deal stronger than he looked and his ball had a capacity for ranging itself to all intents and purposes alongside the apparently unapproachable swipe which elicits the tribute of a long-drawn "oh". He was a very good iron player indeed and he became gradually a very good putter. It may be fancy but I think his putting improved from the day on which he gave up that last look at the hole in which most players indulge, and struck at once after grounding his club behind the ball.

In his manner of playing he affected a rather bleak detachment from the world and had clearly great power of concentration. His confidence as a match player perceptibly increased with his successes. The way in which at one time he won the President's Putter at Rye almost as a matter of course—he won for four years running—was a great testimony to his match-playing powers, and when at last in 1924 he was beaten by O. C. Bristowe in an early round it hardly seemed credible to those struggling on other parts of the course. It may be a wholly fantastic suggestion but I have always thought that one putt, by somebody else, gave Holderness just the little fillip he wanted to carry him to the highest honours. At Prestwick in 1922 he met in the semi-final W. I. Hunter, then the holder of the Championship and looking very likely to win it again. Going to the fifteenth hole, the first of the famous Loop, Hunter was one up and he had a putt of a yard or so, perhaps four feet, to win the hole and be two up and three to play. He was playing with the greatest confidence and perhaps he struck that putt a little too boldly, but it seemed impish and malignant in the ball to hit the tin and come back in such a way as to leave its owner with a dead stymie. There were those who said the hole was badly cut; I have no evidence whatever to that effect, but there was the stymie; Hunter lost the hole which one brief moment before had seemed more than half in his pocket, and all square at the fifteenth is a very different thing from two up. Holderness took his chance and won the match, as he also won the final next day against John Caven, and I think from the moment that putt of Hunter's came leaping out the hole, he became a permanently stronger and more confident golfer.

Out of the first five Championships after the war this amateur Triumvirate won four, Tolley in 1920, Holderness in 1922 and 1924, Wethered in 1923. Of these the most dramatic victory was Tolley's. It had all the ingredients of excitement; the winner himself had but lately burst on the world, and though of course older than the average freshman, for he was a warrior with the Military Cross, had not yet quite finished his first year at Oxford. Moreover he had the honour of his country to defend again in the final against an American invader, R. A. Gardner. There was a considerable number of American entrants that year, for a party of delegates—I think that was what they were called—had come over for the discussion of golfing politics. They all entered for the Championship, but most of them in a spirit of light-hearted frolic and one of them was rather ruthlessly beaten 10 and 8. Incidentally there entered two young golfers destined afterwards to be famous professionals in America, Tommy Armour and Bobby Cruikshank, but they were Scottish amateurs then and Gardner was the sole foreign menace. He was very young as political delegates go and was a golfer to be taken with all seriousness; he had won the American Amateur Championship when hardly more than a boy in 1909, and had reached the final again in 1916. He was an exceptional all-round athlete, having held the pole-jumping record of the world and won the double rackets championship of America. He had not quite the beautiful golfing swing we connect with American amateurs; it was rather the style of one who can hit any kind of ball well, but there was no doubt he could hit a golf ball very well. When at the beginning of the tournament he was only one out of a field of 165 his chances were perhaps too lightly esteemed, but he went on quietly winning, and by the time he had beaten first Gordon Lockhart and then Michael Scott in the semi-final there was no question about our acute peril.

Tolley too had been playing very well; only Cruikshank had pushed him hard and he was playing moreover with great discretion. Muirfield has comparatively narrow fairways with very definite rough, though not so tenacious as it once was, on either hand, and Tolley finding his driver a little unruly had kept the ball in play and hit it quite far enough with his spoon. All the other memories of this final fade away before those of the last four holes which were agonising beyond words, and the thirty-seventh, which brought relief and joy. Tolley had progressed steadily towards victory till he became three up with four to play. Muirfield has since been altered, but many will remember the old fifteenth, an admirable drive-and-pitch hole, with a difficult approach shot to a green with a bunker behind it. Gardner played the odd, and as I remember it, only reached the edge of the green so that he would have to putt well to get his four. There seemed a reasonable chance that our man would win by 4 and 3 for he had hit a fine tee shot. Rightly he hardened his heart to be up, but he hardened it a little too much; over went the ball into the bunker behind. That hole was lost for the ball lay badly in the bunker, and so was the sixteenth. Down to one. Tolley played the seventeenth well and got his four and his half, both players holing out bravely, and the rot had been momentarily stopped; but at the home hole Tolley pushed his drive out a little and got a poor lie. Gardner always played that hole well, with a push cleek shot for his second, and he got his impeccable four. All square and on to the thirty-seventh. The first was then a one-shot hole and Gardner put his ball on the green, a little to the left but a fine shot at a crisis and a very nasty one to follow. I remember losing sight of Tolley's ball in the air and crying out wildly for information. The ball supplied it by coming plump down on the green, dead straight, perhaps four yards or so short of the hole.

Here was a situation—I have made the comparison before but will make it again—resembling that at the thirty-seventh hole in the famous Prestwick final between John Ball and Freddie Tait. A fine iron shot on to the green had been countered by one still better; the relative distances from the hole were much the same and so were the strokes that ensued. Gardner, like Tait, played in the circumstances a truly excellent approach putt and laid the ball virtually dead. Tolley played the part of John Ball to perfection; he walked straight up to his ball and hit it straight in. There are always

39

legends about historic shots and there is one about this putt, of which I will not guarantee the truth though I honestly believe it to be true. Tolley had provided himself with a five-pound note to give his caddie in case of victory. Before playing this putt he took it out of his pocket and handed it to him.

In 1921 the Championship went to a very fine golfer, Willie Hunter, and I shall come back to him, but at the moment I am dealing with my particular trinity, and Holderness was the next of them to win at Prestwick in 1922. I have talked of that putt at the fifteenth hole there, which, to my mind, made all the difference to Ernest Holderness, even the difference possibly between a champion and one who never quite won. That was to my mind the important point at Prestwick and not the final between Holderness and Caven, though it was a very good one in which both men stuck to it admirably to the end. The way in which one after the other holed an eminently missable putt on the thirty-sixth green was most inspiriting and John Caven showed himself a brave and excellent player.

Perhaps in looking back it suffers a little in interest because in the following year we had the Americans down upon us in force for the first Walker Cup match in this country and though the match was lost the Championship was not. 1923 is likewise a notable year in my memory because I hold that no one who did not watch that Championship has seen quite the best Roger Wethered. That is a strong thing to say considering all that he has done and won, and especially considering that he had two years before tied for the Open Championship, but I shall continue to maintain it, even as I say that Tolley's best achievement has never been in our Amateur Championship, but in twice winning the French Open against a field of professional talent. That was the truest measure of the highest quality.

Turning over an old scrap-book I chanced the other day on an article I had written at the time for an American magazine. It seems now a little ecstatic and perhaps it was, but at any rate it represented what a lot of other people as well as I thought at the time. We believed that even as Braid had gone to bed a short driver and woken up a long one, Roger had gone to bed a rather crooked driver and had woken up a faultlessly straight one for evermore. In fact that was a partially delusive hope, but by re-reading my rather flamboyant remarks I am confirmed in my recollection that he did drive most magnificently at Deal. He looked easier and he played more easily; he did not seem to be trying to hit at all hard but he hit the ball as far as any human being could want and with great accuracy. For that week and for some little time afterwards the whole secret of driving, whatever it may be, had been revealed to him. In that same article I quoted a remark of his sister's which I had completely forgotten. She having for the only time in her life been beaten in the semi-final of a Ladies' Championship, had travelled all through the night from Burnham to Deal and—such at any rate is my story—after watching her brother play a hole or two she exclaimed, "Why, this is a new Roger!"

Apart from his great long game he had become a better putter than ever before, a step forward from which there was no going back, and as he had always been an iron player of the first water, the combination of all these gifts was terrifying indeed. It was an altogether outstanding display of the kind of golf that beats the other man down and does not allow him to play his game against it. Robert Harris played quite well, in the ordinary sense of the words, against Roger in the final, but he came near to being crushed; his opponent was too good and there was no more to be said about it.

The really exciting match—excitement only flared up for some three holes but was desperate while it lasted—was in the semi-final between Wethered and Francis Ouimet. Ouimet had played beautifully up to the green in the morning against Tolley and had holed most of the putts when he got there. In the afternoon he was just about as good up to the green but he did not hole the putts. As a result Wethered was four up with five to play; he was on the green at the short four-teenth and Ouimet was not; 5 and 4 seemed a probable ending and then the horrid fun began. Ouimet laid a masterly chip dead and Roger took three putts; down to three. At the fifteenth Roger was bunkered and Ouimet this time holed a chip; down to two. At the sixteenth Ouimet with his enemy on the lip and having only half a hole to go for, was in and out with his putt for the hole. It was out, how-ever, and with that the strain was over; Wethered made no mistake and got his half and the match at the seventeenth. It had been a hot burst while it lasted.

Holderness's second win was not the last win for this unofficial triumvirate, but it was the last for some time since Tolley did not win his second Championship till five years later at Sandwich. Meanwhile I must go back a little to an interesting Championship of 1921 and a very good and interesting player who won it, W. I. Hunter. A year or so later he disappeared to America and became a professional. If he had stayed at home he would, humanly speaking, have been one of the outstanding amateurs for some time. He came of a good golfing family and had a grand golfing education, for he was the son of Harry Hunter, a professional affectionately remembered by all who played at Deal. So all his boyhood's golf had been on that course, as fine a school as could be imagined. He had something of the indefinable professional touch about his game, especially in the crispness and firmness of his iron play. His swing was rather a short one; he was not outstandingly long though quite long enough, and all his shots, played with refreshing quickness, dash and confidence, proclaimed him a golfer. He had done well, as I remember, at Muirfield for several rounds and then came down with rather a bump, but at Hoylake in the following year he had clearly made a stride forward and was more sure of himself and his game. It was not in the least odd that Hunter should win that Championship for he was playing very good golf, but nearly everything else about it was odd. The ground was very hard and fast; the shorter drivers were helped in reaching the long Hoylake holes in two, but only he who had the touch of his putter absolutely true could hope to get down at all regularly in two putts when he had reached those icy greens. It was a state of things likely to produce unexpected results, and it did from the very start. The Americans had just trounced our men in the international match and were supposed to be going to carry all before them. Yet almost at once they began to disappear. Cyril Tolley set the good example; he had beaten Chick Evans in the international and now he beat Jesse Guilford. He did not long survive, but he had begun the good work which was enthusiastically taken up. Hodgson, a good little golfer from Yorkshire, though perhaps hardly powerful enough for so big a course, putted like an angel and beat Ouimet. Evans and Fownes had by bad luck to meet each other; Fownes won and so another most alarming invader had gone. Then came the most resounding crash of all. Bobby Jones after struggling through an absurd game with Hamlet, had recovered himself and played brilliantly against Robert Harris. He seemed immensely dangerous when he relapsed again and, in his own words, "A genial, sandy-haired gentleman, Allan Graham, fairly beat me to death with a queer brass putter." The words admirably describe the event, for Allan won by 6 and 5 and he was by all accounts holing most things. Allan Graham was not in the class of his brother Jack and had, for one brought up in a classical school, rather a loose and straggling swing; but he was a naturally good player of ball games; he had, unlike Jack, an ideally placid temperament, and he was a magnificent putter. He hit the ball so smoothly with that crook-necked putter of gun-metal (I have never seen one cast in the same mould) that in certain moods he would follow through in a long putt so that the club-head would end over his left shoulder as in a full shot. He did not take golf too seriously but at the same time had plenty of resolution. Having beaten Bobby so surprisingly, he played most of the afternoon round in a happy post-prandial dream. Towards the end he enquired of his caddie —this was his own story—how the match stood, and finding that he was, I think, two up with four to play against Hezlet, declared that in that case he had better go on and win. He did win accordingly and contrived to win till he reached the final.

Meanwhile the disintegration of the American team had continued. In the last sixteen there were only two, Paul Hunter and Fred Wright, feeling no doubt a little lonely, and Hunter lost. Next morning Wright was beaten likewise and the terror was surprisingly over. W. I. Hunter had not chanced to meet any of the invaders and so his career had not been noticed, but he was playing very well, as I know to my cost, and by the time he reached the final he was marked out for the Championship. Allan Graham had played the week's golf under the stress of a great private anxiety over his father's illness and he was tired out one day too soon. He could not hold up over thirty-six holes against Hunter, who murdered

43

him with professional precision by a vast number of holes.

Hunter was emphatically a worthy champion and he showed it later in the summer in the American Amateur Championship at St. Louis when he beat Bobby Jones, who had been going great guns, by 2 and 1 over thirty-six holes. He beat him by sheer doggedness too, hanging on and on till his opponent grew worried by not being able to draw away, with the inevitable result. Hunter was playing very well again at Prestwick in 1922, as I said in describing that match of his with Holderness, and then came the end of his amateur career. He had not, I suppose, quite the power to keep up with the big professionals in America, but he was a thoroughly good golfer.

1926 at St. Andrews did not, as I recall it, provide anything quite on a par with Wethered's golf at Deal, but it did provide Holderness with the opportunity of winning for the second time in three years which only an exceptional player can do. If his win at Prestwick had been a little bit of a surprise there was no surprise this time; it seemed a perfectly natural thing to happen, which is probably why it has left no very abiding memories. His opponent in the final was Eustace Storey, still in his fourth year at Cambridge, and I have an oddly clear vision of him looking very wet and bedraggled, for it was an odiously rainy final, and wearing a tie of light blue and white stripes. If that was a challenge to Oxford it was unsuccessful, but he made a hard fight of it and only lost by 3 and 2. Storey was not then, I think, quite such a good golfer as he was a few years later and certainly not so long a driver, but he was perhaps at his best as a putter. He had perfected his unique stance, with the ball at his right toe and his left foot tucked away behind his right in apparent anguish, and much regular practice on the floor of his rooms at Cambridge had made him as nearly dead at five or six feet as it is ever given to fallible man to be.

Chapter 5

THE PASSING OF A GENERATION

*" How for everything there is a time and a season, and then how does the
glory of a thing pass from it, even like the flower of the grass."*

IT is always hard to put ourselves into other people's places
and enter into their feelings, and perhaps it is never harder
than in imagining that those who are young now feel much
the same and with the same intensity as we did when we
were in their case. Thus, strive as I will, I cannot wholly
convince myself that young golfers of today stare with quite
such reverential eyes at Mr. Tolley and Mr. Wethered as I
did when, as a small boy, I first beheld Mr. Mure Fergusson
and Mr. Horace Hutchinson, or, at a later date, Mr. John
Ball and Mr. Laidlay. I accept it as a fact that they do,
but there is this to be said for my doubts, that once upon
a time there were fewer of these heroic figures among the
amateurs and that therefore they seemed to stand out in the
more towering grandeur.

I am thinking particularly of those in the earlier days of
the Amateur Championship in the middle eighties, even
before the time of two players, then boys of 15 or 16, whose
names were within a few years to become very famous, Harold
Hilton and Freddie Tait. There was a small and select body
at the top of the tree amounting, appropriately, to the sacred
number of seven : Mr. John Ball, Mr. Horace Hutchinson,
Mr. J. E. Laidlay, Mr. Leslie Balfour-Melville (then Balfour),
Mr. S. Mure Fergusson, Mr. Alexander Stuart and Mr.
A. F. Macfie. All survived till more than half-way through
the period between wars, and I never cease to wonder that
it can be really true that with the first five of them, I, *moi
qui vous parle*, played in the first international match between
England and Scotland. It still seems to me a monstrous
presumption, a piece of incredible growing up. Nearly all
have now departed, but one, I am glad to say, remains.
Mr. 'Andy' Stuart, who played with Horace for Oxford in
the first University match, is today the *Ultimus Romanorum*.

He is, as Borrow wrote of Tom Spring, "the last of all that strong family still above the sod", and long may he be so! This was a mighty band of amateur golfers, and since they were my first and greatest heroes, and I came to know them all, I must pay them a humble tribute.

The seven were not of course of an exactly equal degree of merit. Their names may be bracketed together, but there are brackets within brackets. It is written in Horace's book of memories that the late Sir Alexander Kinloch once exclaimed at a general meeting of the Royal and Ancient: "What's the good of all this talk about first-class players? There are only three first-class amateurs, Johnny Ball, Johnny Laidlay and Horace Hutchinson." That was plain speaking with a vengeance and it did something less than justice to the other four, but it had in it this much truth that those three were the best. When I used to talk to Horace about his early days he always assumed this as a fact, just as he also assumed that Johnny Ball at his best occupied a solitary pinnacle, a verdict which history will unquestionably endorse. Since no feelings can now be hurt, I may add that next to those three he put Mr. Stuart. These things are matters of opinion; Mr. Stuart retired earlier from the game than did the others and his achievements are not so imposing, but I put Horace's view on record as an interesting one which might otherwise be lost. I like to do so too because Mr. Stuart's name occurs in a passage from the old Badminton volume on the St Andrews swingers which, as a boy, I knew by heart, and now copy out from mere sensual pleasure: "O duffer! ill will it fare with you if you strive to emulate their supple elasticity. This is but the fruit of a boyhood spent golf club in hand. Swing with their young insolent fearlessness—it is but a caricature. . . . Look rather at Mr. Alexander Stuart. . . . His is a free long supple swing, indeed, but formed upon quieter methods. There is more repose—less fascinating dash, may-be; but more apparent absence of effort. His is the safer style for your model."

Let us take the seven in order of their Amateur Championships, and first comes Mr. Allan Fullarton Macfie, the first champion, who died quite lately when well advanced in the eighties. The tournament which he won at Hoylake in 1885, beating Horace by a surprising number of holes in the final, was not at the time called a championship, though it was so in the quality of the entrants. It was only by a graceful act on the part of the Championship Committee that he was retrospectively canonised as the first champion. It was in that character that he sat on the platform when the Walker Cup was handed to the British captain, unable to hear a sound of all the tumult and cheering, since he was quite deaf, but smiling pleasantly and perfectly well aware of the references made to him.

It is one of the regrets of my golfing life that I never saw Mr. Macfie play. By the time that I went at all regularly to St. Andrews, where he lived for the latter part of his life, he had practically given up the game, and I never saw him do more than take a walk with a single iron and chip casually at a daisy as he went along. By all accounts he must have been as accurate a player as ever lived, for he was light and slightly built and, though wiry enough no doubt, never possessed any great power. He used to asseverate most solemnly that never in his life had he been over the Swilcan burn in two at the first hole. Perhaps this was not strictly true but he was thinking, I imagine, of gutty days when the carrying of the burn in two was a much greater feat than people can now believe. At the best of times then he was not long, but he was appallingly straight and the Badminton credits him with hitting full wooden club shots up to the seventeenth green, which is certainly a test of straightness. Not only was he the most accurate of players but he is also generally deemed to have been the most energetic and scientific of all practisers, his only possible rival among amateurs in that respect being, I suppose, Mr. Walter Travis. The story is well known how he used to practise at Hoylake in the gathering dusk, so that when the caddies found the links strewn with balls next morning, like so many magically arisen mushrooms, they always knew that Mr. Macfie had been out the night before. His great accuracy and also, I have no doubt, his habit of practising, extended to his putting, for he was famous in his day as a putter. The pictures of him show him standing with the ball far back, almost behind his right toe, but he was a player of changing moods, theories and attitudes, and declared that he putted on a new principle every day. He had theories about everything to do with golf including clubs,

47

being skilled in the use of tools and sometimes making his own club heads. By the kindness of his niece I now possess one or two specimens of his art and also a curious driver that he had made to his order with a bamboo shaft.

As Mr. Macfie grew older he became more and more an affectionately regarded 'character' at St. Andrews. His high voice with its tone of gentle lamentation was a test or diploma piece for all the budding mimics in the club. Though he had early in life become stone deaf, through, I believe, a fall from a horse, he was an expert lip-reader and conversation with him was as easy as it was pleasant. Indeed he was so skilful that he would now and then pretend to confuse one word, which he had read perfectly well, for another similar to it, a proceeding which suited a rather impish and mischievous sense of humour. Thus on a pompous gentleman whom he disliked, saying that he was going to put his son into the diplomatic service, Mr. Macfie is alleged to have answered, "Domestic Service?", and then, having expressed his approval of the choice, to have passed serenely on his way. There was in his voice, as I said, a perpetual suggestion of mourning and this was mingled with scorn as he spoke of some new thing in golf which displeased him; but, though strongly conservative, he remained always interested and ready to watch and to admire what was admirable. Any gap in a comparatively small community such as that of St. Andrews seems perhaps disproportionately large, but, whether or no, Mr. Macfie's place is one that nobody else can possibly fill.

In 1886 the Amateur Championship was officially founded; the tournament was played that year at St. Andrews and in 1887 at Hoylake, Mr. Horace Hutchinson winning each time, in the first year by the length of the street against Mr. Henry Lamb, in the second after a battle of Titans against Mr. John Ball. He never won again, but many years later in 1903 he strolled on to Muirfield to play his first round in the Championship after no preliminary practice and went right through to the final, when he found Mr. Maxwell, as did other people, rather too good. It was given to Horace to be something of a pioneer. He was the first Amateur Champion, until that place was awarded to Mr. Macfie many years after the event; he was the first Englishman to be Captain of the Royal and Ancient; he was the first good player to write regularly about golf and to do so with skill and style. Thus from his early days he was essentially a leader and a notable and picturesque one, whose name was more widely known to the outside world than that of any other golfer except Mr. Arthur Balfour.

After his two championship victories, at the ages of 27 and 28, he was hardly seen so much perhaps as were some of his chief rivals. For one reason his health was never robust and for another he had many interests and many friends outside the golfing world. So though a great figure in that world he was never, in my recollection, quite of it, and there was about his appearances in the field something of a god stepping down from Olympus to visit the earth. This suggestion was enhanced by his aloof and fastidious nature, which made him a greatly admired rather than a popular or familiar personage. Under this slightly distant aspect there was not only a wonderful charm of manner but, as it well befits me to say, great friendliness and kindness of heart. This his many friends knew well; so, I think, did many whose only acquaintance with him was through his books, but the golfing crowd did not to my mind wholly understand him.

Horace wrote so much and that not only about golf, always pleasantly and with a sense of humour, sometimes a little casually and hurriedly with his small, stumpy pencil, sometimes also with real grace and charm, that people nowadays are apt, as I jealously fancy, to think too much of him as a generally noteworthy figure and not enough of him as a very fine and accomplished golfer and one, moreover, that was very unlike any other. The pictures in the Badminton book, which were drawn from photographs not instantaneous but deliberately posed, do no kind of justice to a style that was hardly a model for other people but most attractive in itself. They greatly exaggerate the much criticised lift of the right elbow; indeed they deceived him himself on this point; they convey little either of his artistry or his almost bombastic freedom and dash. He was essentially loose and flexible, judged by normal standards too flexible; he held his club loosely and in certain shots such as his high pitches would let the club 'flop' into the web at the base of a thumb with, to quote his own words again, a "young, insolent fearlessness". Nobody had a freer, looser wrist in putting and he was generally, though not invariably, a very fine putter. His strongest point was, however, his skill and ingenuity in every form of recovering shot in which that free and not rigidly "grooved" swing was a great help to him.   In the Badminton is a drawing called "A champion in difficulties", which represents Horace contemplating with some dismay a ball teed up in the branches of a small tree.   If anybody could have got that ball out he could, for his shots from such un-promising places seemed to his disconcerted adversary in the nature of witchery.   When I knew his game best, it was always possible that he would miss the easy, bread-and-butter shot, because he was tired or mildly bored or out of practice; but set him, in a favourite phrase of Mr. John Ball's, to scratch his head, and as far as success was possible he never failed.

Horace's was not an easy or serene temperament.   He knew this well himself and so had a kindly sympathy, as again it befits me to say, with others who grew cross over their game. He perhaps played his best in a state of cold, restrained anger. Once he was roused he was, I think it not unfair to say, an essentially hostile golfer.   He had been brought up in a school of fierce singles against the comparatively few really dangerous opponents of his day, between whom there was a more than suspected touch of jealousy.   They were very good friends but they did not at all like being beaten by each other.   "I'm a very disappointed man," said Mr. Laidlay after a match at Muirfield, when he and his opponent were both past their prime.   "I knew I was no good now, but I thought I could beat poor old Horace."   The fire of ancient rivalry had flamed up again in those words, spoken as they were with a rueful smile.   The school had been a hard and a good one and had made of Horace a most resolute match player, always capable of putting in a desperate thrust at a crucial instant. Such was a certain niblick shot laid nearly dead out of the bunker at the nineteenth hole at Sandwich against Mr. Maxwell in 1904.   Equally typical was the fact that in the afternoon against Mr. Travis he was a palpably exhausted man.   Fine as his record was, it would have contained many more victories but for the ill health which dogged him.   It was while we were waiting to watch the start of that afternoon match that an American friend, pointing at Mr. Travis, said to me in solemn tones: "You may not believe it but this man is one of the great golfers."   So was Horace Hutchinson.

Next came Mr. John Ball, "a player", to quote a fine tortuous sentence from John Nyren, "between whom and all other comparison must fail". If I write less about him than about some others it is because so much has been said so often, and I am conscious of having said a good deal of it. The beauty of any particular player's style must, like his exact place in the golfing firmament, be a matter of individual feeling, and I can only say that I have derived greater aesthetic and emotional pleasure from watching Mr. Ball than from any other spectacle in any game. Beyond all question his was a very beautiful style, round, smooth and rhythmic, with a big turn of the body so utterly unforced that, as in the case of Bobby Jones, at a first glance it escaped attention. Some very fine players have a big turn of the body but it is in the nature of a wrench and is instantly perceptible. Mr. Ball's looked, and no doubt was, a perfectly natural movement and it ran through his whole game. Once upon a time it was deemed immoral to swing an iron club; the stroke was to be more in the nature of a hit. "As soon as you begin to swing an iron you go wrong" was a dictum of Mr. Laidlay, a very great iron player. John, likewise tremendous with iron clubs, always seemed to me to have more of swing in his iron shots than any other of his contemporaries and it gave them an added attraction.

The trueness of his swing was a prop and stay in many of those close finishes for which he was famous, and which he seemed almost to enjoy. It is curious to recall that in his earliest days he lacked the power of doing himself justice on the big occasion, and was the despair of his Hoylake friends, who rightly thought unutterable things of him. This period did not last long; once he had tasted success he never looked back, and became more and more famous as the man for a forlorn hope. Yet he could be quite humanly nervous and I have seen him about to play a nineteenth hole at Hoylake when his fingers almost refused their office in tearing the paper off a new ball. Yet at the very same hole he hit a brassey shot (I remember how he always pronounced that word with a short *a*) of the most dazzling quality right up to the pin. He could not swing the club otherwise than well, and this, combined with a silent dogged resolution, pulled him successfully out of all manner of desperate situations.

I was too young to have seen him till a little something of crushing brilliancy had gone out of his game, so that he relied rather on a lovely and almost monotonous accuracy. He had been the first player, before the days of J. H. Taylor, to set up a new standard in playing long shots straight up to the pin, and this power stayed with him wonderfully, though the shots might not be quite so long nor hit with quite so much dash. As he grew older he became in a sense rather a lazy player in that he was difficult to rouse at the start of a match and wanted the incentive of a hole or two down. Yet now and again he could be stirred into ferocious action from the start. In one championship that he won at Hoylake he had. to meet quite early a comparatively young golfer. John was as a rule very merciful to the young, but this particular player had said or done something to annoy him and John went out obviously meaning venom and murdered the offender. He had in him, as a good match player must, a strong vein of hostility and if he wanted a particular player's blood he would fight his way through a tournament with the sole object of getting at him. That was not a personal hostility but rather a desire to measure himself against a foeman really worthy of him. It was a trait on which his adoring supporters used sometimes to play adroitly in order to awake in him the pugnacious mood they wanted.

John was a fine instinctive judge of golfers with an almost cruelly high standard; if he could be induced to express an opinion, it was apparent that he "reckoned"—his own word— only a select few. I think he was a good judge of men, and here also he had an austere standard. He once saw a man, a very fine player, commit an act of which he did not approve. What it was I do not know for he merely spoke of it as something not to be named, but he declared from that moment that one who could so demean himself could never win a championship, a prophecy which proved true. His whole conception of the game was austere, for he wanted it as difficult as possible with no concessions to weaker brethren. Raked bunkers, which he called "geranium beds", roused him to articulate anger and in his heart I think he would have liked to see fairways some twenty-five yards wide flanked by hayfields. This sounds very grim and there was a grim side to his reserved nature, but at the same time there was no one more delightful to play with in any form of game, particularly a foursome, which he did not deem important.   Then he unbent wonderfully and revealed a sense of humour which, had he been a Scotsman, would have been called 'pawky', endeavouring to undermine the enemy's *moral* by small, sly jokes.   Even so he would suddenly bestir himself with disastrous effect to the other side. "Now," said one of his adversaries who had become dormy two in a four-ball match, "Now you'll see John save his half-crown," and he did so accordingly with a three and a four. That is only one mild little story from among the numberless ones, most of them too well known for repetition, that grew up round his name.   No man ever came to be more of a legend in his own lifetime, and this was the more remarkable because to most people he scarcely opened his lips.   What he did say had some quality of sticking in men's minds, particularly in the hero-worshipping minds of Hoylake.   Somewhere deep down in him there was, I suppose, a liking for being a hero, but the only outward sign of it was in a reserve bordering on shyness, and an appearance of wanting to run away if anyone made as if to speak to him.   The last time I met him was on one day of the Amateur Championship at Hoylake shortly before this war, when he came over from Wales to look on, hid himself as far as possible, talked to a few friends and vanished swiftly away afterwards.   I wondered, and still wonder, whether he was thinking at all of his past glories.

Next come Mr. Laidlay and Mr. Balfour-Melville, and I put them together not only because they were the two most conspicuous Scottish amateurs of their day, but for a purely personal reason.   One of the most amusing things I ever saw, though I do not hope to convey the fun of it, was in an Ayrshire garden where, Mr. Balfour-Melville being present, Mr. Laidlay gave an imitation of him playing in a big match. He fidgeted about on the tee; he shouted several loud and ferocious 'Fores' to the spectators; he turned with a sweet smile and an exaggerated gallantry to ask two imaginary ladies to stand away from behind; he returned more stormily than ever to shouting to the offenders in front; finally he topped the ball hard along the ground.   It was an admirably mischievous impersonation at which Mr. Balfour-Melville looked on, not severely, but with a slightly puzzled air, as if wondering at such frivolity.   I never fail to recall that small scene when I think

53

of the two men, both very keen golfers and utterly different
from one another; Mr. Laidlay a little puckish and incalculable with a flavour very much his own; Mr. Balfour-Melville
by comparison slow, earnest and orthodox. Mr. Laidlay was
a player of genius, a very unorthodox genius. "His miserable
imitators swarm on every links in the Lothians", wrote Sir
Walter Simpson, and never was there a player less easy to
imitate save in mere external characteristics. The ball was
almost in front of his left foot, and was addressed with the
extreme heel of the club, the feet very wide apart, the right
foot drawn far back, the club held at the very bottom of the
grip,—it would be hard to imagine an address to the ball
more entirely *sui generis*. Moreover he was the originator of a
modern orthodoxy, once deemed another eccentricity, namely,
the overlapping grip. The swing itself was not, I think,
peculiar. When he died some people who obviously knew
very little about him, wrote of his extremely short swing.
It was not a very long one, since with so wide a straddle no
one could swing the club to any great length, but it was really
to my mind a normal swing, made to appear abnormal by
the striker's stance, even as is that of a very good player of a
later generation, Major Hezlet. He was not, judged by the
severest standards, an entirely trustworthy wooden club
player, partly perhaps because he was not constantly in
practice; he had lots of other interests and odd unexpected
talents, from modelling to photographing gannets on the
Bass, and would pop up and win a medal at St. Andrews or
Muirfield or North Berwick (he had a prodigious collection
of medals) and then vanish from the links again till the next
occasion. His iron club play, on the other hand, in or out of
practice, was nearly always admirable; he had learnt pitching
on the old short course at North Berwick and till Taylor
arrived he was deemed the best of all mashie players. He was
likewise a very fine putter with a little lofted cleek, a friend of
his boyhood at Loretto, and his putts had a way of coming on
and on and dropping in when the enemy hoped that they
would be well short. Many outstanding putters boldly hit
the back of the tin, but Mr. Laidlay's was a more insinuating
method. The now disused expression 'a long steal' seemed
eminently applicable to him; there was something stealthy, as
also menacing, about the sight of him getting down to the

ball, with hands held low on the grip of that little cleek. Towards the end of his time he took to an aluminium putter which he said was an easier club to play with, and ungratefully abandoned his old comrade, but whatever he used nobody was better able, in his phrase so often quoted by East Lothian friends, to trust to a pitch and a putt.

Mr. Laidlay's two victories in the Amateur Championship came in 1889 and 1891, when he beat Mr. Ball and Mr. Hilton respectively; he also lost two finals to Mr. Ball and one to Mr. Peter Anderson at Prestwick, which he would in all human probability have won if he had not after a prosperous start gratuitously topped his second from a good lie into the Cardinal. That was in 1893, but he kept almost his best game for a long time afterwards and played regularly for Scotland from 1902 till 1911. Altogether he was a very fine and very interesting golfer—perhaps today he would be called "intriguing"—with a gift of saying odd, entertaining things.

Mr. Laidlay was, as I said, a golfer of genius. Mr. Balfour-Melville was rather one of great talent, talent for playing every kind of game, carefully and enthusiastically cultivated. His swing was as good a model as anyone could want, up-standing, firm, strong and steady with a certain air of rigidity which was compensated for by a big free follow-through. Mr. Everard prophesied that of all the leading amateurs of the eighties Mr. Balfour-Melville's style was that which promised to serve him best and longest in later life, and this forecast was on the whole well borne out. He went on playing and playing well for a long time and his simple-minded, boyish enthusiasm never deserted him; he never ceased trying experiments, one being the purchase of a peculiarly heavy driver, such as Abe Mitchell was using; he was always full of hope and did not, I think, fully realise that for some mysterious reason the ball did not go so far as it had once done; he would walk on and on still hopefully looking for it. His iron play was sound and good, his putting less so; he could indeed miss very short ones but, though he never looked very comfortable on the green, he could often putt well, as it seemed by sheer, resolute concentration. As Mr. Laidlay had hinted in his impersonation, Mr. Balfour-Melville was rather fidgety and fussy when he was playing a big match, but there was no doubt about his determination and his victory in the Championship

55

at St. Andrews in 1895 was evidence of his lasting power. In all his last three matches against those two stalwarts of the St. Andrews Club, Willie Greig and Laurence Auchterlonie, and against John Ball himself, he had to go to the nineteenth hole, and against Auchterlonie he only got so far by laying a full wooden club shot dead at the home hole. At each one of those nineteenths he pitched his third safely over the burn and the other man pitched in, a curious symmetry of ending that must have made the winner believe in some higher power.

Mr. Mure Fergusson never won the Championship though he was twice in the final, losing once at the last hole to John Ball after a match made famous for ever at Hoylake by its hero's great carry over the Dun bunker, and once, by rather a large margin to Freddie Tait. There was another which by all accounts he ought to have won, Mr. Peter Anderson's Championship at Prestwick; he was playing the best golf there until in the semi-final he was virulently attacked by gout in the toe. There always seems to me something typical about that fact. Mure was not a man to be dictated to, and if he suspected his toe the last thing he would have thought of was giving up his port wine: he would never submit to a toe; rather he would "larn" it to be a toe. Never was there a man more resolutely set in his own ways; he never, so he told me once, had played a practice shot before a round and he never would; if he was stiff and topped it, very well then he would top it. He was a fine, strong, dour golfer who could be very charming and very terrifying, but always commanded respect.

He was big and square, burly and red-faced. He might have been painted by Raeburn as one of the Senators of the College of Justice and I sometimes even fancied that there was a touch of Braxfield about him—formidable, a little over-bearing, going undeterred on his own way, with a tongue both terse and forcible. If one had never seen him play before, I think one would have expected from such a figure a rather short controlled swing. In fact it was a very long, almost exuberant one with a very free movement of the body, and an equally long follow-through. There was, however, another stroke of his, eminently characteristic and, I thought, better suited to him. This was his push shot with an iron, not the shot usually so called, but a genuine push played with a stiff wrist, a short take-back of the club and free follow-through. It was most effective, especially in a wind, and I never saw anyone else play a shot like it. It was fascinating to watch but his putting was still more so, for not only was he a fine and bold putter, but his look, as he stood up to the ball, was that of a master who would brook no disobedience from a slave; that ball had got to go in. It was written by one of the old cricketers that "his air was erect and appalling"; it might have been written of Mure.

He was a St. Andrews golfer, but his business took him to London and he played at Felixstowe, where as a small boy I first saw and trembled before him, later at Sandwich, and constantly too at New Zealand (which is Byfleet), a delightful club and course over which he ruled on totalitarian principles. The very fir trees there must have learned to obey him, for if his tee shot plunged into the woods, as it occasionally did, the trunks seemed to align themselves as if by docile magic and out came the ball, crashing its way through to the green. To think you were going to win a hole because Mure was in the trees was like entertaining similar hopes at Ashdown when Horace was in the heather; it was to dwell in a fool's paradise. He kept his fine game for a long while and won a St. Andrews medal with a particularly good score at 56, but when he grew a good deal older his back became very sore and stiff. He treated it with a fine contempt, even as he had his toe at Prestwick, taking pleasure in the game, content to accept strokes from those to whom he had once given them, grimly amused when a caddie told him he might be a good player if he could learn not to drop his shoulder. To play as he did then, humbly enjoying himself, uncomplaining as to his twinges, was surely "a sundown splendid and serene", and had a touching quality that one would not naturally have associated with him. I always wish he had won a Championship.

Finally, there is Mr. Alexander Stuart, but he might conceivably, though it is very unlikely, read what I write and moreover he had given up serious golf by the time I began to see it. I did see him play once at Muirfield against Miss Rhona Adair when he tried under protest to give her a third, and his protest proved perfectly justified. I have quoted Horace's opinion of him and it would be foolish to add anything more of my own. Let me end, however, with a little story that he told me himself on a, to me, very pleasant walk round St. Andrews. It sheds an amusing light on the past. Mr. Leslie Balfour-Melville had finished with a score deemed good enough to win the medal; Mr. Stuart was playing the seventeenth hole and had hit a good tee shot. To him appeared Leslie's younger brother, always called Itie, who announced what Leslie had done and enquired Mr. Stuart's score. Mr. Stuart, reckoning it up, answered that he had a 5 and a 4 to tie with Leslie. "Have you?" said the loyal brother. "Then I hope to God you'll top your second." The second *was* topped and the family honour was safe.

Chapter 6

THE IMMORTAL BOBBY

STILL sticking to the amateurs I come now with faltering pen to the greatest of them all. As far as the United States are concerned the Bobby Jones era began, I suppose, in 1916 when at the age of 14½ he reached the third round of the American National Championship at Merion and went down after a hard match before an ex-champion, Robert Gardner. From this time onward till he retired full of honours if not of years, he was a great figure in American golf. For us, however, his era began somewhat later, since he came here first in 1922 and did not show us his full powers till 1926 when he had reached the immense age of 24. He then won our Open Championship for the first time and perhaps this is the best place to set out his record in the barest and briefest outline. In his own country he won the Open Championship four times (he also tied for it twice and lost the play-off) and the Amateur Championship five times. Here he won one Amateur and three Open Championships. In 1930 he established what has been picturesquely called "the impregnable quadrilateral" by winning the Open and Amateur Championships of both countries in a single summer. He played against Britain in six International matches, five of them for the Walker Cup; he won his single every time, sometimes by immense margins, and he won his foursome five times and lost once by a single hole.

Bobby's first appearance here was in the International Match preceding the Amateur Championship at Hoylake in 1921. He won both his single and his foursome handsomely and impressed everybody, as he could not fail to do. Then came anticlimax. His career in the Amateur Championship was short and rather chequered. He began well enough against a good Scottish player, Mr. Manford, and there followed that rather farcical encounter with Mr. Hamlet of Wrexham. Whatever he might be at Wrexham it is pardonable to say that Mr. Hamlet was not of the stature to face Hoylake, even though it was made less formidably long than

59

usual by the hard ground. Yet with the match all square going to the Royal, which is the seventeenth, it really seemed as if he were going to beat Bobby, which, as Euclid might remark, would have been absurd. This was not due to any great golf of his but to a sort of general futility and paralysis on the greens on Bobby's part. However, the crisis passed, Bobby scrambled through with a score nearer ninety than eighty and proceeded to play devastatingly well in his next match against Mr. Robert Harris. He had got his bad round over, he was going to win—and then he relapsed again and was beaten by many holes by Mr. Allan Graham. There was a chance of redeeming himself in the Open at St. Andrews but all went ill; he felt a puzzled hatred for the links which he came afterwards to love and at the eleventh hole in the third round he picked up his ball. Legend declares that he relieved his feelings by teeing it up and driving it far out into the Eden. If he did it was a gesture deserving of sympathy, and if he did not I am very sure he wanted to.

In 1921, at the age of 19, Bobby was already a magnificent golfer, as great a hitter of the ball though not as great a player of matches or medal rounds as he ever was. Several years before Mr. Walter Travis had said he could never improve his strokes, and that was true enough; there was, humanly speaking, no room for improvement; it was simply a matter of stringing them together more successfully. There could be no more fascinating player to watch not only for the free and rhythmic character of his swing but for the swiftness with which he played. He had as brief a preliminary address as Duncan himself, but there was nothing hurried or slapdash about it and the swing itself, if not positively slow, had a certain drowsy beauty which gave the feeling of slowness. There was nothing that could conceivably be called a weak spot. The utmost that could be said—and this may be a purely personal impression—was that he did not seem quite so supremely happy with a mashie-niblick as when playing approaches with longer irons.

People liked Bobby at once, and that not only for his natural pleasantness of manner; they discerned in him a very human quality; he was no cold machine but took his game very much to heart as did humbler people. In his almost infantile days he had been inclined to throw his clubs about.

This we were told since the American press had once emphasised it rather unkindly; otherwise we should never have guessed it, for he had already tamed his naturally fiery temperament into betraying no outward signs. Those indeed who knew him well professed to know the symptoms which showed the flames leaping up within. I remember once watching him at an Open Championship, it may have been at St. Anne's, in company with that fine American golfer, the late Mr. J. G. Anderson; Bobby missed a shortish putt and "Now, he's mad," said my companion. I could detect nothing, but doubtless Mr. Anderson knew his man and Bobby did hate missing a shot. Perhaps that was why he missed so few, for in the end that highly-strung nervous temperament, if it had never been his master, became his invaluable servant. In his most youthful and tempestuous days he had never been angry with his opponent and not often, I think, with Fate, but he had been furiously angry with himself. He set himself an almost impossibly high standard; he thought it an act of incredible folly if not a positive crime to make a stroke that was not exactly as it ought to be made and as he knew he could make it. If he ever derogated from that standard he may even in his most mature days have been "mad" in the recesses of his heart, but he became outwardly a man of ice, with the very best of golfing manners.

How much other people have suffered over their golf we do not always know; the light of fame has not beaten on them so fiercely and they have not possessed such a friend and *vates sacer* combined as Bobby had in Mr. O. B. Keeler. Of Bobby we do know that he suffered greatly. How he could scarcely eat anything till the day's play was over; how on occasion he felt that he could not even button his shirt collar for fear of the direst consequences; how he could lose a stone in weight during a championship; how he was capable of breaking down to the point of tears not from any distress but from pure emotional over-strain—these things are now well known and may be found in Mr. Keeler's admirable and Boswellian pages. No doubt his capacity for an emotional outlet was at that time a relief and a help to him, but there must be a limit. I was in his company soon after he had finished his fourth round when he won the last of his three Open Championships here in 1930, and seeing him nearly past speech I thought that the time had come for him to call a halt and that this game could not much longer be worth such an agonising candle. He had great courage and great ambition, and these not only pulled him through but probably made him a more successful player than he would have been had he been gifted with a more placid temperament. There is much to be said for the stolid, phlegmatic player, but the great golfers have never had what I once heard Jack White call a dead nerve. It is worth remembering that James Braid, most rock-like and apparently impassive of men, has said that he "liked to be a wee bit nervous" before a big game. The steady-going and un-imaginative will often beat the more eager champion and they will get very near the top, but there, I think, they will stop. The prose labourer must yield to the poet and Bobby as a golfer had a strain of poetry in him. He stands for ever as the greatest encourager of the highly-strung player who is bent on conquering himself.

In 1926 we saw Bobby on his second visit. Four years had passed since he had been here before and he had now, as the Americans called it, "broken through"; the lean years were over. In 1923 he had won the American Open after a tie with Cruikshank, thus emulating Mr. Hilton here in winning the Open before the Amateur. In the following year he had put this to rights by winning the Amateur with triumphant ease and had been runner-up in the Open. In 1925 he had won the Amateur again and had tied in the Open, to lose rather surprisingly after a protracted play-off with Willie Macfarlane. He was in the plenitude of his powers and who should stand before him? And yet there was a moment when it seemed as if his second visit, like his first, would end in disappointment. All went swimmingly in the Amateur Championship at Muirfield till he reached the fifth round and then out he went and that with a resounding crash, for he was well and truly beaten by Mr. Andrew Jamieson who was then hardly known outside Scotland. I believe that Bobby woke with a stiff neck that morning though he was most anxious to conceal it. Certainly he seemed to lack something of his usual ease, but Jamieson, a very neat, unobtrusive, efficient golfer, did play uncommonly well, well enough to beat anybody if anybody gave him, as Bobby did, the very slightest opening. What was more, having got away with a lead he never grew frightened of it but played with victorious confidence. I saw only odd holes of the match but I remember one vividly. This was the short thirteenth called "The Postage Stamp", though whether it or the hole at Troon has the prior right to the title I do not know. The hole as it then was, had a long narrow green with a drop to perdition on the right, and on the left a high rough bank. Jamieson, with victory firmly in his grasp, if he could keep steady, had the honour and he made a slip; he hooked his tee shot and the ball lighted on the top of the left-hand bank. Would it stay there? It hovered for a moment and then, audibly encouraged by the crowd, began to topple downward by stages, almost coming to rest and then moving on again till at last it ended its rather nefarious career on the green. That was the final blow and Jamieson, having had his little bit of luck, went on to win calmly and easily by 4 and 3.

Mrs. Gamp has remarked how little we know "what lays before us". If Bobby had won that championship he has said that he would have sailed straight for home after the Walker Cup match. As it was he decided to give himself another chance in the Open at St. Anne's. So, after duly doing his deadly stuff at St. Andrews in the Walker Cup—he beat Cyril Tolley by 12 and 11—he went to Sunningdale for the qualifying rounds of the Open and proceeded to play there what was by common consent as nearly flawless a round as ever had been played. He went round in 66 and he may be said to have holed only one putt worthy of mention, one of eight yards or so for a three on the fifth. Otherwise if he missed nothing short—and there were one or two putts missed to be called shortish—he holed nothing that could conceivably be called long. He simply went on and on with exact perfection. There was indeed one slip, an iron shot pushed out into a bunker at the short thirteenth, but it cost the player nothing since he chipped the ball out dead. It probably brought relief to him as it did to the spectators, who had been feeling that they must scream if perfection endured much longer. It was Mr. Keeler, I think, who once wrote, "They wound up the mechanical man of golf yesterday and set him clicking round the East Lake course". All great golfers at their best are more or less mechanical, for they do the same thing over and over again, but I doubt if any of

63

them save perhaps one has given quite such an impression of well-oiled, impeccable machinery as Bobby did from tee to green. The notions of beauty and machinery do not go well together; the word 'clicking' may suggest something done 'by numbers' and so far it is inappropriate; but Mr. Keeler's was nevertheless an apt and memorable phrase. Harry Vardon and Bobby Jones combined exquisiteness of art with utterly relentless precision in a way not quite given to any other golfers.

Few joys in this world are unalloyed, and though Bobby was naturally and humanly pleased with that 66 he was a trifle worried because he had "reached the peak" rather too soon before going to St. Anne's. His second round of 68, with, if I remember, one innocuous misunderstanding with a tree, did nothing to reassure him on this point and he was so far right that, though he won at St. Anne's, his play there was not quite of the same unrippled smoothness as at Sunningdale. The game was by contrast "aye fechtin'" against him and he had to work hard for his scores. That was as exciting a championship as any between wars, save only for this, that from the very start it seemed that no Briton was likely to win it. Mitchell ended fifth but he only accomplished so much by two very fine rounds on the last day; as far as winning was concerned he had put himself out of court by beginning with two 78's. So to the narrowly patriotic this championship was merely a brilliant, alien exhibition contest.

The invaders went off with a bang: Hagen had a 68 and the powerful, broad-backed, rough-hewn Mehlhorn, said to have graduated as hod-carrier to the champion bricklayer of America, had a 70. Then came M'Leod, an expatriated Scot, and Al Watrous with 71 and then Bobby in the position he liked, lying well up but not prematurely leading, with a 72. It was a good round but he had to fight for it, since at each one of the last four holes he made some sort of a slip and had, in Mr. Laidlay's phrase, to "trust to a pitch and a putt" to get his four. In the second round Hagen had a compensating and disastrous 77 and at the end of it Mehlhorn with 70 and 74 and Bobby with two 72's led the field. Watrous, 71 and 75, was two shots behind them.

On the last day Bobby and Watrous were drawn together, and as it turned out this chance involved just such a strain on

Bobby Jones

R. A. Whitcombe

them and just such a terrific duel for first place as Vardon and Taylor had endured at Prestwick ten years earlier. Watrous was a very good player who has left no very distinct image on my mind; he had no tremendous power, but he had all the American virtue of smoothness and rhythm and he was a very fine putter, bang on his putting. Bobby was two strokes ahead when they set out and he had a 73 in a good fresh wind, but Watrous playing perfectly had a 69 and so—again this brought back memories of Vardon and Taylor—turned the deficit of two into a lead of two. Hagen took 74 and Mehlhorn began to fade. So the battle was to be fought out between these two and they were fully conscious of it as they went back to their hotel together, lunched together and even lay down to rest in the same room—a pleasant picture of friendly rivalry.

When it was all over and Mr. Topping, who had been in charge of this couple, gave away the prizes he declared that Bobby had made but one remark to him in the course of the last round, "My golf is terrible." In fact it was terribly good except in one important respect; he was taking too many putts. By his own account he took 39 of them and what he gained on Watrous in length he certainly threw away on the greens. The short ninth which had consistently bothered him beat him again and he was still two down with five to play; in what was in effect a match the language of match play may be used. Then at last the strokes came back one at a time and the pair were all square with three to play. At the seventeenth came Bobby's historic second, which I must presently describe yet again, but before that on the sixteenth came an incident of which a friend has lately reminded me; it gives force to the ruthless doctrine that someone ought to murder a photographer *pour encourager les autres*. Watrous had played his second to the green and Bobby had got half-way up with some pitching club when a fiend with a camera stepped out and tried to snap him. Bobby stopped and began again, and again the photographer tried. This time he was metaphorically lynched; he was shooed out of the way, and Bobby, by a considerable display of control, pitched safely to the green and the hole was halved in four.

Now for the seventeenth, a hole a little over 400 yards in

length. The course of the hole bends to the left and the line is well out to the right, in order to get a clear view of the hole and avoid the sandhills guarding the left-hand side of the green. Nor is that the only reason for keeping to the right, for on the left of the fairway is a wilderness of sandy, scrubby country dotted here and there with bunkers. Bobby with the honour, drew his tee shot, not badly but badly enough to be obviously in some form of trouble; Watrous went straight and playing the odd reached the green; he was some way from the hole but he was on the green and that looked good enough. Bobby's ball lay in a shallow bunker and it lay clean, but he was 170 yards or more from the flag and between him and it were the sandhills. He took what I think he called his mashie-iron (it now reposes a sacred relic in the St. Anne's Club) and hit the ball perfectly clean, playing it somewhat out into the wind so that it came in to finish on the green and nearer the hole than his opponent. Admittedly the ball lay as clean as clean could be and this was the kind of shot that he might very well have played in a practice game, but in the circumstances, when a teaspoonful too much sand might have meant irretrievable ruin, it was a staggering shot, and it staggered poor Al Watrous. He took three putts, Bobby got down in two and everybody felt that that shot had settled it. Watrous was bunkered at the home hole, Bobby nearly bunkered but not quite; he got a four against a five and finished in 74 against 78, 291 against 293.

There still remained Hagen and George Von Elm, both of whom were rumoured to be doing well. Hagen arrived on the last tee wanting a four for 74 and a two to tie. He could doubtless have tied for second place with Watrous but Hagen was never interested in second prizes. After a fine drive, he walked some way forward and then with a characteristic gesture had the flag taken out. His ball very nearly pitched into the hole and ran on into the bunker behind the green. *Aut Caesar*, etc. His effort had failed and he took four more to get down, so that Von Elm coming with a wet sheet and a 72 tied with him for third place. Let me add as a postscript that the Council of the Royal Lytham and St. Anne's Club have now decided to mark, as far as it can exactly be done, the spot at the seventeenth from which Bobby played his shot. This is a precedent that could not often be followed, but here the geographical conditions are favourable and if now and then someone has to lift a drop from behind the monument he will do so in a reverent rather than an exasperated spirit.

I have written at perhaps excessive length about the St. Anne's Championship both because it was Bobby's first and because it was so dramatic. When he came back next year to defend his title at St. Andrews, having in the meanwhile won the American Open at Scioto, he played unquestionably better; he enjoyed the greatest single triumph he ever had here, but there seems much less to say about it, for the reason that it was 'his' championship, he was winning all the while. By this time St. Andrews had taken a thorough hold on him. He was amused by its problems; he knew whereabouts were its hidden bunkers and was not annoyed by them, as some people never cease to be, because they are hidden; he had devised some three different ways of playing the Long Hole In according to the wind; he had realised that for a player of his parts the Road Hole need hold no excessive terrors, unless he is over-ambitious. In short he had proved the truth of Mrs. Malaprop's saying that "'Tis safest in matrimony to begin with a little aversion", for he was now thoroughly in love with the Old Course and played it as if he loved it.

Bobby's four rounds were 68, 72, 73 and 72 and he led from the start. I do not know that he played any better for his 68 than in any of the other three rounds; it was simply that everything came off for him, as for example a putt holed for three at the Hole o' Cross going out. It is by far the biggest green in the world and if this was not the longest putt ever holed it must have been very nearly so. Mr. Keeler's brow was a little knitted, for he was not sure how his man would like to be "in the lead" straight away instead of lying a stroke or two behind, but the general impression was that there would be no holding Bobby. After two rounds he only led Hodson by two strokes, but good player as Hodson was he could scarcely hope to give the leader two strokes; in fact the third round destroyed him as far as winning was concerned and those who were more likely to hold on were several shots further behind. At the end of the third round Bobby led Fred Robson, who had just done a splendid 69, by four shots and Aubrey Boomer by six, and it was for him to set the pace.

Only at the beginning of the last round was there a moment's doubt, for Bobby frittered away a couple of shots in the first four holes, and so with an orthodox five at the fifth his score was three over fours—a definitely vulnerable star. At that point I left him to look at other people, meaning to pick him up again at the thirteenth on the way home. Some bursts of clapping from the neighbourhood of the 'loop' suggested that he was doing well, but how well no one of us waiting on the big double green knew. The advanced guard of his crowd came towards us, in the van one who trotted briskly, as if big with news to impart. I have a well-grounded distrust of spectators' tales but this one looked a man of good counsel, sober and unimaginative; so I buttonholed him and asked his tidings. When he said that Bobby was now two under fours I thought he was only the usual liar, but what he said was true, for Bobby had done the holes from the sixth to the twelfth in 24 shots. After that the round was a triumphal procession. His second to the last hole was a little cautious and ended in the Valley of Sin. Thence he ran it up dead and as he scaled the bank the crowd stormed up after him and lined the edge of the green, barely restraining themselves. He holed his short one and the next instant there was no green visible, only a dark seething mass, in the midst of which was Bobby hoisted on fervent shoulders and holding his putter, "Calamity Jane", at arm's length over his head lest she be crushed to death. Calamity Jane had two pieces of whipping bound round her shaft where she had been broken, not we may trust in anger but by some mischance. When some years later the market was flooded with exact models of her, each of them duly bore two superfluous black bands. Did ever imitation pay sincerer flattery than that?

Only once more, in 1930, were we destined to see Bobby here in battle array, though he has returned once since his retirement and in playing a friendly round of the Old Course took the major part of St. Andrews round with him. It was at St. Andrews in 1930, the year of the "impregnable quadrilateral", that he realised almost his last unachieved ambition and won our Amateur Championship. He did not win it without his bad moments, for he had never concealed his dislike of eighteen-hole matches. In the American Championship the first two rounds, which were of eighteen holes only, had at least once brought him to grief and he had had, in the words of old Beldham the cricketer, "many an all but". Once safely through them and in the haven of thirty-six holes, where he felt that he had space to manœuvre, he had crushed his men one after the other by murderous margins. Thus in our championship he could never feel really at ease until in the final and he had never yet reached the final. He set out on the enterprise strung up to a high pitch and no one who saw the beginning of his match against a good Nottinghamshire golfer, Mr. Roper, will forget it. On the first green he holed a long putt for a three, the ball going in with an almost suspicious rattle against the back of the tin. Bobby looked a little apologetic and made several little practice movements of his club. I remember Mr. Hilton whispering to me that he was trying to get the swing of his putter smooth; that first putt, successful as it was, had shown signs of tension. After a four at the second he holed another and shorter putt for a three at the Cartgate and then at the fourth hit a very long tee shot rather to the left into the Cottage bunker. Thence, a culminating atrocity, he holed out, a full shot of 150 yards or so, with some sort of iron, for a two.

After this astonishing display Bobby became comparatively quiescent and had to struggle as hard to get through as many less gifted players have done. Two of his most close-run things were against compatriots, Mr. Harrison Johnston and Mr. George Voigt. Mr. Johnston, after being several holes down, chased him to the last gasp and Mr. Voigt, if I may permit myself an 'if', ought to have beaten him. Bobby was obviously struggling and when Mr. Voigt, very cool and steady and putting beautifully, stood two up with five to go, he looked like a winner. And then he committed what the onlooker, who has nothing to do but criticise, felt inclined to call a gratuitous folly. With the broad space of the Elysian Fields to drive into he cut his tee shot over the wall and out of bounds. It was a heaven-sent reprieve; Bobby took it and fought his way home to win by a hole.

Yet even this paled before his battle with Cyril Tolley. Every man, woman and child in St. Andrews went out to watch it, and Mr. Gerard Fairley was quite right to set the scene of the murder in one of his stories on the afternoon of that match. There would have been ample opportunity to commit several murders and escape undetected through the lonely streets, though stained with the marks of crime. Never was there more perceptible the silence of expectation, that lull before the storm in which men speak instinctively in whispers, and Cyril gave it if possible a more thrilling emphasis, since he began with a full-blooded top from the first tee. It was ominous but it was no presage of disaster for he played finely afterwards and a dog-fight on a magnificent scale ensued, which delighted everyone save other poor wretches who were trying to play their own insignificant matches. Each man seeing the mighty flood approach him must needs crouch over his ball guarding it as best he might and pick himself up again when the torrent has swept over him. The most discussed shot in the match was Bobby's second to the Road Hole, as to which hundreds are prepared to take their oath that the ball would have been on the road if it had not hit a spectator and an equal number of witnesses are quite certain that it would not. I was there but was running for my life with my head well down at the moment and can offer no opinion. The hole was halved; so was the last and Bobby won at the nineteenth, where his adversary played a rather loose second and was punished by a stymie. Exactly how good the golf was I cannot now remember for there are occasions when that is of secondary importance. It was the devil of a match.

At last Bobby was in the final—against Mr. Wethered; his chance had come and he did not mean to waste it; he was on his favourite long trail of thirty-six holes. At the very first hole a shudder of surprise went through the crowd as he entirely missed his pitch and stayed short of the burn, but from there he chipped dead and got his four; nor did he ever exceed that figure till he put his second into the Road bunker at the seventeenth. I can see him very clearly now, as the stewards are moving away the crowd at the back of the green. He is gently smiling a protest to the effect that he does not mean to go on to the road. In fact his explosion shot gave him quite a good chance of a four but the putt did not drop; there was to be no fiveless round for him. His opponent fought manfully but without avail and Bobby won by 7 and 6.

Now for the last lap, the Open at Hoylake, which was won in the end as had been that at St. Anne's by sheer, hard fighting. As at St. Andrews Bobby jumped away with the lead with a 70 which was equalled by Macdonald Smith. He added a 72 while Mac Smith took 77 and his nearest pursuer was now Fred Robson with 143. The third round was sound enough, 74, but meanwhile another British hope had arisen. Compston, who had begun with 74 and 73, added to these a tremendous 68 and led Bobby by a stroke. Diegel was not far behind with a 71, giving him a total of 228; but Diegel, though having an astonishing game in him, has been in championships one of those unfortunates who can never quite do it. He has said bitterly himself that however hard the other fellows try to give it him he will not take it. This may be partly due to his highly artificial method of putting, "contorted almost to anguish", as was written of a fine putter of a much older generation. Such styles are always apt to break down under strain, and apart from this Diegel was cursed with a temperament the most highly strung possible. Walter Hagen, once sitting up cheerfully late before a final against Diegel, was told in a tone of mild reproach that his adversary had been in bed for hours. " Ah," said Hagen, "but he's not asleep." I have seen Diegel, as "crazy" as ever was Duncan, and as brilliant as anyone I ever did see, but somehow he did not quite seem the man to stop Bobby, and in any case it was with Compston that were all British hearts.

I went out to see him play the first hole in the last round. His drive was perfect; his iron shot adequate, to the edge of the green, and he took three putts. One five meant nothing to be sure but there came other fives and the final 82 was heartbreaking. So out again in search of Bobby. All went if not perfectly according to plan at least reasonably well until he came to the eighth or Far Hole, which measures according to the books 527 yards, two shots and a pitch for Bobby in ordinary conditions with the ground fairly fast. The two shots were entirely satisfactory but the pitch was weak and the ball rolled back from the plateau; the next was nothing to boast of and at the last he missed a shortish putt; result, a horrid seven without touching a bunker. As Ben Sayers might have said, "It was no possible but it was a fact." The news of that seven quickly spread all over the links bringing consternation or encouragement. To Bobby himself it must have been a cruel blow but he pulled himself together and fought his way home, much, I imagine, in the frame of mind of a runner running himself blind, not seeing the tape but determined to get there. He was round in 75 and now we knew what had to be done. Compston was dead and buried; Diegel did a 75, good but not quite good enough for he had started two strokes behind. Those of us who were with him in one of the smaller rooms of the clubhouse united in assuring Bobby that all was well, as he wandered restlessly about holding a glass in two hands. And then there came a suggestion that all might not be well since Mac Smith was doing great things. To be sure he had to do a 69 to tie and that to an impartial judgment seemed very unlikely, but at such moments judgments can scarcely be impartial.

I remember very well going out to meet him. I could not go far for I had to broadcast and time was getting hideously short, but I *must* know. He holed out at the Dun taking to my jaundiced eye a very long time over it, and then we knew; two threes to tie. It was almost but not quite impossible. I saw him play the Royal—I was to broadcast from a house not far off—and his putt for three did not go in. Two to tie and that was surely impossible, but with an obstinate fidelity to duty I waited till his second had pitched on the home green and had palpably not holed out. Then I ran and ran and arrived just in time to announce in breathless tones to an expectant world that Bobby had won again.

I will not follow him home to America. He won the Open at Interlaken and the Amateur at Merion where he had played in his first championship at 14 and won his first Amateur Championship at 22. But as far as this country is concerned he departed in a blaze of glory from Hoylake.

He retired at the right time and could say with Charles Lamb, "I have worked task work and have the rest of the day to myself." After Tom Cribb had beaten Molineaux for the second time in the great battle of Thistleton Gap it was decided that he need never fight again but should bear the title of Champion to the end of his days. I think that most golfers in their hearts grant the same privilege to Bobby Jones.

Chapter 7

DARKEST BEFORE THE DAWN

FROM 1924 to 1930, except in one single year, the Open Championship was won by Walter Hagen or Bobby Jones. They did not both come every year; each seemed rather in the nature of a mouse playing when the cat was away and it was only at St. Anne's in 1925, when Bobby won and Hagen was third, that we saw them opposed to one another. Of these two I have said a good deal already and so let me turn to the single one in those seven years when neither came over and Jim Barnes won, namely 1925 at Prestwick. This too must be reckoned an American victory, but it possessed at least this circumstance a little soothing to national pride, that Barnes was not only born in this country but "in spite of all temptation had remained an Englishman". He had sturdily refused to be an American citizen; he was still above everything an intensely patriotic Cornishman and this, apart from his many other pleasant qualities, endeared him to us.

I had first seen Barnes, I suppose, though without realising that he was a future champion, when he was a lanky boy in Whiting's shop at Lelant and I spent a never-to-be-forgotten week at Christmas there, in which we lay basking on the grass while the rest of England was in the grip of fog and frost. Next I had seen him in Francis Ouimet's year at Brookline when he had a chance of winning in the last round but faded a little away. He had been sixth in Duncan's year, at Deal; third to Hagen and Duncan at Sandwich; ninth when Hagen won at Hoylake; and he had won the American Open in 1921, won it easily, which is a difficult thing to do. So he had certainly earned his turn at Prestwick. He was not only a very fine player but technically a very interesting one by reason of his height. Of all the champions I can think of he must be decidedly the tallest, and great height combined with slimness of build is not an unmixed advantage. Bobby Jones is a good example of a comparatively small man using all his height by standing up to the ball; Barnes is an example of the tall man who must needs cancel some of his height and gets well down to the ball without undue stooping. Get down he

73

did; he seemed to use rather short clubs and had a fairly wide stance, but he kept his legs taut and was firmly propped upon them; his stance was the very opposite of that broken-kneed old cab-horse stance (I speak feelingly) noticeable in some stoopers. Moreover if he got down well he kept down superbly well; his finish was a model for the tall man who is inclined to spring up too soon after the ball is hit. Everything he did was pleasant to watch, not least his putting with a cleek and again, as was natural, a wide stance.

This Prestwick Championship has come to be regarded in retrospect as a duel between two exiles, Barnes from England and Macdonald Smith from Scotland, and so in the end it proved; but this is a view unjust to Ray and Compston who each finished one stroke behind Barnes and two ahead of Smith. Still it is hard to fight against abiding impressions and it is to those two figures from America that memory clings. It was they who set the pace in the first rounds, changing places with startling rapidity. Barnes began with a 70, streaking right ahead of the field, while Mac Smith was in the ruck of the other likely ones with a 76. In the second round Barnes fell away with a 77 and Mac Smith to the unbounded joy of the Scottish crowd had a wonderful 69 and led by two strokes. On the last day Barnes was among the early starters, a fact that was to be of great advantage to him, but he made little use of it at first, for he fell away again for a 79. He had come back to his horses, for Compston had caught him and Ray and Abe Mitchell were but two behind him. As for Mac Smith, with an eminently sound third round of 76 he now seemed to be out by himself.

Barnes again was off early, before the bulk of the crowd could catch him, and this time he did get his blow in first; he played very well indeed for 74. It was a good last round but Barnes was convinced that it was not good enough, and certainly the prospect of such a player as Mac Smith wanting only a 78 to win was not too encouraging. J. H. Taylor would have none of this hopelessness; Barnes had got his card in and the other fellows would know what they had to do; he shook his head; he was very emphatic about it and he was right. Compston had a 75, very good but not good enough by that one fatal stroke; Ray had a gallant 73 to tie with Compston. Out went Macdonald Smith with 79 to tie and

78 to win and the whole turbulent, enthusiastic Scottish crowd went with him.

Poor Macdonald Smith was not unnaturally sad and bitter at the end of the day and blamed the crowd for his failure. They may have stopped him from winning, but assuredly that was the last thing they intended to do. They wanted the Scotsman to win and all that was wrong was that too many of them wanted it too much. It has to be admitted that Prestwick is not a good course for spectators. The crowds are very big and very keen and some of their number are imbued with the spirit of the miner on his holiday who traditionally remarked "Players be d——d. I've come to see." Moreover the ground especially near the clubhouse is very ill adapted for the purpose since the spectators watching one player get inextricably mixed with those watching another. The Loop becomes as a whirlpool of people, and the steering them round the great width of the Cardinal bunker is a problem in itself. There used to be one member of the club who regularly took charge of the Cardinal and was supposed to know more about it than any man alive; his was an awful task.

This crowd of Macdonald Smith's meant unquestionably well, but despite all the stewards could do they did sometimes press very close. Other people, Vardon and Taylor for instance in 1914, have endured as much and played their game, but that is not to say that Mac Smith had not a good deal to bear. It is unnecessary to follow the round in any detail; it was a tragedy of frittering and some time before he had ended in 82, Barnes was practically safe in his haven. Nor is it necessary to speculate on what might have happened in other conditions. From what I have seen of Macdonald Smith, for whom I have a great admiration, he seems to me a player who can play a great last round when the chance of winning has almost gone, and not such a great one when the chance is there for the taking. The whole affair was unfortunate and the Prestwick Club, not over-fond of the storm and stress of an Open Championship, has never, I think, asked for one since. That is sad, for here was the original home of the Championship Belt, but the greatest number recorded as entering for the Belt was seventeen and a modern Championship does make very stern demands alike on a club and its course.

The tale of Champions from America does not end with Bobby's last win in 1930. There were three more to come in a row, Armour, Sarazen and Densmore Shute. 1931 saw the Open Championship played for the first time at Carnoustie, the nursery of many famous Scottish golfers, and it seemed a pity that Bobby Jones should not be there to play on the home green of his boyhood's model, Stewart Maiden. It has every qualification for a championship course; it is long, interesting and difficult and it possesses in particular a fine, crucial finish amid the lethal windings of the Barry Burn. Save where the crowd is apt to get a little entangled amid the loops of that famous and ubiquitous stream, it possesses plenty of space in which spectators can be and are well controlled. It was not quite so long and fierce in 1931, as it was when Cotton won there seven years later, but it was stern enough. Incidentally it was made fiercer for some people and kinder for others by a rather inconstant wind which twice changed in the course of the day. It was kind to Armour who won, unkind to Sarazen, who philosophically remarked that "you must have the breaks".

Armour, who had been Open Champion of America in 1927, won this Championship in the most gallant possible way by coming up from behind with a last round of 71. It was particularly interesting to see him play again, since we had seen him play as an amateur in the Amateur Championships of 1920 and 1921 and for Britain in the first unofficial international at Hoylake. I had also met him, still as an amateur, in the United States in the summer of the first Walker Cup match. He had in those days possessed a fine and notably rhythmic swing; he looked like a golfer of high class but he had been, judged by expectations formed of him, just a little bit disappointing. When he returned in his new capacity it was apparent how much professional training had done. His style as graceful as ever appeared more strictly workmanlike, stripped of all superfluities and exuberances, and the high standard of American putting had made a far better player of him on the green. There are certain remarks which it becomes for a time the correct thing to make about certain players. One commentator adopts them from another till there swells up a great chorus of voices repeating the same strain. At about this time it was eminently the right thing to see that Armour was the best iron player in the world; it was an opinion to be taken as read. Beyond doubt he was a very fine one, hitting the ball a beautifully crisp blow, "like the shutting of a knife" to use another well-worn simile; but whether he was notably better than several other players I do not know. Enough that he was thoroughly well armed at all points.

One thing I do recall distinctly about him; it made his victory the more meritorious because it must have increased the strain on him; he was suffering from that waggling disease of which John de Forest was a victim when he reached the final of the Amateur Championship in 1931 and won it in 1932. He was not completely a victim; he could play his long shots confidently enough with the minimum of preliminaries but when he came to short pitches and even to putting he could not make up his mind to take the plunge but must hover shivering on the brink, postponing the decisive moment. I recollect one shot, I think, in his last round, at a short hole on the way home. He had put his tee shot just off the green and was left with a short and not very easy chip. He took so many rapid little waggles as to induce in the onlooker a tendency to scream aloud; it seemed as if there could be no end and that he could "Tire the sun with waggling and send him down the sky". Yet he went on till, as I suppose, he felt the right instant had come and he laid that most important chip dead. If he had not the mastery over his waggles he had it over himself, and that is what counts.

Armour was deservedly champion but the most memorable figure at Carnoustie and the one that drew the greatest crowds and evoked the greatest sympathy was the Argentine, José Jurado. The Duke of Windsor, then Prince of Wales, came to watch the Championship and had scarcely eyes for anyone else. Jurado was a most attractive player as well as a very fine one: small, dapper, agreeably smiling, with a swing like a flash of greased lightning and altogether a dashing and pleasant way with him. He had played in the Championship at Sandwich three years before when he had been for three rounds in the very forefront of the battle and had tailed off rather sadly in the fourth with 80, as compared with the 72's and 73's of the five players who finished ahead of him. Now he was more mature by three years; he was not a stranger in a

strange land but had many friends and admirers here, and
almost from the start he made the pace. He began steadily
with a 76 and followed this up with a brilliant 71 which put
him at the head of the field, with a formidable cluster close at
his heels, Armour with 72 and 75, Farrell 72 and 77, Sarazen
74 and 76, Macdonald Smith, who had been practising steadily
for a long while on his native heath, 75 and 77. Nor, though
he gradually faded from our view on the last day, must Henry
Cotton be omitted, for he shared the lead with Jurado. He
had returned from a long visit to the United States a profound
believer in the "from inside out" swing. He had hardly ob-
tained that complete mastery over it which he later attained
and bent the ball much more pronouncedly to the left than
he does today, when the turn of the ball in the air is rather
a suggestion than a fact. That turn was very plain to see at
Carnoustie and looked a little as if it might get out of hand,
but he played truly admirable golf for those first two rounds
and cheered all patriotic hearts.

On the morning of the last day Cotton was disappointing
with a 79 and as a winner must be written off. Alliss, with
a 73 had come up to take his place as chief British hope, but
once more the cup seemed destined to go abroad, for the
invaders were bunched thick round the top of the tree.
Jurado had shown not a sign of being afraid of his own score
and a 73 put him at the head with 220. Mac Smith had made
his effort with a 71 and was 223. Armour, Sarazen and our
own Alliss were at 225 and there was no need to look further.
I did not myself see Armour again after he had laid that vital
chip dead but news came back of fine fours at the long home-
coming holes near the end and presently his 71 was bruited all
over the course. Now Jurado must be watched above all
others, Jurado, with a 75 to win, a score very well within his
powers but leaving little margin. Nobody knew whether
Jurado knew; the general impression was that he did and this
turned out to be wrong. He had not heard of Armour's score,
but as he drew near home the strain was obviously telling and
there came one or two rather wild strokes and one tee shot
puffed high in the air and a very short way. Still he struggled
bravely on with no major disaster and on the last tee wanted a
four for a 76 to tie. Two long, very long, shots were needed
to carry the burn guarding the home green, but he would

surely go for it if there was a chance. He hit a fine tee shot; then played short with an iron, pitched home in three, tried hard for his four but did not get it. There was a general sigh of sympathy, and only after he had holed out was it realised that he had not known what he had to do. Here is one of those baffling and utterly unsatisfactory 'ifs'. If he had known he might have gone for the green, and further he might have played better or he might have played worse before he came to that last hole. The only thing that one can say is that, humanly speaking, he would have played differently. After that came the almost inevitable spectacle of Macdonald Smith not quite doing it (I watched his drive at the sixteenth plump into a bunker with the sound of a death knell) and Armour had won, with Jurado second and Sarazen and Alliss (with another brave 73) equal third.

In 1932 the Championship was played for the first time on Prince's, Sandwich, a worthy battlefield, which has temporarily through the war ceased to be a golf course but must surely rise again from its ashes when peace comes. About the Championship itself there is not much to say for it was won too easily for excitement, but there will be plenty to say about the winner, Gene Sarazen. He began with a 70 and a 69 and was winning all the time. He had a 70 again in the third round and seemed more safe than ever. True Havers had done a wonderful 68 in that third round (this was a very low scoring Championship) and when Sarazen, with no more than a little human faltering, had finished in 74, there was I suppose a chance; but 68's do not happen twice at such a juncture and it was a very small chance indeed. Vividly do I recall a tall, fat gentleman among the spectators who said to me optimistically, "Havers only wants a 69 to win." I replied with some emphasis, "Only." "What!" he exclaimed. "Don't you think he'll do it?" and we parted for ever. Havers in fact took 76 and was ousted from second place by Macdonald Smith, who finished with the courage of hopelessness, in 70. Charles Whitcombe and Padgham were close behind Havers. Armour, the holder, was a long way down the list, but still the cup could avail itself of its regular return ticket.

Gene Sarazen has been one of the most faithful and, to me, one of the most engaging of our visitors from across the Atlantic. He is a wise little, strong little man, with a round

79

olive face and a charming grin which is never far away, beaming when he holes a long putt, still there though perhaps with a wry twist to it when the ball hits the hole and stays out. Perhaps it is pure fancy on my part but of all our invaders I should put him down as in method most like one of our own golfers. I should have guessed that he had learnt his game in some British caddie shed. His swing seems to me to have nothing typically American about it, save its merits; there is something care-free and casual about his game, more especially about his way of tackling a putt, which reminds me of generations of boys whom I have seen chipping round English club-houses with their master's clubs. He is in fact of pure Italian blood, though he was born in the State of New York and began life as a caddie at Apawamis, a course the name of which recalls a certain famous and fortunate shot of Harold Hilton's which won him the American Championship at the thirty-seventh hole. Gene may have seen it for he was then nine years old and was already an experienced person who had carried for a whole year.

It was in 1922 when he was 20 years old that he suddenly brought fame to himself and to Titusville by winning the American Open by means of a fourth round of 68. Nobody had then heard of him and not many perhaps of Titusville. It was really little more than a trial run for him and he did not take it too seriously. He was sleeping, as he once told me, in a sort of dormitory of his fellow professionals. They all went to bed early, but Gene, not realising the solemnity of the occasion and liking to amuse himself, used to come home late and pick his way circumspectly through the sleepers. If his win was surprising he soon gave evidence that it was no accident, for he proceeded to win the Professional Championship and then to do what perhaps no else could then have done, win a set match of seventy-two holes against Walter Hagen, a match that Hagen had no intention of losing if he could help it. It was in the autumn of that year that I first met him in a hotel at Boston, when he grinned pleasantly and rather shyly, and said (it is the one thing I remember), "I have a very *very* great respect for Walter Hagen's golf." No doubt the sentiment was mutual.

With the glory of these victories upon him Sarazen came here in 1923 to play in the Championship at Troon, impressed

Lawson Little with W. Tweddell

Henry Cotton with A. Perry and W. G. Oke

everybody in the qualifying rounds and then failed to qualify. It must have been a blow but he said he would come back if he had to swim across, and a few years later he became one of our regular visitors. In the meantime his game had for a while suffered a slight set-back, perhaps because he had originally played entirely by the light of nature and then set himself, as any wise player must at some time, to think about the game. He had experimented with the overlapping grip in place of his natural interlocking grip, which is also that of Francis Ouimet and the Whitcombes. From this unavoidable sickness of thought, from which some good young players never wholly recover, he emerged a sounder and better player than ever before and in 1928 was second to Hagen at Sandwich. That time he might almost have won, but for one little outbreak of a naturally excitable Latin temperament, usually kept under stern control, which made him dash too swiftly at a ball in the rough with his wooden club at the Suez Canal hole. At Muirfield in the following year he was ninth: then at Carnoustie he was fourth and at last at Prince's he won. He made no sort of mistake about it, for his winning score of 283 was the best yet recorded and has since been equalled but never beaten.

All through that Championship he played with victorious confidence but he also played with his head. With the ground fast and full of running he several times took his spoon off the tee lest he should go too far. At one hole, the fifteenth, he regularly did so, that he might have a longer pitch to play and so with a higher shot have a better chance of stopping the ball on that perilous little plateau. He putted throughout very well and so boldly that he almost seemed unlucky in often hitting the hole without the ball dropping. In short it was just about as convincing a win as I remember to have seen and the inspiration of it abided with him, for he went home and won the American Open, finishing with a 66 to beat the unlucky Perkins, who had been hailed the victor, by three whole shots.

Still one more Championship remains before the tide turns, that at St. Andrews in 1933. It may seem ungracious to set it down as rather a dull one, and yet that is my impression. It appears quite unjustifiable for it ended in a tie between two players who were in the hunt up to the last moment. Yet I cannot rid myself of the feeling and can only think that we had grown heart-sick and that five Americans out of the first six—after we had won the Ryder Cup too—made the last straw. The play was interesting enough to be sure, with the ground hard which makes St. Andrews more typically itself, and a strong wind which blew against the players homewards and was rather too much for many of them in the fourth round. How hard the ground was and what strength there was in the wind at times was shown by a single shot, which will be remembered, and perhaps disbelieved in, when the rest is forgotten. In one of his rounds Craig Wood playing the long hole out (the fifth) drove his ball from the tee into one of the bunkers in the face of the hill in front of the green. The hole as played that day was 530 yards long and the ball ended about 100 yards from the hole. That the thing happened there is no shadow of doubt, and as to how it happened I give it up.

I begin to wonder why I called this a dull Championship for, as I look at the scores and recall more of my feelings at the time, there seems plenty of excitement. With the last round to go three men led at 216 and two of them Englishmen, Cotton, Easterbrook and Diegel. Craig Wood was 217, Sarazen 218 and Shute with three consecutive 73's 219. No doubt it was the disappointment of the last round that soured me, for Cotton was very disappointing with 79, and though Easterbrook was in it till the end his 77 was too high by that one fatal stroke. Trying rightly for a four at the seventeenth, a desperate enterprise, he went over the green, over the road and on to the patch of grass under the stone wall. He retrieved himself very well but there could be no four. Shute once again a model of steadiness had a fourth 73, and Craig Wood, not quite so consistent—one of his rounds was 68—tied with a 75. Both had played finely but I cannot get it out of my head that Sarazen ought to have won that Championship for he played the best golf there. In his second round he played out so brilliantly that he could take a six at the eleventh and yet finish in 73. He got into the Hill bunker, and that is still a bunker, deep, horrible and precipitous, to strike terror into any man. It was a crooked tee shot and there was no bad luck, but still three niblick shots to get out—it rends the heart. There had moreover been a question raised by a spectator as to whether he had not in fact taken seven. Both markers, for he had two, were quite positive and there was an end of the question, but it naturally distressed Sarazen. Even so on the last day he might well have won but for one or two mistakes, as I thought, of judgment, in particular an attempt to carry Hell when it was entirely unnecessary.

There is another man who no doubt thought that he ought to have won, Leo Diegel. At last Will-o'-the-Wisp seemed honourably and faithfully to be leading him to the pot of gold. He was getting very restive in the fourth round but still he looked as if he would do it. I remember at one green on the way home he made a deplorably short approach putt and then banged the next one in. "Now he'll surely win," said I, for that was just the thing to hearten any man, a shocking mistake greatly retrieved, but it was not to be. On the home green the very converse happened; with two to tie he laid a fine long approach putt close to the hole and utterly failed to hit the next. Poor Diegel! he could never quite take what the gods gave him.

The next day's golf felt very flat by contrast and was from the onlookers' point of view not much more than an exhibition. It had an amusing start when Wood, having put his second into the burn, waded in and played it out—an almost fool-hardy thing to do so early, and bringing no particular profit. The game did not live up to its start. Shute got a lead and kept it, playing again very steadily: he won with 149 against Wood's 154. It is darkest before the dawn and it felt very dark after that Championship.

Chapter 8

THE TURNING OF THE TIDE

WITH 1934 I come with a feeling of relief to what, ringing the changes on familiar metaphors, I may call the turning of the tide. It was then for the first time after ten years that a British golfer succeeded in winning the British Open Championship. Let me try to be scrupulously honest in this matter. The renewal of British victories did synchronise with a slackening of the foreign attack. The invaders were for a while less numerous and less formidable, but nothing can alter the fact that our men did begin to win again and that moreover in 1937, when the American invasion was at least as menacing as ever before, and there came the severest possible test of our golfing renascence, the cup remained at home.

It is the first step that counts and the first Briton to win again as also to win in that most testing year was Henry Cotton, unquestionably the outstanding figure in our golf during the last few years. He has been so not only because of his merits as a player, but because he has so intensely applied a naturally acute mind to attaining success in his profession. He possessed the gift of exploiting an interesting and complex personality to the furthest advantage, as a player, as a speaker, as an entertaining writer, and even on the music-hall stage. He realised that there was a great body of golfers ready to reward golf in many directions more richly than golf had rewarded his predecessors. Without any apparent attempt to conciliate public opinion—indeed in some respects he appeared rather to disregard it—he had and has a magnetic attraction for the public. By force of character he dominated it and whether people wanted to see him win or to see him beaten they could not help themselves; they must watch him.

From the very start of his career he interested the world because he had not the professional's normal background. He had played as an amateur and a schoolboy before he determined to be a professional golfer, a determination encouraged by J. H. Taylor, whom his father consulted. He had not perhaps quite the natural gifts of some of his contemporaries and rivals who had graduated as caddies, but he had an energy, a power of sticking to it, and a resolution to get on in his chosen line of life which could hardly be surpassed. There have been other great practisers, several of the most famous being among the amateurs; some will claim the palm for Mr. Macfie, some for Mr. Travis, some for Mr. Hilton. Many professionals too have practised assiduously and none perhaps more than Harry Vardon in his early years; but I doubt whether anyone has devoted as many backbreaking, hand-smarting, brain-tiring hours to the acquiring of golfing shots as has Cotton. There are all sorts of legends about him, such as that he went home to practise putting after a tournament instead of remaining on the ground to receive the prize. I know not whether they are true; some of them probably are, and at any rate they are essentially true in that they depict one prepared to live the most laborious days in quest of success.

Moreover Cotton's practising was not merely a mechanical grind, though perhaps nobody tried harder to turn himself into a machine, for it was reinforced by constant thought and a willingness to try every kind of experiment, such as that of learning to hit the ball with the left hand alone, in which I believe he is extraordinarily expert. He made a prolonged visit to the United States in order to sit at the feet of the best players there, and returned a zealous convert of the " inside out " method of swinging a club. All the while that he was wrestling with these technical problems he was likewise wrestling with a not naturally easy or ideal temperament and gradually reducing it to order. And so step by step, going on his rather lonely way, undeterred by criticism and unwavering in hard resolve, he built himself up into a remarkable figure, one which to the man in the street stands for golf in a way that no other in this country has quite done since the days of Harry Vardon. Today, and especially since all his good work in exhibition matches for the Red Cross, Henry Cotton is an essentially popular figure. He was not always that, but popular or unpopular he was not to be disregarded ; he compelled the attention which he now attracts.

In 1933, thinking a little perhaps of the prophet that has not honour in his own country, Cotton had gone to Belgium as professional to the Waterloo Club, and it was thence that

he came to Sandwich for this memorable Championship of
1934. One thinks of it now, even after his rather agonising
last round, as of Eclipse first and the rest nowhere; but apart
from our other home players—and Padgham and the Whitcombes had now fully come into their own—there were
some dangerous visitors to maintain the overseas menace, the
persistent Macdonald Smith, and Kirkwood from America;
Dallemagne from France, a magnificently athletic figure
of a man and a fine dashing player; Brews, an Englishman
but for some time settled in South Africa and known to be
uncommonly good.

From the start it was Cotton, Cotton all the way. In one
of the qualifying rounds he had broken all records for the
course, which is over 6700 yards long, with a 66 and now in
the real thing he set such a tune to dance to as had perhaps
never been heard before. 67 for the first round was stunning
enough and he followed it up with a 65. His long game was
not only immensely powerful but most rhythmic and beautiful,
for he had now reduced the "inside out" flight of the ball to
an artistic minimum. At the same time his putting, if not
beautiful, was deadly. He was using a wooden putter,
wielding it, as I remember, in an attitude of some apparent
stiffness and discomfort, with his elbows notably crooked.
Here was that mechanisation of putting, which it has always
been thought must break down in the end; but the machine
worked and kept on working. For those who do not know
Sandwich his card is merely a general and blinding scintilla-
tion of threes and fours; for those who do it is a standing
marvel, and here it is:—Out, 4 3 3 4 4 4 3 4 4. Home, 4 3 4
4 4 4 3 3 3. The outgoing nine represents the finest conceiv-
able start with one stroke gained at the second hole and one
lost, actually lost, by a four at Hades which is the eighth.
The homecoming in 32 over nine holes measuring 3551 yards
is fantastic and indecent. So was a total of 132 for thirty-six
holes, and it left Cotton nine strokes ahead of Padgham who
had done 72 and 70. The most dangerous invaders then
appeared to be Kirkwood and Dallemagne each with 143.

Cotton continued to play finely in the third and usually
deemed most critical round. It was impossible to keep up
sixties, and this was an unpleasant day with a strong wind and
some squalls of rain and hail, so that 72 was eminently satisfy-

ing. Kirkwood had a 71, but what did a gain of one stroke matter? Brews had done 70 but he had been four strokes behind Kirkwood. Padgham with the worst of luck in the matter of the weather had taken 75. Cotton's position was more secure than ever but it had narrowly escaped a peril which perhaps he did not know of himself, which is mentioned in no history books but which I have the best of reasons for knowing.

Cecil Hutchison and I had taken shelter from the hail in a hut full of green-keeping tools near the eighth green. Just then "a scout came flying all wild with haste and fear", and seeing our blue rosettes poured out his tale which was grim enough. The seventh hole (in the shallowest of tiny hollows, but they are the most dangerous ones) was under water and the approaching players could not hole out. We rushed out, or, Cecil did and I hobbled, with awful visions of the Championship being null and void, and somehow or other men with squeegees were mobilised and the green swept clear while the couple near to the green waited with patient good-humour and the couples began to silt up behind them. It did not take very long though it seemed an age, but for that time the course had been technically unfit for play and if anyone had lodged an appeal—O heaven! Everyone behaved admirably, nobody complained and all was well, and when Cotton started out on his last round it seemed over bar the shouting.

It was all over but not until the players and spectators alike had endured agonies. Cotton, who has never had the strongest of insides (witness the serious illness from which he is fortunately recovering as I write), is said to have eaten something that disagreed with him, but it is never necessary to seek specific causes for nervous misery at such a moment. Certainly he looked pale and drawn and for twelve holes he kept us on tenterhooks. Not at first, for after a scrambling five at the first hole, 4, 3, 4 for the next three was perfect golf. There came a horrid six at the hole before the Maiden, a stroke wasted at the Maiden itself and then another six. A three and a five made 40 to the turn. It made everyone uneasy, but that which was really depressing was the row of three horrid fives at the tenth, eleventh and twelfth, where fours seem essential before facing the longer holes coming home. Cotton's iron shots to the green would keep drifting away to the left in the wind and I think we knew by then that Brews had done another 70. Everyone was making frenzied calculations and J. H. Taylor was gesticulating with his umbrella, as Sir Horace Mann used to cut down the daisies with his stick when he watched some agonising old cricket match at Hambledon. And then suddenly as I suppose Cotton felt better. At any rate he took a pull and began to play magnificently. Two grand shots and a well-played third gave him a four at the thirteenth, and we too began to feel better. A four at the Suez Canal and he was surely home. A third four at the fifteenth and it was a certainty. Never a slip did he make till he dropped a stroke and took five to the home hole. He had the lowest aggregate ever done in a Championship, equalling Sarazen's 283 at Prince's; he had won by five shots from Brews; he had followed Taylor's saying that the way to win a Championship is to win it easily— but "easily" seemed at the moment somehow not quite the right word.

Next year at Muirfield saw another new British Champion, Alfred Perry. He had often played well before and had reached the final of the 'News of the World' to be heavily beaten by Cotton, but it would be absurd to say that his win was not a surprise. Yet though he has never as yet won again, no one who has watched him would say that he was not worthy to win. He is not an elegant player; there is something at first sight a little bucolic about him and he has a curious grip of the right hand which, by riveting the eyes on itself, distracts attention from the essential soundness and trueness of the swing. It is rather a forcing style perhaps, but there is a fine quality about it which for want of a better word I may call roundness. He attacks the ball with the greatest dash; his club comes right through and he pitches and putts with the almost insolent confidence of a small boy with his master's iron on a caddie's miniature course. About his game, as there was about Ray's, there is something which looks a little uncertain until the results are scrutinised.

Perry began at Muirfield with a 69, but even that score did not for the moment attract any vast attention since all eyes were on the holder, Cotton, and until he had played seventeen holes in his first round he was in invincible form. He stood on the last tee with a four for 66 and seemed incapable of a mistake. He made a slight one, drawing a long tee shot into a bunker on the left of the course. Thence he might conceivably have got home and he went out for the shot. Whether or not he tried for too much he failed, and in the end was hard put to it to get a manful six. Heaven knows 68 was good enough and it led the field, but that six must have been an unforgettable splash of cold water, for Cotton was not the same player afterwards; his putting began to fail him, and the Muirfield greens demand very true putting; slowly but surely he faded and the Championship was left to others.

There were strong invaders in the field: Lawson Little, then still an amateur and Amateur Champion of two counties; Picard, an eminently dangerous player always likely to be there or thereabouts; and Macdonald Smith who began with a 69, only to fall steadily away. Yet somehow Sandwich had heartened us and I do not think there was any American terror. After two rounds Charles Whitcombe seemed the man, for he had done 71 and 68. His 73 in the third round was full of fine golf but his putting had begun to be a little too cautious, whereas Perry, having comparatively relapsed with a 75 in the second round, had slashed his way round in 67 and equalled Hagen's record. With a round to go Perry's total was 211, Whitcombe's 212 and Whitcombe's putting was not regaining its victorious touch; in the end he took 76. Here suddenly was the road to victory open wide for Perry. I watched him start and it was a lamentable start, for being very near the first green in two he took six to hole out. Yet he appeared wholly unmoved and the way he played the second, just missing his three, was a restorative. I did not see him again or only for a moment till he had some seven or eight holes to play, and then he was playing with such glorious confidence and abandon as to make one think better of human nature in general. At the fourteenth with the Championship in his pocket, he pulled his drive into a bunker, took a spoon with superb audacity and hit the ball right home. He hit another gorgeous spoon shot, from no bunker this time, bang home at the eighteenth. The sight of the winner breaking through the crowd on to the home green is always thrilling, but somehow or other it seemed to me this time more than usually charged with excitement. Perry got his four for 72 to win by four strokes and rolled off the green as cheerfully and unconcernedly as he had rolled round the course.

Every year is remembered to a greater or less extent as the Open Champion's year, but if ever one year belonged to one man then 1936 belonged to Alfred Padgham, for he not only won the Championship but nearly everything else besides. In fact by the time he came to Hoylake there was an uneasy feeling that this sort of thing could not go on and he must have shot his bolt. He had of course won many things before, and had been runner-up at Muirfield, but this was his wonderful year and it was "aye the putting"; he came to Hoylake with such a record of counting putts holed as would have frightened a less placid nature into a belief that his ration was exhausted. All the rest of his game is at once extremely orthodox and beautifully easy; I remember to have heard Sandy Herd say that Padgham reminded him of Harry Vardon and this was as if one Admiral should say of another that Nelson had come again. His putting, on the other hand, though pleasant enough to look at, is by comparison unorthodox; he stands very upright, a good long way from the ball and hits it rather as if he were playing a short chip from off the green. I have seen other fine putters stand as far or even farther from the ball, Mr. Mure Fergusson for instance, but his was a genuine putting stroke whereas Padgham's seems to be hardly that. That handsome is as handsome does is at least as true of putting as anything else and Padgham has holed many putts in his time, but it is not the part of his game which gives me most pleasure. I like best the almost sleepy power of his long game, particularly of his long iron shots up to the hole. No man could be as placid as Padgham looks, and he is in fact a shrewd and observant man, but his appearance of almost bovine serenity, whatever the situation, adds a piquant quality to his game.

Padgham comes of one of those golfing families which are the pride of the Forest (need it be said that I mean Ashdown Forest?) which has produced the whole tangled cousinhood of the Mitchells, and the Seymours, and Jack Smith, who not only won Long Driving Competitions but was a very fine golfer into the bargain. A strict regard for truth compels the admission that Padgham was born not in Sussex but in Surrey and that he played some of his earlier golf near Birmingham, but he was later assistant to John Rowe at Ashdown Forest.

It was there that I first heard of him from an enthusiastic friend who rightly prophesied that here was a future champion. Anyhow his father was an Ashdown man; he has the right blood in his veins and it would be both unjust and unromantic to deny his glory to that heathery land, which has produced golfers as the fens used once to produce the great skating families of the Smarts and the Sees.

That Championship must have been hard work for Padgham, if only because there was so universal a feeling that it was marked down for him in the book of fate. I remember watching some of his play in the qualifying rounds and thinking that he seemed a little aware of the burden. However when the real thing began he was his best self again and right in the hunt from the start. There were foreign invaders of distinction: Dallemagne again; Sarazen, a thought less spritely perhaps, using Allan Graham's famous brazen putter borrowed for the occasion; two fine amateurs from the Dominions, Bobby Locke of South Africa and Ferrier of Australia, who had just lost an exciting final of the Amateur Championship to Hector Thomson on the thirty-sixth green. Dallemagne was the most threatening after two rounds but fell off a little in the third and even a 69 in the last could not quite win for him. The gravest danger to Padgham came from a player new to most people, James Adams, then of Romford, but born and bred at Troon, where as a small boy he had carried the clubs of the great Willie Fernie and imbibed a proper admiration of that lovely, easy swing.

Adams is an interesting player—he is likewise a very good one—for two reasons. First in these days of curtailed swings he has a very long one. It would have been deemed so even when swings were far longer than now, and since he is big and burly of build it suggests a quite extraordinary lissomeness and flexibility of body. Secondly he is a beautiful putter with a smoothness of "stroking", to use an Americanism, which no American could exceed, and one of those stances on the green which instantly inspire confidence in the ensuing putt. At the end of the first day he led with 71 and 73, one stroke ahead of Padgham, Cotton and Dallemagne. After three rounds he still led Padgham by one shot, since each had a 71. Padgham had the advantage of starting first of the two and once again it told. He did not play his last round like a

plaster saint but like a human man, very strong and cour-
ageous, fighting for his life; there were slips in his 37 to the
turn and it hardly seemed good enough, with all the wolf
pack of his pursuers at his heels. Then he buckled to and
came home in 34, beginning—and it is essential to begin well
over the last nine at Hoylake—with 4, 3, 4, 2. He made slips
after that but saved himself magnificently. Two fives at the
Lake and the Dun were a little ominous, but were compensated
for by a four and a three (with a five-yards putt holed) for the
last two. Adams had a 72 to tie, a cheerless prospect, and
when he had taken 38 to turn it seemed almost a hopeless one.
But he had a great home-coming, beginning with a couple of
very long putts at the Dee and Alps for a three and two.
They put him right in the hunt again and he was left with two
fours to tie. With the old Royal Hole that would not have
been asking overmuch but the new Royal is a different
matter; he was bunkered and took five. He was in and out
of the last hole for three but the rule held good, the early
starter was not to be caught, and the putt stayed out. Padgham had started first and Padgham won. Cotton and
Dallemagne finished one shot behind Adams and two strokes
behind them came Sarazen.

The leaders' scores were amazingly consistent. Padgham
and Adams varied only to the extent of two strokes in their
four rounds, between 71 and 73. Cotton's worst round was
74 and Dallemagne's 75. And Hoylake was oh! so long, to
the eyes of the short and the elderly almost insufferably long.
The big men sailed over the carries of course but even for them
length is cumulative and will tell. If ever there was a battlefield for giants this was it. So no doubt was Carnoustie in
1937, and there the giants were further teased by certain
newly added bunkers, something on the model of the Prin-
cipal's Nose, right in the middle of the fairway at just the
distance from the tee that a giant's drive can compass.
Cotton who won got into one or two of them and nothing
showed his control, nothing perhaps more directly contributed
to his victory, than the philosophical spirit in which he
accepted them. This, his second win, was, to my mind at any
rate, a much more satisfying one than his first. At Sandwich
it was impossible not to be made a little unhappy by that fourth
round, even though it was so bravely retrieved in the last six

holes. At Carnoustie three fine rounds led up to one super-latively good; the winner was not being caught but was himself coming up from behind to finish in a blaze of glory.

Carnoustie further provided the most satisfying of modern championships not for any one man but for the body of British golfers, because the invaders had never been more formidable and they were not merely repelled but sent flying. The whole of the American Ryder Cup side was there and they had just won the match at Southport. That victory did not unduly frighten us, but when they one and all did almost fantastically good scores in the qualifying rounds, our confidence in our own men was admittedly a little shaken. All the more cheering was the state of things at the end of the first two rounds. Of all that invading host only Dudley was left in the forefront with 70 and 74 and he was two strokes behind Reggie Whitcombe. The rest if they were not out of the hunt had yet a great deal of leeway to make up, and good player though Dudley is, nobody was very much afraid of him as a lone crusader. The American terror departed almost as suddenly as it had arisen. It is true that C. Lacey ended third, and his 70 and 72 on the last day meant in the conditions probably as fine golf as ever was played in a championship; but in the first place he had been so far behind that nobody watched him and so nobody had much time to grow afraid of him, and in the second place he was, if the worst came to the worst, an Englishman born and brother of our own A. J. Lacey.

The only unsatisfactory thing about Carnoustie was the weather which was on the last day appalling. It seems to be a matter of touch and go with Cotton's championships whether the play will have to be declared void, and as at Sandwich, there came a dreadful moment at Carnoustie when the first hole was said to be unplayable. The green there lies in a hollow and the hole was moved as far as possible to the side, and yet there had to be a pause for the rescue squad. At any instant it seemed that a complaint might come in from some far-out hole that the course was unplayable, and in fact I have not often seen a course more nearly in that condition from the rain. For almost the whole of that long, drenching, miserable but in the end glorious day everyone was on tenterhooks.

Apart from Charles Lacey's astonishing spurt—and I am ashamed to say I did not see him play a shot— there were two outstanding players, Cotton and R. A. Whitcombe. Cotton won by two strokes and entirely deserved to, but Whitcombe played so well that it seemed a pity that there could not be two champions. He made a great stride forward that year. Always a fine player and a strong man, with a style of fascinating dash and rapidity, he had perhaps never done himself full justice before and he had not been chosen for the Ryder Cup team. If he wanted to prove the selectors wrong he certainly made out his case. At the end of the first two rounds he led Cotton by four strokes, 72 and 70 against 74 and 72. He was the first of the two to start on the last day and had a 74 in all that wind and rain. Cotton gained one stroke on him and his brother Charles was a stroke behind Cotton. It would perhaps be invidious to pick out any one time of day when the weather was at its worst, but certainly no one had to face a heavier storm that did R. A. Whitcombe. At one hole his club slipped clean out of his hands and I have a vivid recollection of seeing him at the last hole bending down as best he could to get a little shelter and wiping his hands on a sopping towel before hitting a brassey shot right home over the burn. He finished in 76, which seemed to me in the circumstances a magnificent score and a winning one; this was to be another illustration of the old rule; I could hardly see Cotton giving him three shots. And yet he gave him five, for he went round in 71 and won by two.

Towards the end of the round Cotton's weather was not quite so bad, but he had had a hard time earlier, and heaven knows that at the end it was bad enough. It was only the end I witnessed, and that imperfectly through a forest of wavering umbrellas, but I can still see Cotton very clearly in his favourite dark-red jersey with a handkerchief knotted round his neck, a dominating figure that seemed to "ride in the whirlwind and direct the storm". 71 is as nearly as maybe a perfect score at Carnoustie, but nobody could get it perfectly in such weather. At those long "four" holes— fives for humbler mortals—he had to do it by chipping and putting of marvellous consistency. As I remember it he did at last fail with a putt at the fifteenth, but when he had got his three at the sixteenth he was virtually home. There was one moment of anxiety when he put his second safely over the burn at the eighteenth but into a bunker at the right of the green. It is at such a moment that the tortured imagination conjures up fearful suppositions. Suppose he hit the ball too cleanly and hit it right over the green and out of bounds! Suppose he stayed in the bunker! Of course he did nothing of the kind; he got safely out and was down in two putts for his five, but that bare possibility of disaster in the very moment of victory had been full of anguish.

I believe Cotton drove his car himself through a good part of his journey home that night. Victory is no doubt an encouraging thing but even so that was a remarkable testimony to his fitness, and when only a few days later he had to face Densmore Shute in a 72-hole match over a Walton Heath of monstrous length, he was suffering from none of the almost inevitable reaction. For one day Shute hung on splendidly and there was nothing in it, but he could not quite do it for a second against such big hitting on such a big course. In the end his long game grew a little ragged, and when at the fourteenth hole in the morning he hooked his tee shot into deepest heather Braid remarked with an almost malicious smile, "He'll want all his dynamiters there."

That was a remarkable match (Cotton won by 6 and 5) but I must get on to another Championship, Sandwich in 1938, in which the weather also played a noteworthy part. For two days it was on its most seraphic summer behaviour; as far as it can now be easy Sandwich was easy and the scores were astonishingly low. Busson, Cox and Burton, I think led at 140; Adams was only a stroke behind them with R. A. Whitcombe on his tail. Then in the night there rose a mighty hurricane and next morning the surroundings of the club-house were as a devastated area, with flags rent to tatters and exhibition tents sheer hulks; and still the wind blew, if possible harder than ever. As a single example of its force Padgham drove the eleventh green, 380 yards away, and then holed his putt for two. Those at least rejoiced who had been "bears" in the popular form of Stock Exchange speculation which consists, in untechnical language, in betting about the winning score. I am a child in these matters but I believe a certain score is fixed and, according as you think it will be beaten or not, so you buy or you sell, and in the end you receive or you pay differences. It has always seemed to me in my innocence that the seller has the best of it for the score is fixed so low that it will scarcely be beaten by many strokes and liability is therefore comparatively limited, whereas if the weather be really bad the fixed score becomes unapproachable and the bears reap a rich harvest. If some of them were kept awake by the tempest that night at least they had a pleasing occupation in counting their prospective winnings. There may have been some players who rejoiced likewise. Years before on the eve of a Championship Arnaud Massy had expressed the pious hope that the wind would blow hard enough to blow down every tree in Sandwich. So perhaps one or two of the big men were glad, knowing that they could fight their way through the storm, which would treat many of their rivals like shuttlecocks. Some players of indisputable quality could make nothing of it. Burton, destined to be next year's champion (to be sure he had notably improved by then), had his long high shots carried to the uttermost parts of the rough; Rees, a great little golfer but without the weight for such an ordeal, was almost literally blown off his feet and so, though he struggled nobly, was Bobby Locke. It was a day almost to suspend criticism and how the leaders got round in such scores as they did I cannot imagine.

Professional opinion, than which there is none shrewder, was that this was the day for Reggie Whitcombe, so strong, firm and compact, with his short swing. Clearly he was a man to watch, especially as he was coupled with Adams, who led him by a stroke, and they started early. And these two were worth watching, for they produced that best of gladiatorial thrills, a fight between partners one of whom is going to win the Championship. It was fit to be compared with that between Vardon and Taylor at Prestwick or Bobby Jones and Watrous at St. Anne's. Here were at once the cut and thrust of match play and the long-drawn-out agony of scoring, in which some terrible disaster in a bunker may always lie in wait. This likelihood of sudden calamity, with the lopping-off of several strokes at one hole and the ensuing kaleidoscopic change of situation, was naturally increased by the wind. In fact the two did lose strokes to one another almost in handfuls in a way very unusual among players of the highest class in ordinary circumstances.

The weather was so bad that I could scarcely make a guess at the sort of scores which could conceivably be done. When I first came across Whitcombe and Adams drawing near the ninth green and was told that Whitcombe's score for eight holes was two under four I was struck dumb with incredulous amazement. Before I had had time to recover there occurred one of the most dramatic loppings of a lead in the whole day. Whitcombe, being on the verge of the ninth green in two, somehow contrived to take four more to hole out. Even so he was out in 36 but Adams, at the back of the green with his second, holed out with his third and bang went three whole shots at one swoop.

In the end Whitcombe with 75 led Adams, 78, by two shots, and the afternoon's round was fuller of drama than the morning's. On the first green Whitcombe had another fit of amiable insanity and took four putts. Adams got his four and they were square. At the Maiden Adams led, but after that he fell away a little and with four holes to go Whitcombe was four shots ahead. That sounds like the end of all things, but let the reader wait! it was only the beginning of the most excruciating fun.

At the fifteenth Whitcombe had a perfect copy-book four but he lost a stroke, for Adams holed out from the back of beyond, below the bank, for a three. Adams wisely put his tee shot—with wood mind you—at the back of the sixteenth green; Whitcombe unwisely under-clubbed himself, went from one bunker to another and took five. That lead of four was now a lead of one and anything might happen, but at this horrid crisis Whitcombe played a really great seventeenth, two fierce bangs in the teeth of the gale, a long run-up and a putt holed. That settled it, for Adams was heavily bunkered and took six. The lead was back to three and a carefully played five by Whitcombe beat the gallant Adams by two shots. What a gorgeous duel it had been!

There was one thrill remaining when Cotton went out to do a 71 to tie and really looked at one time as if he could accomplish the wholly impossible. He drove the second green (370 yards, so the book tells me) and he was out in 35. That was supremely good but not good enough. He began homeward 4, 3, 3, and that did seem good enough. And yet the thing was beyond human power. There was bound to come some one fatal blow and there did come two. At the fifteenth a putt for four went right into the hole and out again. At the sixteenth from a great high iron shot the ball looked, while we all gazed upward, as if it must come plumping down on to the middle of the green. Then the wind got it as it hovered, and it began to turn; it pitched just on the green and relentlessly rolled into a bunker. No doubt a 71 round Sandwich that day would have been an impious act and the gods did not mean it to be done, but there had been moments when it seemed vividly possible.

The last year before the war produced another new champion and an interesting one, Richard Burton. Very tall and strong, with immense power and a suspicion of looseness in his swing, he had several times been brilliant and threatening, but had never quite lasted it out, and he had gained a reputation, not wholly undeserved, for being erratic in a high wind. There was plenty of wind on the decisive day at St. Andrews and Burton did hit one or two wild shots, but no more than anyone might have done. As regards the wind he cleared his character. I was pleased at his winning for a selfish reason of my own. I had always thought Burton a fine putter. I said, and say, that no one had a smoother delivery of the club and that he struck the ball quite beautifully. When I said this to some who knew his game much better than I did they would not wholly agree with me; and so my vanity was tickled when Burton won the Championship in the final round more than by any other one thing by admirable holing-out.

Our national vanity, which had been steadily rising with better times, very nearly received a nasty jolt this year. Lawson Little, now a professional, was brilliant in the qualifying rounds but faltered in the real thing. Bobby Locke could not quite do it, though he played one of the greatest rounds ever seen at St. Andrews; a 70 with an eight at the fourteenth hole, now made far more formidable by a back tee which brought the Beardies back into play. Pose, the South American, a truly grand golfer if ever I saw one, was a little shattered by a disastrous eight at the Road Hole. He unluckily incurred a penalty for grounding his club on the grass beneath the wall, due to his imperfect knowledge of our language and his caddie's inability to explain in dumb show.

These alarming persons were safely out of the way and then suddenly there came danger, desperate, imminent and unexpected, from another American, Bulla. Before we knew where we were we realised that unless Perry or Shankland or Burton could stop him Bulla would inevitably have the Championship. In due course Perry and Shankland just failed and only Burton stood between us and humiliation.

Bulla had come over, I believe, as in some way representing a new and cheaper American ball. Whether he played with it in the Championship I know not but he played uncommonly well with something. He was a mountain of a man, with a rapid swing and great strength. Luckily for us he had trouble with his putting, on the first day great trouble; then he bought yet another new club—he had according to legend been buying them in sheaves—and he must have putted better; he must, I think, have putted pretty well, for his last two rounds were 71 and 73 and he left Burton—O horror!—with a 73 to tie.

Burton was far away at the end of the course and I only heard he was out in 35, which was eminently hopeful. I heard of an astonishing second out of heather at the tenth, played with his 'blaster' with the face turned in on the ball, which gave him a four. I heard too with great joy of a two at the eleventh, and then all is a blank till I see him in memory coming to the fifteenth with two fives and two fours for a 72 which would win by a shot. I remember dimly a four at the fifteenth, with a very long run-up and an eight-footer holed. With dreadful clearness and a mixture of horror and relief there comes back the sixteenth—a drive hooked nearly into the whins, a second short, a chip fluffed, a fourth weak and then—heaven be praised!—another good putt at the bottom of the tin.

After that all was serene. He steered his second to the Road Hole to just the right place and George Duncan exclaimed, "It's all right. He must do it now." He pitched nicely up and got his five, and he had a fine wind to blow him home at the last. Tee shots are not often cheered but there came a roar of cheering as Burton hit a vast drive almost to the Valley of Sin. There was only one way in which he could lose and that was by completely missing his second. A scuffle with a putter seemed the shot, but Burton said afterwards he never thought of that. In a ghastly silence he took some much-lofted niblick and played a beautiful little pitch. Two putts to win now. I was walking with Gordon Simpson, not generally deemed an emotional person; we could not see exactly where the hole was, and when Burton struck his putt, a little downhill, with what looked like too free and bold a stroke, Gordon gave a sharp cry of agony, as of a hunted creature. But it was all right; the ball vanished into the hole for a three and a 71. The curtain could not have been rung down with a more splendid gesture on pre-war golf.

Chapter 9

THE RISE OF THE MIDLANDS

PERHAPS nowhere in England has golf, especially amateur golf, been more keenly played during comparatively modern times than in the Midlands. By that I mean the counties of Warwickshire, Staffordshire and Worcestershire and in particular the neighbourhood of Birmingham. It is a part of the country not so rich as some others in the soil that makes the best inland courses though it has several that are naturally very good; but it has largely made up by art and by enthusiasm for what it lacked by nature, and it has produced a number of good players, who have by serious application to the game made the best of their chances and themselves. I may perhaps claim to have seen a little more of the rise of Midland golf than have most Southerners through the accident of my playing regularly at Aberdovey, the nearest seaside course to Birmingham and so from its early days the holiday ground of many Midland players. I remember the late C. A. Palmer very well there from the last year or two of the nineteenth century. A little later I played with both Frank Woolley and Frank Carr when they were schoolboys, and I think it is true to say that these three, though golfers of very different ages—for Palmer was many years older than the other two—were in a great measure the founders of the Midland school.

Charles Palmer had made his athletic name as a famous amateur racing bicyclist, a fact commemorated by the name of Palmer tyres, and had only taken to golf as a comparatively middle-aged man, when he had prospered in business and so had leisure to play. He quickly made up for lost time, being a man with immense powers of taking pains, very shrewd and very determined, with an ideal game-playing temperament, tranquil and yet with the right spark of pugnacity, not in any circumstances to be daunted. His defeat of Jerome Travers in an Amateur Championship at Sandwich, a Travers to be sure strangely off his game, when he was himself partially crippled with lumbago, was typical of him.

With his rather short swing and without youth to help him, he might never have had quite the power to climb so high as he did had it not been for the coming of the rubber-cored ball in 1902, just when he was becoming a good player. It helped to promote him to a higher class and in 1907 he reached the final of the Amateur Championship at St. Andrews. This is ancient history and outside my limits but it is worth mentioning, not only because Palmer was a remarkable golfer, but because by his successes and his tireless enthusiasm, to which Handsworth is in some sort a monument, he did, I am convinced, a great deal to fire Midland golf.

The other two, the two young Franks, Woolley and Carr, were of another generation and another type; they had begun to play as boys and had all the advantages that a boyhood spent golf-club in hand can give. Both were fine, natural swingers of a club, though Woolley beginning with a very long swing cut it down, without knowing how or why, into a very short one, compensated for by a notably full follow-through. Both played in the English team which beat Scotland at Hoylake in 1910, making their first appearance at the same time as Abe Mitchell, and both seemed likely to do so for years to come. Their careers were, however, sadly short for Carr fell in the war and Woolley became early a martyr to arthritis. However, they had helped to sow the seed which was to bear full fruit a good many years later when the Midlands were to win two Amateur Championships running with players comparatively little known save to their admirers at home: Dr. William Tweddell in 1927 and T. P. Perkins in 1928.

Scotland has some claim to Tweddell, though he is an Englishman born in Durham, for he learnt much of his golf at Aberdeen University where he had played for the University side for three years. Immediately after the war he had won the Cruden Bay tournament, for which a number of good Scottish players enter, but still he was little known to the general public when he came to Hoylake for the Championship and won it. There was nothing particular about his methods to attract attention, save their idiosyncrasies and the excellent results they produced, particularly in his high iron shots to the green, and he certainly betrayed nothing of the honour of a Scottish upbringing. He had a curious stance, with his arms rather stiff and held far out from his body, his right hand noticeably over the club; he played for a big hook or rather he appeared to aim to long off and hit the ball over the bowler's head. It was a decidedly original style and the success that it would achieve was not immediately apparent, as witness this true story. A golfer, now dead, who had not been to Hoylake, was at Prestwick in the following year to play in the Championship, and on one of the practice days was waiting for his turn on the first tee. After one player had struck off he remarked, "Well, thank goodness, there's one man in this tournament I *can* beat," and was disconcerted on hearing that he had pitched on the then reigning Champion.

Tweddell played very well at Hoylake, gradually gaining supporters as he went along. In the final he met Eustace Landale, who knew Hoylake intimately, was a steady and resolute golfer who could make the ball run, and a really admirable putter on those big greens, as on any others, with the big-headed wooden putter that goes by the name of Gassiat. Thirty-six holes are apt to emphasise a difference in merit and I think Landale was nearly as tired by the time he reached that final as Allan Graham had been in 1921. At any rate he was rather out-hit and out-played by Tweddell who won with great comfort by 7 and 6. From that time onwards Tweddell was always a player to be reckoned with and perhaps his greatest achievement, though in the end an unsuccessful one, was his fight against Lawson Little at St. Anne's eight years later, which is described in another chapter. Meanwhile in that same year another outstanding amateur golfer from the Midlands, an entirely home-made product, born at West Bromwich, the seat of the far-famed Albion, had made his first appearance, not in the Amateur but the English Championship. It was played that year in his own county at Little Aston, a pleasant park course of excellent turf. I remember the occasion well for one particular reason, that neither for the first nor the last time I formed on insufficient premises a thoroughly bad judgment. Before the Championship began somebody asked me to come and look at a young man called Perkins, who had been doing various good things in the neighbourhood and was thought promising. I went and saw, and to my shame was not conquered. It was not a very engaging style; unless I am merely excusing myself it grew much more polished afterwards; at any rate

I was not particularly impressed. However, I soon had cause to recant as he reached the final against another Midlander, J. B. Beddard, and I believe I refereed the match. Beddard was by far the more experienced of the two, a very neat and compact player who had already played for England. He played well, but so did his opponent who had a little more power to help him and Perkins won a very good match on the thirty-fifth green.

I was wrong when I said a little while back that Perkins was comparatively little known when he won the Amateur Championship in 1928, for he had become known by name to the general golfing public, but not many had seen him play before Prestwick. He had beyond all doubt come on since Little Aston; he now gave more feeling of control and his iron play in particular was very fine and had a masterly, professional touch. He was too a very sound putter. Only in one early round was he pushed hard, when he was, if I remember, taken to the last hole by Rankin from Sunningdale. Otherwise he strode victoriously through the field from the start and was the best player there. Prestwick was rather dry and burnt, and as evidence of this I remember that Perkins used to play the Cardinal Hole, 505 yards long, with a No. 1 iron from the tee, a club with which he was very strong, and a spoon to the green. His opponent in the final was Roger Wethered, not the best of Wethereds by any means but one who had struggled bravely through by sheer sticking power and the ability to play an occasional very good shot when it was needed. Several times he had been in jeopardy and when in the last eight he met Lord Wardington, whom it is hard to call anything but Montie Pease, he had appeared doomed. Lord Wardington, then at what would have been deemed for anyone else the mature age of 59, was one up going to the home hole; that hole is an easy four and a difficult three and who more likely to do a steady four when it was wanted? However, for once he did not quite hit his drive, the ball was caught in some benty country; and the hole cost him a five. I have a disgraceful recollection of retiring to lunch at a hospitable house near by and seeing those two struggle away into the distance, where Wethered ultimately won at the twenty-first hole. He had once again hacked his way through, but that sort of golf of gallant patches was not quite good enough for the game that Perkins was consistently playing and the younger man won by 6 and 4.

In that same summer Perkins played very well in America; but he had a severe dose of Bobby Jones. At Wheaton Bobby beat him in the Walker Cup match by 13 and 12. Then in the Championship at Braeburn, after Perkins had done nobly in reaching the final, Bobby was just a little more merciful, to the tune of 10 and 9. Bobby was doing that sort of murderous thing to anybody and everybody about that time; the best of golfers might lose to him by double figures and leave the court without a stain on his character. Perkins was almost beyond doubt the favourite for the Amateur Championship of 1929 at Sandwich. He was playing formidably well beforehand but he had developed the habit of playing unconscionably slow with an altogether too leisurely painstaking. This led to an incident unique in the annals of the Championship; an occasionally fire-eating old friend of mine, playing behind him and his partner, demanded the right to go through on the ground that they had lost, as was beyond dispute, more than one clear hole on the couple in front of them. What Mr. Yellowplush might have called a "holtercation" ensued and the papers fell greedily on such a delicious titbit of news. Perhaps this had an effect on Perkins's golf; he may have been conscious of a certain lack of sympathy; at any rate his game decidedly fell away and he was beaten after a desperate struggle at the twenty-second hole by that good Scottish golfer A. A. MacNair.

That was in effect the end of his career in his own country, for he presently went to the United States, where in 1932 he became a professional. No doubt an intensive course of American golf had made him a still better player than before, when in 1932, his first year as a professional, he tied for second place in the U.S. Open Championship. So certainly did he appear to have won when he had holed his last putt, that the photographers made him hole it again in order that the authentic scene should be immortalised. However Gene Sarazen came in with a terrific last round of 66, to beat Perkins and Bobby Cruikshank, who had tied with him, by three strokes. That was a hard fate. From that moment we have heard little of him over here though the books tell me that he won the Ohio Open in 1937. He was not for some inscrutable reason a very attractive player but there could be no two opinions about his merits.

The names I have set down by no means exhaust the list of those who have brought distinction to golf in the Midlands. The game seems·to run in families there. Witness C. F. Bretherton, an adopted son of Charles Palmer (I remember him the smallest of boys at Aberdovey) who played four years for England; Stanley Lunt, one of the most graceful of players, an English Champion and a nephew of Frank Carr; Eric Fiddian, English Champion and runner-up in the Amateur, and his brother. Nor must I forget A. S. Newey, Dr. Robb, a Scottish international and a Midlander by adoption, and Chris Buckley, formerly a famous Association football player and later a most sturdy and resolute golfer. And these are but some of the many who have kept the torch of golf burning brightly in the three counties.

Chapter 10

MORE AMATEUR CHAMPIONS

FROM my excursion into Midland golf and its two Amateur Champions I must retrace my steps a little to 1925 and take a rapid look at the other Amateur Champions between that year and the coming of war. It was a noteworthy year on two accounts, that the Championship was played for the second time at Westward Ho! and that it was won by Robert Harris, without whose name the list of worthy Champions would have been incomplete. He had twice reached the final; he had won the 'Dundee Evening Telegraph' Cup, then something in the nature of a Scottish Amateur Championship, twenty-three years before; he had been known as an outstanding player since in the early years of the century London golfers had discovered that there was a young gentleman playing at Acton who was alarmingly good. He had won all sorts of things but the Championship had escaped him till he was 43, and then just when people had begun to say regretfully that he never would win it now, he came out and won it in the most convincing possible manner. He was definitely a player of pre-war vintage (I shall come presently to one considerably more crusted and cobwebbed in Michael Scott who also won after the war) and he had, as his contemporaries and elders thought, the pre-war virtues. I have already quoted his dictum that the way to play golf is to learn it first and think about it afterwards. Few people have followed their own advice so well. He learned as a boy at Carnoustie, that home of fine swings, a style at once free and admirably compact, and there is no shrewder and more observant judge of golf. He is now one of the wisest of the elder statesmen and at the same time is possessed in some directions of a fine youthful enthusiasm. I seem seldom to have met him without his having just acquired a brand-new set of clubs of peculiarly magical quality, and no one is happier in judicious tinkering at old ones amid the fragrant surroundings of leather and cobbler's wax in the professional's shop. He is a good golfer in every possible sense of the words.

1926 was a Walker Cup year and so that happened which was always likely though it surprisingly had not happened since Mr. Travis's day, two-and-twenty years before; an American golfer won the Amateur Championship. This was Jesse Sweetser at Muirfield and his victory was certainly not surprising to those of us who had been at Brookline in 1922 and watched him win perhaps the most overwhelming of all Amateur Championship victories in history, unless it was that of Freddie Tait at Sandwich 'way back' in 1896. Just as Tait had done at Sandwich Sweetser had mown his way through the hardest part of the draw, knocking out one fine player after another by big margins and being scarcely pressed throughout the whole week. He is big, strong and essentially athletic—he was a quarter-mile runner at Yale—having a conspicuously "grooved" swing, not exactly pretty, with a touch of mechanism about it, so that one might imagine it set clicking by a penny in the slot, but obviously sound and most impressive. If he was not quite so clearly inspired at Muirfield as at the Country Club, that was the sort of thing that could scarcely happen twice in a lifetime; he played formidably well and, as I remember, was only once in danger, namely against Brownlow (now Lord Lurgan) in the semi-final. Brownlow, with his unruffled calm and the extreme tidiness which suggests that he has emerged magically from a band-box, played shot for shot with him and holed out impeccably with his Gassiat putter. The match went to the twenty-first hole and I, having lately had small objects cut out of my knee, must needs rest exhausted by the home green, so that I did not see the end. I believe that at one of those three holes a chip and a Gassiat putt would have brought victory, but this may not be true and there are always might-have-beens. Nobody could conceivably say that Sweetser did not deserve to win and in the final he won with perfect comfort against a good Edinburgh golfer, A. F. Simpson, who palpably did not carry quite enough guns for him. How well do I recollect the fine impersonal patriotism of a Scottish friend, whom I heard telephoning from the clubhouse at luncheon and uttering in a tone of unspeakable gloom the words "Scotland four down"!

Next come the Tweddell and Perkins years already dealt with and after them I may skip again, for in 1929 Tolley won for a second time at Sandwich and I have said plenty about

him. In 1930 came Bobby Jones who has had a whole chapter.
1931 saw the Championship again at Westward Ho! than
which there is no better battlefield and no more delightful
one for those who go there, but having this disadvantage that
the Scottish players will not go there, at any rate in any
proper quantity. It is to be sure a long way off. It can be
speciously argued by the aid of Bradshaw that it is no further
off than Sandwich or Deal, but they will not listen, and there
is this to be said that Sandwich is at any rate much nearer
London, where a defeated entrant may find consolation and
amusement more easily than in Devon. It is a great pity, for
Scotland is so full of good young amateurs that a field is not
representative without at least an adequate number of them.

   This particular Championship produced two brand-new
finalists, Eric Martin Smith and John de Forest, now Count
John de Bendern. Martin Smith won by a hole and that his
victory was a surprise it would be idle to deny. One who had
lately played with him in the Cambridge side telegraphed to
him on the morning of the final in some such terms as these:
"Quite ridiculous but keep at it". And yet it was not at all
ridiculous on the week's golf, for he played very well and
steadily and obeyed that sovereign rule for winning championships, to which so few have ever managed to adhere, the rule
which enjoins the not playing a bad round. A player may of
course be swept away by an overwhelmingly brilliant round
by his opponent; that is just "too bad", but he is far more
likely to be beaten through playing a poor round himself, and
wonderful things can be achieved by the man who keeps
throughout to a steady level of the pretty good. Martin Smith
was very consistent and putted very well indeed. He drove
far enough with a well-controlled swing, which he later turned
into a much longer one, gaining something in length but losing
in accuracy. He never grew frightened of winning and in a
close finish he avoided all the grosser forms of sin and was
admirably cool and steady. It was an odd win but not an
ill-deserved one.

   His opponent, John de Forest, was perhaps the most
interesting figure in this Championship, for a reason which
aroused the sympathy of all who watched him and now and
then, especially when the breeze blew chill, the irritation of
all who played behind him. He was suffering from the

waggling disease in its most aggravated form. Most of us have had it at times in a milder shape and it is not so lethal as the disease, christened by Horace Hutchinson from a familiar Greek verb "atupsia", which allows the patient to get the club up but will by no manner of means permit him to get it down again, though he tug at it as at a recalcitrant bell-rope. The victim of the waggling disease can get the club both up and down if only he can stop waggling, but this he cannot do for a most unconscionable time. Even when poor de Forest could make up his mind to go back there was a suspicion of a hitch in the swing, and on the green his putter went back by numbers. Yet he kept control of himself nobly, humouring his ailment since he could not exorcise it, resolute not to hit till he was ready. It must have been desperately hard work for him, and it is fair to add that it was also rather hard work for other people.

To reach the final one year and win the Championship the next is an achievement that only a really good golfer can compass and that is what John de Forest did, for he won at Muirfield in 1932, though his waggling symptoms were as pronounced as ever. A little while later he made a complete recovery and became a particularly quick and attractive player, but though he looked better he never did nearly so well again. It almost seemed as if the game had become too simple and the fact of having to wrestle with that waggling demon had given him the extra something that is wanted for victory. He had one very close shave at Muirfield when he met in the semi-final that grand Irish golfer of pre-war vintage, Lionel Munn. Going to the home hole it seemed to be Munn's match and then suddenly, and to the general consternation, he lobbed his second from a perfect lie into a bunker not such a very long way in front of his illustrious nose. The match went on for several additional holes as Munn's matches have a habit of doing; he once lost to C. A. Palmer at the twenty-eighth at Sandwich, and now he lost again though not so unreasonably far from home. In the final de Forest met Eric-Fiddian, a powerful and attractive player with a tendency amid a number of perfect tee shots to hit one or two hard on the head. That final took a very, very long time; it seemed to go on for ever and when I staggered to the microphone to describe it I was told that my voice sounded weak and weary. If it did it did not belie me. John de Forest won by 3 and 1 and he undoubtedly earned his Championship, but though the match was "long-drawn-out" I should hesitate to call it "a bout of linked sweetness".

1933 at Hoylake saw one of the most notable wins of the whole series, that of Michael Scott. Since he was born in 1878 his victory was generally acclaimed as one for the Senior Golfer's Society, for which the qualifying age is 55, but honesty compels the statement that he was still at the time a stripling of 54. It was a wonderful win and the winner seemed as fresh as a daisy after it, which will strike most people of 54 as almost more wonderful still. Incidentally he broke the record set up also at Hoylake in 1902, when Charles Hutchings won at the age of 53, a record that most people thought impregnable. Michael Scott had been for years and years more than good enough to win, but somehow or other he never had, perhaps because he had tried too hard. Now the mellowing passage of the years had brought just the needed touch of relaxation, without weakening his belief in his own powers. At any rate after barely scrambling through the first round he went on growing stronger with every round and reached his 'peak' at just the right moment, when he quitely crushed the life out of the American Dunlap, who was beginning to look very dangerous. In the final he was always too steady for Dale Bourn. Once or twice his lead dwindled a little uncomfortably, but it always came back and he 'snodded' his man at the Lake. His putting had much to do with it, for he had a week of really good trustworthy putting, and that had not habitually been his strong point. What he had always been was a very straight driver, especially good in a wind, and a beautifully crisp player of iron shots, bearing all over them the hallmark of that indefinable thing called "class".

Of all the golfing families I doubt if any have been keener than the Scotts—the three brothers Osmund, Denys and Michael and their sister, the once peerless Lady Margaret. The family tradition was being carried on by Kenneth who was killed, to the sorrow of all who knew him, in Sicily. Two years or so ago when I was in Gloucestershire I made a pilgrimage to Stowell to see the course in the park where in youth they had been used to play. It had fallen sadly out of repair but most of the greens could be discerned; indeed some holes still possessed rather rusty and lackadaisical flags, and I amused myself, reverently amused myself, by trying to trace the sequence of the holes and imagining a family foursome or three-ball rushing out for one more wild dash, one more nine holes before dinner. It is pleasant that Michael accomplished what Osmund just failed to do, namely put the family name on the roll of champions, as long before their sister had done.

Now for 1934 and 1935 and two American victories running won by the same player who was in the same two years Amateur Champion of his own country. I feel that the brush should be dipped in earthquake and eclipse to do justice to Lawson Little, for here was a player for whom my too hard-worked epithet 'formidable' is scarcely strong enough: Lawson was intimidating. Not very tall but enormously broad and enormously strong, capable of a daunting pugnacity of expression, he was as a bull in the long game, and yet no dove could be gentler near the hole, so persuasive was his touch. The power of his rather shut-faced swing was immense, not only in fact but in appearance; at the top of the swing, with everything at full stretch, he looked as if he must surely kill the ball, and he was essentially a killer in match play. After winning those four championships he turned professional in 1936 and has since won the Open Championship of the United States. Doubtless the change added something more both of polish and consistency, as it always must; but if he lives to be a hundred he will never play better golf, never, I venture to think, such devastatingly good golf as he did in the final at Prestwick in 1936. He arrived there in the full tide of success, for in the Walker Cup at St. Andrews, a course of which he has a just appreciation, he had with Goodman beaten Tolley and a sadly erratic Wethered in the foursomes by 8 and 7, and had been by only one hole more merciful to Tolley in the singles. At Prestwick he was pressed very hard once by that meteoric player L. G. Garnett, who holed a great and curly putt to save the match on the eighteenth green only to lose at the nineteenth. In the final Lawson met Wallace, a good West of Scotland player since turned professional, who had been putting beautifully and had won a "local Derby" (the crowd seemed to think it was Celtic and Glasgow Rangers) against Jack McLean.

Poor Wallace had a sore time of it. He wanted a good start and his putting forsook him on the first green, so that he took three putts. It was, though we did not then fully appreciate it, the writing on the wall. Little was home with two mighty blows at the Cardinal and holed his putt for three: Wallace made mistakes at the next two holes, and then when he played the sixth perfectly well his enemy holed another inhuman putt for another three. Scotland five down in six holes and so it went on. Little did put two shots into bunkers but got his five and his half in each case and here is the fantastic score which made him twelve up at lunch:

Out, 4 3 3 4 3 3 5 4 4—33
Home, 4 3 5 4 3 4 3 4 3—33

Did lunch have the least mollifying effect? Far from it; it only made him more tigerish. He began with yet another putt holed for a three at the first hole, and there was nothing for it but to laugh. He had another three at the famous Pow Burn, the fourth; in five holes he only had one hole over three, a perfect four at the Cardinal, and he won at the Himalayas by 14 up and 13 to play.

Very different was Lawson Little's next final at St. Anne's, a wonderful match which saw him fighting with his back to the wall against a truly heroic Tweddell, to emerge victorious at the last hole. St. Anne's was far from being that year the velvety expanse of perfect lies and greens which all its visitors know. It had been cruelly attacked, I think by leather-jackets, and a somewhat ruthless chemical treatment had left it rather bare and brown and unsightly. It was truly hard on the club to have such bad luck on the occasion, for which the members had longed, of a first Amateur Championship. The course was a sound test but it was temporarily not St. Anne's. It was well enough suited to Lawson Little, with his great power and his capacity for the forcing shot, but, till the final was reached at any rate, he was by no means the Little of the year before, and from the start he let himself be harried by players whom at Prestwick he would have trampled under-foot. Still by sheer fighting power and by the great golfer's ability to play the counting shot, he won through, and when the final started it seemed that his troubles were over. Full of menace he attacked his man as soon as the bell rang; he won the first two holes perfectly, he looked as if he would win the third but slipped and only got a half, he did win the fourth. "There is no standing this," I exclaimed in Hazlitt's words, as he saw the Gas-man's blows playing like lightning round Bill Neate's head, but Hazlitt was wrong and so was I. Never have I admired a golfer more than I did Tweddell in the disastrous beginning of that match; his serenity and cheerfulness, the care that he took, and it is so much easier to take care when you are up, his whole demeanour were beyond praise. He was outdriven, as was inevitable, but he recovered his long game which had begun rather shakily, and he had the touch of his putter very true. Even so he was two more holes down by the time the eleventh was reached, for Little continued to play commanding golf, and five holes is a heavy deficit. Tweddell hung on splendidly and two came back by lunch-time—a fine effort but could it avail?

In the Prestwick final of 1899 Freddie Tait had at one time in the morning been five up on John Ball; two holes had come back by lunch and John Ball won in the end at the thirty-seventh. Here was a glorious precedent, and it was nearly but not quite followed. Tweddell was still three down at the eighth in the afternoon; then he holed a putt for two to win the ninth; then he won the eleventh and twelfth to square the match; then he had a putt of nine or ten feet to win the thirteenth and he had been putting beautifully with his wooden putter. It was a breath-catching moment big with fate, but this one beat him; the ball just died away. Now it was the time for a counter-attack and Little did attack vigorously, winning both the fourteenth and fifteenth, the first by a very fine chip. Hope never died but it was almost gone. Tweddell looked as if he could win the sixteenth but Little holed a putt. The match looked as if it must end at the seventeenth but Tweddell saved himself with a great shot out of bunker near the green and got his four in the teeth of destiny. Little remained unshaken; he never looked like getting anything but an orthodox four at the home hole; Tweddell never looked like a three though he made no mistake. So ended a great spurt and a great match.

Four more Champions remain for me, and the first is Hector Thomson at St. Andrews in 1937. This was a victory reviving to the spirits, for it was at that moment in the young

Scottish amateurs that our chief hopes seemed to lie, and here was one of them, and he the most promising, coming right to the front. Jack McLean had been their leader for some little while; a grand iron player, a very good putter, lacking only something of length. He had thrice won the Scottish amateur; he had won in Australia; he had been dreadfully near to winning in America; only in our own Amateur he had consistently disappointed. Now here was his most dangerous opponent in Scotland, gifted with just a little more power, doing what Mclean had failed to do. Hector Thomson was that year and indeed in any year a beautiful golfer, with a swing so easy that he could control, when he took a fancy to them, very springy clubs; well armed right through the game, an admirably steady putter. Thomson won but he very nearly didn't and in Ferrier from Australia he had an extremely dangerous opponent. Only perhaps when we watched him steadily in the final did many of us realise how dangerous he was. Superficially he was not a very attractive golfer, for he had a curious, sprawling finish to his shots, due, I believe, to some weakness in his left leg. It gave an air of uncertainty which was not justified by results, and he like Thomson was good all through. Moreover he had a capacity for bursts of brilliant play; he could make long breaks, if one may so describe it, and he began this final by making one. Thomson did not play badly but Ferrier was clearly on the top of his enemy and he was three up in the first round going to the Long Hole In. Then he did exactly what Voigt had done when he seemed on the point of beating Bobby Jones in 1930; he cut his tee shot over the wall out of bounds. It is a superfluous sort of mistake, one to be avoided easily enough by a player who is on his guard against it, but one which a player in full tide of success will scarcely contemplate. I think it cost Ferrier that Championship for it gave Thomson breathing space and confidence. From that point he gained steadily and gradually till he was two up going to the seventeenth in the afternoon. He played, as was right and prudent, a perfect copy-book five: Ferrier, as was also right, went boldly for the green; he stopped his ball on that narrow plateau with a great shot and got his four. At the home hole Ferrier played the odd to the back of the green and Thomson from the right laid a pitch-and-run second absolutely stone dead; a most dramatic tit for tat and a wonderful finish for both players.

Two more American victories followed, but of the first of them, that of Robert Sweeney at Sandwich, the whole credit can scarcely be given to America, for he had, I believe, learned most of his game at Le Touquet and then some more at Oxford, and he was generally thought of as an English golfer just as, to revive an ancient grievance, Jack Graham was a Hoylake golfer though he played for Scotland. He had always had a sound and elegant style and he had been a good but by no means an outstanding player for Oxford. It would not be true to say that he burst suddenly on the world in 1937 because two years before he had reached the semi-final at St. Anne's, but I think it is true that few people realised before what a very, very good golfer he was. He played beautifully at Sandwich and was not only the winner but the dominating figure of the tournament. Many people pinned their faith to Lionel Munn against him in the final, for Munn knew Sandwich as Mowgli knew the *rukh* and had been playing for a long time round after round of consistently good, almost faultless golf. But Sweeney had the legs of him in the long game, Munn being no longer in the first flush of his youth, and it told as it is bound to tell. One crucial instant there was, which all who watched will recall. Munn having been down at lunch had squared the match at the fifth hole in the afternoon and he had the honour at the Maiden. For a man who has been getting his own back there is nothing more propitious than a one-shot hole, *if* he can put his ball on the green and give his perhaps faltering opponent a nasty one to follow. Munn could almost have played the tee shot to the Maiden blindfold but for once in a very long while he failed and cut his ball into the little bunker lurking on the right. Sweeney leaped at his chance and got his three; the moment had gone and did not come back.

It is hard to say what may or may not happen after years of war and the promise of the last years before it may never be quite fulfilled. All I can say therefore is that if there had been no war—what a big if!—the future historian might have thought of that championship chiefly as the first year of James Bruen. He was the reigning Boy Champion, only just over 17, a plump, sturdy schoolboy; he very nearly won the St. George's

Cup against a championship field; he was second against nearly as strong a field at Deal; in the Championship he lost a hard match to Chapman, afterwards an American champion, and there was no sort of doubt that here was a player quite out of the common. He had not a very graceful or orthodox swing, appearing to take the club very much inwards and bring it down with a loop at the top; he was rather a forcing player, but what force there was behind his shots! how consistently he played them and with what a masterful confidence! He was not then quite the player he was in the following spring when he went round St. Andrews apparently at will in 69 or 70 and sent the other candidates in the Walker Cup trials flying like ninepins, but he was, to put it at its lowest, a most encouraging find. If America could constantly produce infant phenomenons, boys who could play like very good men, why couldn't we? That was a question often asked and now here was at least one practical answer. Ireland had done it. How good Bruen may be when golf begins again I know not; perhaps better still; perhaps never quite so good again in having lost that first careless rapture. At any rate he was excitingly good then.

Bruen saved himself for the Walker Cup next year and did not come to Troon for the Championship in which all the American Walker Cup team took part. There was also a former Amateur Champion of the United States, the Canadian Ross Somerville, who had played in our Championship before, at Hoylake, a very fine all-round player of games, golfer, cricketer and ice-hockey player. Style is a matter of individual taste and I rank Somerville very high in the category of stylists; I think of him as the counterpart among men of the American lady Miss Virginia Van Wie. He brings to mind the description of an old cricketer, "Elegance, all elegance, fit to play before the king in his parlour". There was a certain amount of inevitable and internecine warfare among the invaders and the goddess of the draw was certainly unkind in bringing Fischer and Yates together at the very outset. The luck was against Fischer too when he was laid a dead and practically hopeless stymie on the nineteenth green. Another clash, somewhat later, was between Goodman, the reigning American Champion, and Kocsis. A highly distinguished Scottish golfer said to me at the beginning of the tournament, "Goodman will cake-walk this Championship." This seemed to me an excessive view, as I did not think Goodman quite so alarmingly good as he had been on his previous visit. So there was a certain prophetic satisfaction in seeing Kocsis well and truly beat him. Kocsis had a beautiful swing, reminiscent of the smoothness of the Joneses and Ouimets, and with none of the forcing hook that had become more fashionable among the young American players.

Of these forceful hookers Yates, from the moment of his beating Fischer, was obviously to be feared. With a wrench of the shoulders that reminded me of George Von Elm, he hit the ball straight and far and he was a sure and beautiful putter. Cyril Tolley, who was playing finely, was one of the hopes of beating him but Yates got away with a good start and was not to be caught. The chief hopes of the British Empire then rested in Somerville, but when he met the Irishman Cecil Ewing in the semi-final he seemed a tired man and made some mistakes of which one would not have believed him capable. Ewing, who finished the match with one of the longest putts ever seen on the home green, well deserved his win by two holes. He is a very big strong man with a neat, controlled style and a thoroughly good golfer, but, with all respect to him, I do not think many people expected to see him beat Yates. It was quite a good match without ever becoming desperately exciting and Yates never really looked like losing it. There has been no invading Champion more popular than Charlie Yates, whose cheerfulness and humour, of his own particular brand, made everybody like him. When a week or two later we had won the Walker Cup he led our victorious revels with inimitable spirit.

And so to the last year before the long gap and to another new Champion, Alex Kyle, a border Scotsman by birth and almost Yorkshireman by adoption. The North had recognised him as a fine player for some time, but the first that we poor ignorant Southerners really knew of him was when he appeared in the Mixed Foursomes at Worplesdon, playing with Mrs. Rhodes as a partner. Alike in method and result here was one who could not escape notice and he was at once marked down as a future hope for the Walker Cup side. In due course he showed himself to be capable of great brilliance, if not then quite consistent brilliance, in the trials at St. Andrews, and justified expectations by winning his single in the Walker Cup, the single that sealed America's fate. How joyful a sight, never to be forgotten, was Kyle's crowd, pouring home from the fourteenth green to swell Ewing's crowd at the burn!

This last pre-war Championship was the more cheerful for that Walker Cup win of the year before. It had given us a good conceit of ourselves and a new and more admiring interest in our amateurs. Bruen and to a lesser degree Kyle were the players that everyone wanted to watch, and in due course they met. Bruen had been playing in a style to justify his reputation, and his summary manner of disposing of such a powerful player as Leonard Crawley had been particularly impressive. If he was not quite so overpowering when he met Kyle that was because a man can as a rule only play as well as his opponent will let him and Kyle was giving very little licence. Two holes come back to me from that match, the first and the last. At the first Bruen in playing his second took just too bold a line over the corner of the field and went out of bounds. That was a chance of a good start of which Kyle, not as a rule a good starter, availed himself. Coming to the home hole Kyle was one up, but he plumped his second into the cross-bunker before the green whereas Bruen was over and had his four safe. The hole is memorable as showing the great help given by the modern 'dynamiter' niblick. Three times before in the round had Kyle laid his ball as near as might be dead out of bunkers though thrice he had missed the putt. This bunker at the last hole is deep and fierce and once upon a time there was little hope of laying the ball near the flag out of it; from under the face it was rather a matter of scratching the head and getting out anyhow. Now with what Sam Weller might have called his "patent double million magnifyin' gas niblick of hextra power" Kyle laid his ball, roughly speaking, stone dead and got his half in four and the match. It was a magnificent shot at such a moment or indeed any moment, but it was the club that made it possible.

Kyle's opponent in the final was A. A. Duncan, generally called Tony, the Oxford Captain of a year or two before and one of three or four young golfers in Wales who had made the head of the Welsh side as effective as any in the four countries, even though the tail could not quite keep it up. He had not played in the Walker Cup side of the year before, though for myself I should have felt very much inclined to choose him for the foursomes, since it would be hard to imagine a better foursome partner, very straight and accurate, long enough, of a most unruffled calm and above all a truly admirable putter. In the case of some good putters, the observer is a little baffled as to why they are so good; there seems nothing to say but that the ball goes into the hole; but in Tony Duncan's method there is, apart from its smoothness and swift decisiveness, one obvious merit; the club head keeps low and along the ground as it goes through. If this be not all the law and the prophets it is one of the unfailing marks of good putting.

In the semi-final Kyle beat a dangerous American, Holt, while Duncan just beat Stowe who had reached the same point two years before, an essentially slashing player of great power who can be more brilliant than his conqueror but lacks something of his solidity. The final was a capital match to watch, played delightfully, at a brisk pace, with plenty of really good golf and enough mistakes to make it thoroughly human and interesting. Neither could get away from the other and at all square going to the Dun a thirty-seventh hole seemed imminent. Then at that hole Duncan made a mistake; Kyle at the right moment played the Royal perfectly and all was rather unexpectedly over. So at long last is this chapter and we must wait for the first Championship after a second war, with a new Cyril Tolley and another Bob Gardner.

Chapter 11

THE LADIES

IN 1914 at Hunstanton I had watched the last Ladies' Championship before the first war. It was, I am ashamed to say, my first sight of one and mightily impressive it was. Ever since that time I have always thought and said that well as ladies often play against men the onlooker only appreciates their golf at its full value when he sees them playing against each other. He gets his views in better proportion than he ever can when he sees them being out-hit by the greater strength of men. I came away from Hunstanton, I will not say chastened, because I had gone there expecting to admire, but with a distinctly higher view of ladies' golf than I had had before. I have had many more opportunities of watching it since and have never wavered in my admiration.

That Championship of 1914 was a particularly memorable one because it saw Miss Cecil Leitch 'break through'. She had first played in 1908 with her hair down her back and everyone had instantly seen in her a prospective champion, but the victory had taken longer in coming than had been expected; she had seen lean years like Bobby Jones. Now after six of those years she had done it; she was on the crest of the wave and seemed likely to go on winning. The war came and deprived her, humanly speaking, of several victories, but as soon as it was over she was at it again, more dominant than ever. In 1919 she won the English Championship, and in 1920, the first Ladies' Championship to be played after the war, at Newcastle, County Down. Her opponent in the final was that truly excellent golfer Miss Molly Griffiths, now Mrs. Heppel, a player cast in a small mould, but also in a professional mould. I can hardly think of any amateur of either sex who has so well marked that indefinable professional something, as a rule only to be acquired in the caddies' shed, which distinguishes Mrs. Heppel's game. It was no doubt, to adapt a sentence of Horace Hutchinson's, "the fruit of a girlhood spent golf-club in hand", and still gives an unique charm to her golf. Miss Leitch was, however, too long and strong and good for her and it seemed that she would be irresistible as long as she cared to win.

And then, "a strange thing happened". The English Championship was in 1920 played at Sheringham and thither came Miss Leitch fresh from her triumph in Ireland. Perhaps she was not in fact so very fresh but rather tired. However that may be, she crashed her way through to the final. There her adversary was a young lady who had only just made good her place at the bottom of the Surrey side, and had qualified with two strictly moderate scores. She was chiefly known, as far as she was known at all, as Roger Wethered's sister, but she had played very well in this tournament and beaten some strong opponents. I do not suppose that the young lady herself or anyone else thought she had much chance. They thought so less when she was four down at lunch, less still when she played the first two holes in the afternoon very badly and lost them both. Then in the desperate situation of six down with sixteen to play, she unmasked her batteries. Holes seldom melt away "like snow off a dyke" unless the leader does something to help them, and I have no doubt—I was not there—that Miss Leitch made mistakes, but Miss Wethered not only took advantage of them, but put in some fierce thrusts on her own account, such as three threes in a row, two of them not countenanced by Par or Bogey. The holes changed hands so quickly that Miss Wethered was one up with four to play. Miss Leitch rallied to win the fifteenth, but her opponent placidly ran through a bunker at the next and rubbed it in by holing a putt. She likewise won the seventeenth and with it an astonishing match by two up and one to play.

It was by the way near the seventeenth green that there first appeared the traditional railway train which puffed and snorted loudly as Miss Wethered putted and of which she was so entirely unaware, that, on being congratulated on her imperturbability, she is alleged to have asked, "What train?" It has appeared several times since in various versions of the story and I myself incline to place it at Troon. Miss Wethered herself could naturally not give evidence. Miss Leitch herself assigns it to Sheringham and she ought to know. It may be a ghost train that haunts all the links on which the Champion played, but let Sheringham at least have its due!

The new Champion had not yet attained to the full stature of her game nor come into her kingdom. Miss Leitch was destined to reduce her to a proper state of subjection in the following year, but from this match at Sheringham onwards a meeting between the two was that to which the general public looked forward, so that it dwarfed rather unfairly perhaps the doings of all the other excellent lady players. Therefore this is perhaps as good a time as another to try to appraise the most remarkable lady player who has yet appeared, one as outstanding and memorable in her own realm as Bobby Jones in his. Neither she nor Miss Leitch won as many Championships as they were capable of winning. Miss Leitch was in all probability deprived of her full share by the act of the Germans and Miss Wethered by her own act. She went on winning the English Championship till 1924, when she retired sated. She won the Ladies' Championship three times in four years between 1922 and 1924 and then abdicated from the throne till 1929 when a Championship at St. Andrews tempted her back for one more victory. After that she gave a single public performance a year in the Mixed Foursomes at Worplesdon when she showed a kindly catholic taste in partners and generally pulled them through.

What is there new and true to say about Miss Wethered's methods? I really do not know. I should pitch on the qualities, which are perhaps complementary to one another, crispness of hitting and economy of movement. As for the latter she originally stood so still that her left heel stayed glued to the ground, but later she eased it a little, with gain, I think, both in grace and power. This economy of movement was to some extent delusive. She had in fact plenty of body turn, but it was done so quietly and naturally as not to be very noticeable. As a result I believe that when she went to stay and play at one place where she had never been seen before, the reverent ladies who watched decided in awe-stricken conclave that "Miss Wethered did not pivot". They re-modelled their own swings accordingly, with catastrophic effect. Another quality of Miss Wethered's methods was what for lack of a better word I will call its uniformity. There were days, as there must be with anyone, when she seemed to swing a little faster than others, but generally she stuck to a uniform unhurried and rhythmic pace with a consistency that very few other golfers have equalled. Perhaps this accounted for her accuracy, for she was hideously accurate if one were her opponent, blessedly so if her partner. If ever she did go at all crooked her ball seemed to have a knack of keeping just out of the bunker, and indeed even to skirt one was a rare error. It was part of the fun of watching her at Worplesdon that she was to be seen, through the agency of her male partner, in places where she would never have gone on her own account. It was one of the agitating features of being her partner that one was sure to put her there. If I add that she had an admirable temperament, keen, strung up by the great occasion to exactly the right degree, capable of seeing the humour of the most lamentable situation and having a power of pegging away and hoping for things to come round, I have done with eulogy and will come back to history.

The Ladies' Championship of 1924 at Turnberry, which I had the pleasure of watching, was a memorable one, with Miss Leitch the outstanding figure. In the very first round she had to meet Miss Alexa Stirling, a beautiful player, then American Champion, bred at Atlanta, Georgia, where Bobby Jones comes from, and more or less a contemporary of his. It was hard that these two should meet so soon.

> *One of us two, Herminius,*
> *Shall never more go home.*
> *I will lay on for Tusculum,*
> *And lay thou on for Rome.*

That was the thought in everybody's mind. It was one of those matches that produce before hand a breathless hush. 'Breathless' is perhaps hardly the word, for the wind roared and swept before it across the links a storm of rain. I cannot remember watching on a more unpleasant day, and when at last at a late hour I had completed my account of the match on partially sopped pieces of paper it never reached London. Yet as a spectacle it was well worth the wetting. Everybody felt that it was particularly cruel weather for Miss Stirling, and this was perhaps hospitable rather than logical. There was then an impression that American golfers were not at their best in bad weather. This is a complete delusion and some of the most astonishing golf I ever saw was played by American amateurs in appalling rain at the Country Club in 1922.

Themselves soaked to the skin, their club handles dripping sops, the greens covered with rivers in miniature, they did scores that would have been remarkable in perfect conditions. Miss Stirling did not blench; she played well but Miss Leitch was in an irresistible mood. I have a vision of her with her familiar bandeau and some sort of handkerchief knotted round her neck affronting the tempest, revelling in her defiance of it. The wide stance, the little duck of the right knee, the follow-through that sends the club through low as if boring its way through the wind—all the characteristic movements stand out in memory against the grey and lowering background. Think of Madame Defarge leading the women of St. Antoine against the Bastille, think of anything frightfully grand, and you have a picture of Miss Leitch in that match.

Precisely the number of holes by which she won I do not remember and I do not propose to look it up and so spoil my own imaginary picture by superfluous details. Enough that it was by a satisfying margin, and that the invading menace was removed. Not altogether removed because in a later round Miss Marion Hollins, large, strong and cheerful, was only beaten by her at the last hole, but that seemed comparatively unimportant. Meanwhile Miss Wethered was going through in the other half comfortably enough and the two duly met in the final. Miss Wethered played unworthily in the first round. She had, as I remember it, been a little inclined during the previous day to cut her shots, and this she could not afford to do against Miss Leitch. She was out-hit and generally outplayed and was seven down at lunch. No second marvel of Sheringham was vouchsafed: she played up well in the afternoon but her adversary was not letting go and won by 4 and 3, her third successive Championship.

I did not see the Championship in the following year at Prince's, Sandwich, when the draw was again kind, so that the pair met in the final. Miss Wethered had perceptibly strengthened her game by this time, and after a hard struggle to begin with there came a rapid landslide of holes and she won by 9 and 7. Neither was I at Burnham in the following year, since the Ladies' Championship there and the Amateur Championship at Deal took place at the same time. Miss Wethered looked like winning again till in the semi-final she was beaten by a beautiful golfer, lacking nothing but a little power, Mrs. Macbeth, who as Miss Muriel Dodd had been the Champion of 1913. If Miss Wethered had watched the next day's final it would have been the only round in any Championship during her career she ever could have watched as a spectator and not a player. In every other one she reached the final. As it was she did not see it, because she travelled through the night to see her brother win at Deal. It was between two of the three great Cheshire ladies, Mrs. Macbeth and Miss Doris Chambers, 'and Miss Chambers, doing for once full justice to her fine natural powers, won the match.

In 1924 Miss Wethered won again at Portrush. Next year, 1925, saw the fourth and last final between the two dominating figures, this time at Troon, and it was the best of all. It ended on the thirty-seventh green and everyone felt that it was a great pity that the Championship could not be halved and the throne shared for the ensuing year. From the start of the Championship Miss Wethered was clinging to fours and killing her enemies stone dead. There was one big match on the way to the final against that fine American player Miss Glenna Collett (now Mrs. Vare). Miss Collett held her own for a while, but the fours came too consistently at last and the wave passed over her head as it had over all the rest. Meanwhile Miss Leitch was only fighting her way through, as it were by desperate charges at the point of the bayonet. She was full of courage but not full of golf; that blessed confidence that can make the game seem an easy one would not come to her. Several people had a chance of beating her and were perhaps too frightened of their own audacity to administer the *coup de grâce*. So Miss Leitch was in the final at last, but this time there was no general expectation that she could hold her adversary.

The morning, however, saw a complete change in her. The painful ascent to the summit had been laboriously achieved and she emerged on the heights a different golfer. Confidence, dash, rhythm—all had come back, and from the very start she attacked. Miss Wethered was still playing well, not quite so victoriously well as she had been, but even the very best can have their game to some extent dictated to them by their opponents and only play as well as they are allowed. So after ten holes Miss Leitch was quite deservedly though surprisingly three up. She continued to play fine golf, but she could not help losing a little ground to her enemy's great counter-attack. Miss Wethered came home in 35, finishing with a long putt and the match was square.

The more sanguine of Miss Wethered's supporters believed that now she would draw steadily away, but Miss Leitch was "not so tamed" and a grim struggle all the way out saw her one up going to the ninth. Here Miss Wethered had a putt to win but was stymied. She decided to put it to the touch and risk two down; she went out for the shot and lofted it. A risk thus taken and successfully overcome is seldom without its effect and now Miss Wethered did forge ahead, though very slowly. Going to the long sixteenth hole she was two up and had hit two good shots, while her adversary was more or less doomed to take six. Thus she had an iron shot, such as she had been playing perfectly, to reach the green and win the match. "She had only to hit a straight iron shot," as some writers are a little too apt to say, forgetting how much easier these things are for the people who have not got to do them. Perhaps Miss Wethered herself became conscious of how apparently little separated her from victory. At any rate she hooked her ball into some hummocks to the left and the hole was halved in six. That too had its effect, as a let-off does. Miss Wethered played two rather weak holes; Miss Leitch took her chance, won them both and halved the match. That, as I said, ought to have been the end and both players had palpably had all they wanted, but the law is inexorable and out they had to go again with a mighty crowd lining the course all the way to the first hole. Miss Wethered reached the edge of the green with her second and then laid a very long putt stone dead. A very fine putt it was but there are occasions when the extra holes, however many there are of them and however well they may be played, give a feeling of anticlimax and this was one of them.

Miss Wethered now retired for a while to the avocations of her private life and in 1926, at Harlech, Miss Leitch won again, for the fourth and last time, beating Mrs. Garon, once a Girl Champion, a very neat, correct, graceful player, but hardly carrying enough guns for such an adversary. And now with her there come new names in the list and a slightly different generation begins to arrive at the top. For two years in succession the triumph that Arnaud Massy had achieved

at Hoylake in 1907 was repeated by the two young
ladies of France, Mademoiselle Simone de la Chaume and
Mademoiselle Le Blan. I saw neither championship but
I have had the pleasure of meeting and watching both
these ladies at Worplesdon. Mademoiselle Le Blan's was,
I suppose, rather a surprising win though a well-deserved
one. She was a long hitter, dashing rather than consistent. Mademoiselle de la Chaume on the other hand
was soundness itself with a very true swing of the club
and an obvious knowledge of golf, the product both of a
natural turn for games, and of good teaching and hard work.
She came at one time regularly to Worplesdon, one of the most
welcome of all its visitors, and to Worplesdon I shall, if I know
myself, return later.

With 1929 we come back once more to Miss Wethered
unable to resist the lure of St. Andrews and with her return
the great heart of the general public was once more stirred to
its depths by ladies' golf. The authorities, who thought that
in some minor match in an early round she could be left more
or less to her own devices, were rudely awakened. Wherever
she was the crowd went surging and there was one match
which would almost have come to an untimely end had not
Colonel Dalrymple-Hamilton, by a noble exhibition of shouting and his genius for discipline, cowed the onlookers into a
state of order. She was playing as well as ever and her
progress to the final was a triumphal procession. Then she
met Miss Glenna Collett and there ensued a really historic
battle, fit to be compared with that of Troon.

It was like the Troon final in several ways. First of all
everybody knew that Miss Collett was a very good player but
hardly anybody thought that she could hold her opponent
over thirty-six holes. Then she not only held her but gained
at one time a considerable lead, so that all but the most faithful
and fanatical became considerably alarmed. Again after
Miss Wethered had made her spurt and got all the holes back
and more also, Miss Collett put in so fierce a counter-spurt that
it seemed at one time that an incredible thing, in other words
the defeat of the favourite, might possibly happen. It did not
happen and Miss Wethered stopped the rot and pulled through
but there has seldom been a more "damned nice thing."

Miss Collett was and no doubt still is, as Mrs. Vare, a very

Miss Joyce Wethered (Lady Heathcoat-Amory) with Miss Pam Barton, Miss Enid Wilson, Madame Lacoste and Henry Cotton

Miss Glenna Collett (Mrs. Vare)

good player indeed with a rhythmic, well-taught American swing, very orthodox except for an idiosyncratic movement of the left foot which seemed to give an odd flicker—it is the only way I can describe it—at the top of the swing. She lost nothing in length of driving to Miss Wethered and in every other department of the game, especially in putting, she began, if the expression be allowable, by outplaying her. She holed some cruel putts, she did everything well and nothing ill, and she was five up at the turn with a score of 34 or so. She was, as I recollect, very nearly six up but not quite, and then she failed at a putt on the twelfth green and slowly the holes began to come back. Three of them had come back by lunch-time and there was a general impression to the effect, "It's all right now. You'll see. Joyce will win comfortably." Win she did but not comfortably. To the turn she went steadily away to become four up, but just when people were beginning to be sorry for her Miss Collett attacked with magnificent ferocity. Back came the holes the other way and not till Miss Wethered holed an invaluable putt for a half on the fifteenth green was real confidence restored. She won in the end by 3 and 1 and policemen cleared a road home for two heroines.

There "in the glory of the sunset" Miss Wethered, save for Worplesdon, vanishes for good and all, and if I have devoted a disproportionate space to her and her great competitor, it is out of no disrespect to their successors, but because they were in their very different ways dominating players such as only arrive at intervals in any game. Now with these two out of the way Miss Collett's path seemed clear for her when she came to Formby in 1930 and, as was to be expected, reached the final. However, the opportunity makes the hero, in this case the heroine, and in her hour of dire need Providence sent to England's aid, even as it did to America's at Brookline in 1913, a saviour but recently escaped from the schoolroom, Miss Diana Fishwick. From that time onwards Miss Fishwick, now Mrs. Critchley, was a personage in our ladies' golf, and has shown herself a very good player of a decidedly original type. She stands very upright and rather rigid, has a long swing with something in it which, as the reviewers say when they are stumped, "defies analysis". The swing is a little rigid too but the club comes well through and nobody

uses the height that Nature has given her to better advantage.
Even on the green she stands right up, holds the club long,
and pops the ball in with a rather nonchalant air and great
regularity. A good temperament, serious enough but not too
serious for enjoyment of the game as a game, completes her
armament. I was not, alas! at Formby but I imagine that
when this youthful heroine first took the lead the onlookers
thought it a gallant but unavailing effort, and that as she
went on and on and they realised she was going to win they
were overcome by an almost reverential awe. She never grew
frightened of her lead; she won comfortably by 4 and 3 and
was hailed by the press of a grateful country as a second Joan
of Arc.

Miss Fishwick was succeeded by one of the outstanding
figures of ladies' golf, Miss Enid Wilson, who equalled Miss
Leitch's record of three victories in three successive years, and
won all her three finals by substantial margins. Miss Wilson
is, I think, one of those people with the fortunate power of
devoting themselves wholeheartedly to one subject without
losing her interest in others. Carefully taught by Tom
Williamson in her early girlhood, she was a model pupil
willing to undergo the drudgery of hard practice to an extent
that would weary less resolute people, and yet she never fell
into the error of the over-coached or allowed golf to become a
slavery. In short she retained, as I venture to read her, an
admirable sense of proportion. Tall and strong she was not
a particularly graceful player, but she was a thoroughly
sound one and had the really good golfer's power of playing
well enough to win in lesser contests and rising to the important
occasion. She gave up championships young when she might
well have won more of them. She had not the power nor
probably the wish to arouse in her supporters such a state of
enthusiastic worship as some of her predecessors had done,
but she was a very fine player indeed and inspired a most
wholesome respect.

Miss Wilson's opponent in her first final in 1931 was another
very good player, Miss Wanda Morgan who ultimately won
in 1935 and is, I imagine, perfectly capable of winning again
when golf returns, for she has a style which ought to endure,
with something of that professional touch which I have
attributed to Mrs. Heppel. I had early in her career good

and grateful reason to be impressed by her, from a small mixed foursome meeting on the most engaging private course at Leeds Castle. My partner had, I think, forsaken me; at any rate I had not got one and some kind intermediary said that Miss Morgan would play but had no clubs. She was lent Miss Cecil Leitch's, which were a good deal bigger and longer than her own, and holding these strange weapons at the very bottom of the grip proceeded to play so well that we were second in the competition. This power of adapting herself to circumstances marked the real golfer which she afterwards so often showed herself to be.

Before she had won, however, another notable figure had appeared, then in the nature of an infant phenomenon, Miss Pam Barton, gifted with great power if not with great size, and having a fine, natural, flowing swing. Her record till this war began speaks for itself; twice Champion, twice runner-up and, most striking of all, the making of a lone pilgrimage to the United States and winning the Championship there. This last was an achievement which can perhaps only be appreciated by those who have experienced the difficulties of playing as a stranger, however hospitably received, in a strange land. On each of her first two appearances she reached the final to lose to Mrs. Holm at Portrush and to Miss Morgan at Newcastle, County Down. The third time was lucky for she reached the final yet again next year at Southport and Ainsdale and beat Miss Newell, whose death only a year later saddened the community of ladies' golf. I saw the Championship at Southport, made the more interesting by the presence of the members of the American ladies' international side, and have one very clear memory of Miss Barton. She was unhappy over her putting and suffered from not taking her club back straight. Thereupon she went to a vacant green, laid down two clubs so that the shafts made a groove for the head of her putter and practised away relentlessly up and down the straight line. This improvised piece of machinery was effective, for she putted well thereafter and virtue was rewarded.

After that year which also saw her victory in America Miss Barton's play seemed to deteriorate a little and I take leave to think that she became too humble, not trusting enough to her natural gifts and relying too much on coaching. It is perhaps a King Charles's head of mine that too many fine natural players of the last few years have tried too hard to make themselves into machines. If the mechanics go wrong, as they sometimes will, there is nothing left to fall back upon. I watched Miss Barton play in the Burnham Championship of 1938 when I thought something of this kind befell her; an irresistible start of truly imposing shots and then the breakdown of the machinery followed by vain attempts to recover the exact "groove" of the swing. I may be right or wrong; at any rate Miss Barton came back in the following year more at her ease and won again, and she should have more wins before her. I leave this sentence as it was written but sad to say there will be no more wins for to the great sorrow of all who knew her, Miss Barton was killed, when on duty, in a flying accident. Everybody liked to see her play and everybody liked her for her simple, modest and friendly character.

Two other Champions remain to be mentioned, both Scottish ladies, Miss Jessie Anderson and Mrs. Holm. Miss Anderson is the daughter of Joe Anderson of Perth who has the unique record of being a professional player both of golf and cricket. Thus she started life with every advantage and is a truly excellent player in a style sound and leisurely if to the censorious eye a little artificial. She was a national heroine in 1936 when she saved the international match against America by holing a nasty putt on the last green at Gleneagles. She too may go on winning for a long time and keep the new infant phenomenons in their places.

Mrs. Holm won at Porthcawl when I did not see her, and at Burnham when I did and was mightily impressed. Risking the danger of comparisons and giving a purely personal opinion, Mrs. Holm, as I saw her at Burnham, was the most striking lady player since Miss Wethered had left the lists. She was not the most consistent and was capable of unexpected and perhaps light-hearted mistakes, but when in full tide of play she had a majestic power about her game and a capacity for playing the counting shot rarely seen. To use a phrase often on the lips of an old friend of mine, she "stood up to the ball and gave it one"; to watch her tackling the wind-swept stretch of the long outgoing hole at Burnham was to feel puny indeed. It was an awfully grand spectacle. Of Mrs. Holm's golf *je suis le fervent*.

Thus I complete an imperfect survey of the lady Champions between wars, and ought perhaps to add a short postscript on the international matches between the ladies of this country and the United States. There have been four of them, three here, at Sunningdale, Wentworth and Gleneagles, and one in the United States, at Chevy Chase. So our ladies had the best of the venues but not of the results, for the Americans won two out of the four and one was halved. I only saw the 'one at Wentworth in 1932 and my chief memory is of the play of, I am sure, one of the very best lady golfers that has yet appeared, Miss Virginia Van Wie. She won the American Ladies' Championship three times running from 1932 to 1934, and her swing seemed to me as near perfection as a swing could be. My other memory was of seeing, for only the second time in my life, Miss Wethered lose a match against her own sex. She and Miss Wanda Morgan lost their foursome against the first American couple, after a thoroughly depressing finish, at the home hole, and lunch was depressing accordingly. In the afternoon she played very well indeed and polished off Miss Collett (by this time Mrs. Vare) in a most workmanlike manner; but could aught atone? How grateful the humbler of us ought to be that much is not expected of us!

Chapter 12

WORPLESDON

IT is no fun writing a book unless you can write about what pleases yourself and so I mean to have the fun of writing something about the Mixed Foursomes at Worplesdon, which has been one of my favourite meetings of the year, whether as· player or spectator. Had there been no war the meeting would have come of age in 1942. As it is during its seventeen years of life, which ended temporarily in October 1938, it has given the greatest possible pleasure to all its habitués and habituées, and I use that word on purpose because once a Worplesdonian always a Worplesdonian. Nobody ever willingly gives up the meeting and every year there has been a waiting list of those aching and pining to get a place in the draw. When Colonel Bunbury and Captain Ambrose between them originated this tournament they were benefactors of the golfing·race.

The day before a meeting of any consequence produces an agreeable sensation of reunion in which everyone asks heartily how everybody else is, and says how pleasant it is to meet again even those who have almost slipped from the memory during the last twelve months. The day before Worplesdon is a notably friendly gathering of the clans with the added spice of a little not too unfriendly gossip. Why have Miss or Mrs. A and Mr. B dissolved their partnership of the year before, perhaps of several years? Was it the gentleman or the lady who took the decisive step or was there a mutual desire for a new deal? Who are to be their fresh partners? Such are some of the questions which yearly gave a little fillip of excitement. There was a good deal of annual shuffling of partners and there were some very faithful couples that remained together year after year. The question who would be Miss Wethered's partner was always "intriguing". She won with seven different ones in all, so that it was almost painfully apparent to the partner of any particular year that if they did not win it would be his fault, and further that if by any miracle he was not too grossly to blame everybody would say that he was.

The golf was played as seriously as need be and was as a rule extraordinarily good. Constantly the scores made by a couple would be one that the male partner would be proud and delighted to do on his own account. At the same time there was a unique atmosphere, social but not 'garden party', about the meeting. Many kind neighbours kept open house for lunch; the rendezvous behind the pond at the tenth green, with its chance of ghoulishly enjoying a splash or two, was as a grandstand. So was the verandah in front of the clubhouse looking down on the fourth hole. There never was a better course for leisurely and yet comprehensive watching. It is a paradise of short cuts. It was permissible to some extent *desipere in loco* and there were such perfect opportunities. Only the very energetic spectators ever walked the first three holes when so much could be seen from that eyrie at the fourth. Who but a fanatic would ever watch the long eleventh when he could enjoy a breathing space and see two holes at a time from behind the twelfth green?

The tournament came at just the right time too when there was no rival attraction. The ladies had wound themselves up for it at Ranelagh; the men had come back from their holidays not too long for the good of their golf, but long enough to want a little more. Winter was coming but had not yet come: autumn played out the season with a final fanfare of trumpets. The course had still much of its summer quality, made the more attractive by autumnal dews. Only now and again it must be admitted, the weather was a little unchivalrous. As it seems to me in looking back, there were two or three years running when Worplesdon weather became proverbial in an uncomplimentary sense, and it is certain that one year when I reached the final I was wet through every day, and having exhausted my own providently large wardrobe had to fall back on my host's. That time passed, however, and in many of the more recent years we had, unless distance is lending too much enchantment to the view, the most perfect St. Luke's summer weather.

When in dreams I fancy that golf is once more its old self, there is no vision more enchanting that that in which I see myself "brushing with hasty steps the dews away" in company with Captain Ambrose on the first morning of the tournament. We cross the fifteenth fairway, make a little detour perhaps to talk to the green-keeper, have a look at the seventeenth green beautifully swept and garnished, and so up the long eighteenth fairway, risking our lives from the barrage of golf balls dispatched by ardent practisers. The cars are pouring in, the purple-and-green flag is flying from the flagstaff and soon with an agreeable plump the first ball will come down on the fourth green. Yet another Worplesdon is under way and four jovial days stretch away in front of us.

However, this chapter must not wholly degenerate into an egotistical rhapsody. Let me try to recall a few of the outstanding matches. The first winners were Miss Helm and Mr. T. A. Torrance, who had the glory of defeating in an eighteen-hole final (it afterwards became thirty-six holes) Miss Wethered and her brother. Then Miss Wethered began to win, but I have written so much of her in another chapter that here I shall treat her with ungallant brevity, merely setting out the names of her partners in victory: Mr. Roger Wethered, Mr. Tolley (twice), Mr. J. S. F. Morrison, Mr. Michael Scott, Mr. R. H. Oppenheimer, Mr. T. Coke and an elderly gentleman whose name for the moment escapes me. It now only remains for Lady Amory to win with her husband and so make what Mr. Peggotty called a " merry-go-rounder" of it.

If I had to choose two of the most meritorious victories in the history of Worplesdon I think they would be those of Miss Leitch and Mr. Esmond in 1925, with the lady clearly in charge and the gentleman as a docile and admirable second-string, and that in 1935 of Miss Gwen Craddock-Hartopp (now Mrs. John Morrison) and her brother. Both were fine wins in a field containing ostensibly stronger pairs. If I had to choose the most memorable and also the wettest final it would be that of 1929, between Miss Gourlay and Major Hezlet, Miss Joy Winn and Mr. Longstaffe. I am at any rate a good judge of the wetness for I was the referee and had to walk the whole of the thirty-nine holes that were necessary before the match was decided. Indeed it was so wet that I have always had a slightly uneasy conscience as to whether I ought not to have declared the ground unfit for play before the end. Perhaps, so conscience consoles itself, that would have been an excessively solemn step in a friendly tournament, but the thirty-ninth green was more like a lake than a green.

Miss Gourlay and Major Hezlet were beyond doubt the stronger side on paper and had the greater power, but their opponents were essentially a pair; they had played much together among the pleasant whins of Aldeburgh and there was no getting-away from them. The end was a little farcical. Major Hezlet and his partner wisely pitched the ball through the flood on the thirty-ninth green; the other side tried to putt through it and they were not strong enough—nobody would have been—to putt hard enough. The winners, Miss Gourlay and Major Hezlet, took part in another outstanding final in which they lost to Mademoiselle de la Cháume and Mr. Roger Wethered by two holes. Here the referee had, humanly speaking, something to do with the result; it was not I and he shall remain nameless. Going to the fifteenth hole in the second round Miss Gourlay and her partner were leading and this hole seemed theirs for the asking, for Mr. Wethered had sent his second crashing into a wilderness to the left of the green. Major Hezlet thereupon played a safe, wise shot to the opening just short of the green. Mademoiselle de la Chaume's ball was found in the midst of a sea of brambles; in front of it was a spreading oak tree; beyond that was a bunker and beyond that again the green. The referee, being asked what might be done with the ball in the brambles, began to chant in a low tone apparently to himself, "They are entitled to a sight of the ball, they are entitled to a sight of the ball." Under his directions a game of spellicans was then played with the brambles until the ball was fully disclosed. Mademoiselle de la Chaume took an heroic whack at it; it sped through the branches of the oak and ended on the green; Mr. Wethered holed his putt in four and the other pair, not unnaturally flabbergasted, took five. It was a wonderful recovery, but—well, I was not the referee.

Miss Gourlay won twice with Major Hezlet and once with Mr. T. A. Torrance, so that she may fairly claim to be heroine number two of the tournament. For the position of hero number one I should be inclined to choose none of the men who have won twice (not even Mr. Wethered for so nobly taking a cleek to his tee shots to avoid the trees) but Mr. Noel Layton. He won only once with Miss Fowler, in 1924, but he has periodically bobbed up in the final, with a different partner each time, and has been one of the most faithful as he has been one of the most successful supporters of the tournament. One of the most exciting and dampest of finals was that in which Mrs. Gold and he took Miss Wethered and Mr. John Morrison to the thirty-sixth green.

It is a commonplace that in the years between wars driving has grown longer; it is the constant lament of the aged and ageing, but nowhere has it been more noticeable than at Worplesdon and particularly in regard to the ladies' driving. In early years the twelfth hole was definitely, except perhaps for one or two couples at most, a hole requiring two shots and a pitch. Now as I sit on the mound behind that green, only alas! in imagination, I see one spritely couple after another banging their way home in two, and the same phenomenon has become noticeable at other holes. Again, when the tournament began there was a very general opinion, though a few couples resolutely dissented, that the ladies ought to drive at the odd holes. This was largely because the two rather long one-shotters, the fourth and the sixteenth, were within comfortable reach for the men with their irons, while they demanded greater carrying power with any club than many of the ladies possessed. Gradually the pendulum swung the other way because so many ladies could comfortably reach these holes with their spoons and did so with great accuracy. So their partners were only too pleased to leave such responsible shots, to say nothing of the pitch over the pond at the tenth, in trustworthy hands and expend their own energies in aiming at less testing marks. Ladies naturally get more practice with wooden clubs than men do, especially through the green, and they are remarkably accurate with them. The men are decidedly more arboreal in their habits. On the other hand, for I must in honour bound say something for them, I think that on the whole they pitch and putt the better of the two.

When I was at school we used to have a two-a-side single-wicket cricket tournament, for which the entrants were divided into strokes and bows and the pairs were then decided by lot. Generally speaking in a mixed foursome—there are of course exceptions in the case of exceptional ladies—the man is the stroke and the lady the bow and the heaviest work devolves on stroke. It is he who has to get the length and go out if need be for the big shot, and it is only natural that in

138

these efforts he should make a certain number of mistakes; the trees are more easily within his reach. It is the lady's part to keep the noiseless tenor of her way and be content to "make" her partner rather than perform prodigies on her own account. There was once a small boy at North Berwick who in the afternoon was going to play in a foursome competition of mixed children and grown-ups with Miss Wethered as his partner. He disappeared in the morning and came home for lunch rather hot, tired and dishevelled. On being asked what he had been doing he answered, "Practising getting out of bunkers." That was a properly virile point of view; he was ready to carry the chief burden on his back and that is what the man must be prepared to do, but the best lady partners make the burden a very light one. More and more obviously as this tournament has gone on, has there been no question of one partner doing the work; more and more has the play of the best couples approximated both in manner and result to that of a very good male pair.

And so farewell to Worplesdon, but not I hope for long. If I can once again see the dahlias in the garden by the side of the fifteenth fairway and once again read *The Moonstone* under the kind roof which has so often sheltered me, I shall be almost perfectly happy.

Chapter 13

THE WALKER CUP

REGRETFULLY leaving Miss Amaryllis in the shade of the Worplesdon fir trees, I return to more serious business. In 1921 there was played at Hoylake the first amateur international match between Great Britain and the United States, with disastrous results and a considerable jolt to our complacency. In the following year Mr. Walker gave his cup, a British team went out to America to play for it, and the series of Walker Cup matches began. It has been a calamitous series for our side, and but for the fact, so infinitely reviving to the spirits, that at last we did win the match at St. Andrews in 1938 I could hardly have endured to write about it. As we did at long last break the spell it is now possible to look back at the nine matches that have been played in a more cheerful frame of mind, admitting the unquestioned superiority of the American sides frankly and without excuses but not despairingly, and remembering that however gloomy the aggregate results have been for us, the regular interchange of visits between the amateurs of the two countries has been productive of nothing but friendliness and pleasantness, which is by far the most important thing of all. If it is said, and occasionally with truth, that international matches do more harm than good, the Walker Cup series can always and with entire truth be cited to the contrary.

I said I would make no excuses but I think I may be allowed to say this much; the Americans had much the better sides but they were not always quite so overwhelmingly superior as the scores seem to show. We never had a chance of winning in the United States but over here we had chances and did not take them. There is no doubt at all that for some years our tails were permanently between our legs and our players seemed incapable of doing themselves justice on the day. They might or might not play their game and they generally did not, while the Americans apparently had the power of rising to the occasion. Too often we began deplorably and by the time the first round of the foursomes were over—we were supposed to be able to play foursomes—our hopes were shattered. Now that Todgers's has shown that it can do it, I will not say when it chooses, but at least once in a long while, it may be permissible to say these gloomy things, which would otherwise appear too "defeatist". When the match will be played again and what will happen when it does I do not profess to know, but at least we have turned over a new leaf. When once that is done, the old black pages can be re-read without too unbearable pain.

Any account I can give of these matches must be partial and fragmentary, because apart from the first, in which I chanced to play, I have not been present at any of the matches in America, and apart from the briefest references do not propose to tell them at second hand. All the matches played here I have seen. I am naturally tempted to say most about the one in which I played myself. I will try to resist as far as I can, but if I fail, at least it may convey some notion, by analogy, of the other matches, and particularly of the endless kindness and hospitality of American hosts.

Robert Harris (captain), C. J. H. Tolley, R. H. Wethered, J. Caven, C. C. Aylmer, W. B. Torrance, C. V. L. Hooman, Willis Mackenzie; such was the team which sailed from Liverpool on the *Carmania*. I went out to describe the match for *The Times*, travelled with the side and was to be spare man, if one were wanted. Ernest Holderness, then Amateur Champion, could not come but otherwise it was about as good a team as could then be raised. The match was to be played on the National Golf Links at Southampton on Long Island on August 29th and 30th, and we reached New York some considerable time beforehand. Perhaps we got there too soon and stayed too long in New York. I do not suppose that, pleasant as they were, the many good dinners and the excursions to different courses in the neighbourhood involving long motor drives and big lunches in blazing weather constituted the perfect preparation. I am very sure, however, that, if we had retired into our shells and gone at once to the National, we should have been poor guests and that Mr. C. B. Macdonald would never have forgiven us. Moreover in the end we did quite as well as we could have had any right to expect.

After these preliminary entertainments and one dash to

Philadelphia to see tremendous Pine Valley, we settled down at the National and our golf began to improve, though one or two of us took a long time over it. I will not describe that delightful spot again. It is one of the best and most enchanting of courses, ideal for a match from the players' point of view, but rather too remote from the spectators'. A few days before the match our opponents began to drop in, and they were a truly formidable lot. There are some people who have never lost a match to anyone who took over 69 to the round, and it is human and natural to think our own conquerors uncommonly good. Still I must be allowed to say that at least on the evidence of their individual records there has never been such a side as that first American one. Here are their names, written with an awe-stricken pen, and in the order in which they played in the singles: Jesse Guilford, Bobby Jones, Chick Evans, Francis Ouimet, R. Gardner, Jesse Sweetser, Max Marston, W. C. Fownes. Every single one of the eight has at one time or another won the Amateur Championship of his own country; three of them, Ouimet, Evans and Jones, have won its Open; two of them, Jones and Sweetser, our Amateur Championship; and one, Jones, our Open. Granted that the extraordinary capacity of Bobby Jones swells the total, it is a record such as I prophesy no other side will ever approach.

We knew all about them and had no very high hopes. At the last moment Robert Harris fell ill; I had to take his place both as player and captain and was, I fear, a sad encumbrance to Cyril Tolley in the foursomes, though to be sure Ouimet and Guilford played horribly well against us. One foursome, and a very good one, we won; Wethered and Aylmer beat Evans and Gardner by 5 and 4. The others were lost. It was an almost insufferably hot and steamy day and the ground was wet and heavy after one of those American thunderstorms that does not get it over like a burst of temper but comes sullenly back and back again. It was hard on that noble course and the ball occasionally stuck where it pitched. I remember watching the end of a foursome between Bobby Jones and Sweetser, Torrance and Hooman. On the fifteenth green the end seemed certain, but Bobby's ball though quite close to the hole had stuck firm, and when he tried to dislodge it jumped back briskly and hit him on the foot, thus staving off defeat for us for the length of one hole.

I did not see much of the singles since I had my own match to play and came last on the list. For a long time there was no ray of brightness, for after Tolley had just lost a fine match to Guilford on the thirty-fifth, there followed four more American wins in a row. By that time the whole match was more than over but the last three did a little face-saving. Our hero was Hooman. He played very, very well to beat Sweetser at the thirty-seventh and within a few days Sweetser was destined to win the Amateur Championship at the Country Club, trampling his way through the strongest part of the draw like some all-conquering Juggernaut. Inspired by his example Willis Mackenzie and I managed to win too, he by a considerable and most meritorious margin, I more modestly at the thirty-fifth. This was certainly a curious circumstance for Willis will not, I think, resent the statement that neither he nor I could or had hit a ball before the match. However we made the score sheet look a little prettier.

One odd little fact shows with what a pleasant casualness that first match was played. Nobody had considered what was to be done in case of a halved match. When Sweetser and Hooman halved, the two captains, Fownes and I, were away in the dim distance; so Fritz Byers, as President of the U.S.G.A., sent them off to the thirty-seventh, which Hooman won in a sparkling three. Since then more humane counsels have prevailed and heaven knows that when two men have halved a 36-hole match in the Walker Cup, they have earned an immediate drink with no further demands on them. It was a point which I made clear to Bill Fownes when I was two up on the thirty-fifth teeing ground.

The steam yachts of millionaires were then provided to take us to New London *en route* for the Amateur Championship at the Country Club, at Brookline near Boston, where I had last seen Francis Ouimet beat Vardon and Ray. The weather was rather reminiscent of that historic occasion and I am disposed to think that I never in my life saw such good golf in sheets of rain on a waterlogged course as was played by some of those American amateurs in the qualifying rounds. It was so wet that I can still in my mind's eye see Chick Evans pirouetting round and round on the home green in the attempt to find a spot to which to lift his ball so that he might get a dry putt three or four feet in length. Of the British side only Cyril Tolley did much to distinguish himself, and he after two or three victories fell before Knepper at the last hole. That was a disappointment, but Knepper was a very good golfer.

However I am meandering too far and so home in the *Aquitania*. I have only to hum softly to myself the tune of "Mr. Gallagher and Mr. Sheehan", then ravaging the United States, and a hundred scenes now more than twenty-one years old come vividly back to me. We did not think we had done very well and nobody else thought it of us, but we had done distinctly better than any team that has been there since.

The next year saw the Americans pay us a return visit with only three out of their first eight, Ouimet, Gardner and Marston, and with no Bobby Jones. Here seemed a chance to get all square, and we had on paper a very good side: Tolley, Wethered, Mackenzie, Hope, Harris, Hooman, Holderness, W. A. Murray and that admirable golfer from Prestwick St. Nicholas, John Wilson. Hooman played only in the four-somes and Mackenzie in the singles. We were full of a reason-able hope before the match and at the end of the foursomes full of confidence. Wethered and Tolley had given a good lead by winning the first match against Ouimet and Gardner by 6 and 5 and only Harris and Hooman had lost. Two up in the foursomes is an invaluable lead and there seemed every prospect of victory, for we were leading in the majority of singles at lunch, not by much but still leading, and we had that priceless start of two. There was only one disquieting circumstance. At the end of the Long Hole In Willis Mac-kenzie had seemed to have the match won for certain, for he had played brilliantly and was six up. Then his opponent, George Rotan, had made a great spurt and won the last four holes in a row.

Two up is not so good as six; the match turned out un-happily for us, and with it many other things seemed to go wrong. Rotan played magnificently after lunch; his score coruscated with fours and threes and when he reached the point at which he had been six down in the morning he was dormy five and he won by 6 and 4. Roger Wethered, our new Amateur Champion, played very well against Francis Ouimet; he was two up with three to play, and that seemed good enough.

Miss Diana Fishwick (Mrs. Critchley)

Miss Cecil Leitch

James Bruen

He went on playing very well for he ended with three fours, but even that was not good enough for Francis ended 3, 4, 3 and halved the match—in the circumstances surely one of the bravest and best finishes in all golfing history. Wright was similarly two down with three to play against Holderness and went one better for he won all three holes. Gardner got a four from the rough at the back of the last green to beat Harris. Willie Murray found someone steadier even than himself in Dr. Willing, who always looked hopefully inside the hole before he putted and generally put his ball there with the next shot. Tolley beat Sweetser and John Wilson beat Herron, but the Americans had won five singles and the whole match by one point. As a united spurt by a whole team that last round of theirs has never been surpassed; but we ought not quite to have let it happen. At least so the onlookers thought, but theirs is so much the easier part.

The next year I can write of only by hearsay and by the scores and, as Mr. Serjeant Buzfuz once remarked, "the subject presents but few attractions". Tolley, Hezlet, Murray, T. A. Torrance, Storey, Michael Scott, Hope, Denys Kyle, O. C. Bristowe and Robert Scott; that was our side and the Americans had the same eight players as in the first match with the addition of Harrison Johnston and Dr. Willing. The match was played not at the National this time but at Garden City, one of the oldest of American courses, one of the happy hunting-grounds of the late Walter Travis and regarded as a course of classic traditions. It is a thoroughly good course, if not superficially very attractive, and is narrow rather than long; so narrow indeed that when I watched an Amateur Championship there in 1913, many of the players too cautiously took iron clubs from the tee, thereby contributing to the victory of Jerome Travers, who had to take an iron because he was hooking all his wooden club shots round his neck. The last hole, a one-shot hole, over a pool of water is famous and, as will be seen later in this chapter, saw a British golfer just fail to repeat Harold Hilton's feat and win the American Amateur Championship.

The match at Garden City was sadly one-sided in the total result, but not so one-sided in the individual matches, in nearly all of which our men made a reasonably close fight of it. There were none of those tragic 8 and 7's, but the comparatively small scoring was nearly all on one side. In the foursomes Michael Scott and his namesake Robert from Glasgow did what nobody else has done, namely win a Walker Cup match against Bobby Jones; they beat him and Fownes at the last hole. In the singles Tolley won, also at the last hole, against Max Marston, who played first by virtue of being the reigning champion. Michael Scott won again, beating Jesse Sweetser by 7 and 6, a remarkable achievement and the heaviest win of the match.

So far the match had been played every year, but it was now wisely decided that this could not be kept up for ever and that there should be a two-years interval between matches. So it was in 1926 that the next American team appeared, a very strong one with Jones, Guilford, Evans and Sweetser and a new and most formidable player, George Von Elm, who later in the year beat Bobby Jones in the final of the American Amateur. He was hardly a pretty player, having a very marked wrench-round of the body, but he was in the very first class. Before the match had come the Amateur Championship at Muirfield and Sweetser had won it, the first American to do since the now almost legendary Travis. Our side still looks to me almost as good a one as we have ever had: Tolley, Holderness, Wethered, Hezlet, Harris, Storey, Brownlow and Jamieson; the last two having gained their places from heroic deeds at Muirfield, where Jamieson had beaten Bobby Jones, without Bobby winning a hole, and Brownlow had taken Sweetser to the twenty-first in the semi-final and played with a suave dauntlessness peculiar to him.

Once more the foursomes were disappointing and hung a millstone round our neck. The old partnership between Tolley and Wethered was severed. Wethered, who has had a very fine record in all sorts of internationals, played first with Holderness and they beat Ouimet and Guilford handsomely, but the other three matches were lost. One of them was very unluckily lost and, as far as such a statement is permissible, it turned the fate of the entire match. Storey and Brownlow had been down to Gardner and Roland Mackenzie, but they had gallantly squared and going to the Road Hole victory seemed in their grasp, for they were well down the course in two and the Americans were in a horrid place. Mackenzie had something of a desperation shot at the ball and topped it hard along the ground; it ran and it ran and miraculously got on to the green and then Gardner holed a great putt to rub it in. The hole was lost instead of won and the match likewise. These things will happen, but that it was an astonishing piece of luck, admittedly taken noble advantage of, is undeniable.

How much difference it made was seen next day when we won four singles and halved one out of the eight. Even that halved match was a little bitter, as it turned out, though at the time it seemed good enough. Hezlet played very well against the alarming Von Elm and on the last green they were all square, Von Elm not quite dead in three, Hezlet after a capital second having a decidedly holeable putt for a three. He did not know how others were faring, the green was slippery and he wanted to make sure of his half and so he laid his ball stone dead and short. This was eminently natural and human and it was also natural and human to wish later that he had given the hole a chance. As it was, the wins of our last two men Storey and Andrew Jamieson came just too late to save the day. In the first match Bobby Jones gave one of his most murderous displays of faultlessness and beat Tolley by 12 up and 11 to play. All but one hole has faded from my mind, namely the second hole in the first round, which seemed at the time terribly prophetic. Bobby with the honour hit a long tee shot decidedly to the left. Tolley went after it with a will. He hit an immense drive on the same line and, the gate in the wall of the station-master's garden being open, the ball ran through it and out of bounds. To outdrive the enemy is laudable but it is sometimes an honour too dearly bought. Wethered and Harris won their matches against Ouimet and Sweetser and but for that seventeenth hole on the day before—well, well the match was what old Beldham of Hambledon would have called an "all but".

The 1928 match was played on the course of the Chicago Golf Club at Wheaton, a good inland course as I dimly remember it, though it was always unkindly said that Mr. C. B. Macdonald had laid it out for his slice, since the hazards for all the tee shots lay on the left of the course. It has, I believe, been much altered since I saw it. There was no Wethered or Tolley or Holderness on our side, which was: Perkins, Hardman, Hezlet, Hope, Tweddell, Storey, Martin,

T. A. Torrance, Beck and MacCallum. We won the last single in which Torrance, who has done wonderfully well in singles in these matches, beat Chick Evans by a hole. Otherwise our score was a total and absolute blank. Perkins did something to cheer us by reaching the final of the American Championship, but when he got there he found Bobby Jones almost as ruthless an adversary as he had been at Wheaton.

By this time the Walker Cup matches were becoming from our point of view at any rate rather a bad joke and I find myself hurrying over the story in order to get to the more cheerful end. In 1930 there was a change of venue and an English course was chosen: St. George's, Sandwich. We had constantly prayed for a day of cold and of bitter wind, such as we thought would suit our men by freezing the marrow of their adversaries' bones. We never got it and whether it would have done us much good I do not know, for as far as I have observed it is an entire and pitiful delusion that Americans cannot play in bad weather; I have seen very little evidence to support it and a good deal of evidence on the other side. At any rate we did not get what we wanted at Sandwich, for it was perfectly calm, and balmy to the point of excessive hotness. Down we went again and considering that it was in our own country with the most desolating of all crashes. Tolley and Wethered reunited won the first four-some against Von Elm and a new-comer and a very fine putter, George Voigt: Torrance beat Ouimet by 7 and 6 in the singles and all the other matches were lost, some of them by horribly large margins. One player on our side at least deserved much sympathy, J. A. Stout. He went round under 70 in the morning and was a great many holes up on Don Moe. In the afternoon Moe went round still more under 70 and though Stout stuck to his guns very well he was beaten at the last hole. That was an astounding spurt and the whole American side played terribly well. Our side was: Tolley, Wethered, Rex Hartley, Holderness, J. N. Smith, T. A. Torrance, Stout and W. Campbell.

In 1932 it was by comparison a new and young side and Torrance, Stout, Rex Hartley alone remained from the Sandwich disaster and were joined by Lister Hartley, John de Forest, Fiddian, McRuvie, Leonard Crawley and a first representative from Ireland, John Burke. The match was played at the Country Club at Brookline and by all accounts our men played so well in practice that the American critics held that they had a good chance of winning.   Whether they really thought so or were only polite I know not, but if they did they turned out to be wrong.   The American side, also comparatively new and now deprived of Bobby Jones, did just as well as their predecessors and won all four foursomes by the length of the street.   That was the end of all things. We did much better in the singles for Crawley beat Voigt, and Torrance, Burke and Stout all halved their matches but the round O, even when it marks a halved match is not a wildly cheering figure, and but for Crawley's single 1, it would have represented our total score.

Back to St. Andrews in 1934, where we won one single and one foursome.   The Americans had resuscitated a beautiful golfer in one of their earliest champions, Chandler Egan, who had played against the Oxford and Cambridge Society side nearly thirty years before.   They produced two new and formidable players in Goodman and Lawson Little who have won both the Amateur and Open Championships of their country.   We had a leaven of the good young Scottish players who had been doing well in our domestic internationals, McLean, McRuvie and McKinlay.   We had also something of a resuscitation in the form of Roger Wethered who had not been playing very much or very well.   It seemed to me—and I was a selector—that so fine a golfer with so fine a record must be played since he loved St. Andrews, would have plenty of room there and had a great gift of rising to the occasion. Others, not selectors, thought otherwise and I suppose they were right; at any rate poor Roger's driving, which had been getting steadily straighter in practice, showed signs of dis-integration on the last day before the match and did not return to him, so that he stood down from the singles.   Michael Scott, Tolley, Wethered, McLean, McRuvie, Bentley, Fiddian, McKinlay, T. A. Torrance and Crawley were our side. McLean and McRuvie won their foursome to the patriotic joy of the St. Andrews crowd; McRuvie halved his single and the invaluable Torrance won again, against Marston.   Such glory as there was went to Scotland but there was not enough of it. Lawson Little played tremendously against Tolley; Dunlap fairly wore McLean down in a match of very good golf and we saw another fine new player in Fischer, with a very graceful swing, much quicker than the normal, almost drowsy American swing and having something indefinably Scottish about it. We were to see him again and in great form in 1938.

Now, thank heaven, to the last of the lean years, 1934, at Pine Valley, where we attained that which we had several times nearly reached, a perfectly blank score-sheet. Our side was nearly, not quite I think, as good as we could muster. It possessed one very fine new player, Hector Thomson, and it contained four of the nine who were to turn the tide two years later, but not a single match could they win. J. D. A. Langley, who had just left Stowe and had reached the final of the English Championship in his school holidays, was rightly given his chance thus early, and another old Stowe boy, P. B. Lucas, was with the team but found the forests of Pine Valley so magnetically attractive to his ball that he did not play. Thomson and Bentley, McLean and Langley, Peters and Dykes, Hill and Ewing—that was the team as it played in the foursomes, and the foursomes were by far the brightest part of the match for we did halve the last two of them. Hill and Ewing indeed got back almost as many holes as Don Moe had done against the luckless Stout at Sandwich, but even one more half, that of Bentley with Dunlap in the singles, was very cold comfort. We were almost past cheerfulness by this time and yet we were comforted by McLean's great effort to win the Amateur Championship a little while later. Garden City was, I should think, just the course for him, suiting his accurate rather than long hitting and his first-class iron play. He went on winning round after round and he seemed to be going to beat Fischer, at one time almost comfortably, in the final. Then he dropped a valuable hole or two but he was one up coming to that famous eighteenth over the water; he put his tee shot on the green and his first putt, humanly speaking, dead. Fischer had to hole a putt of a good many feet across the sloping green and he put it right in for a two and then won the thirty-seventh. Certainly these American amateurs are hard to beat.

And now 'avay vith melincholly'. We won at St. Andrews in 1938, and for this win credit is due first of course to the players, then to their captain John Beck, and then to the brand-new Selection Committee who took such infinite trouble over their job. There had been a general feeling that this was almost a last chance or the match would become too great a farce; that something must be done. There was a tendency to demand the heads of the Championship Committee on chargers, and the clubhouse at St. Andrews for a day or two before the General Meeting buzzed with conspiracies and the whispered texts of proposed motions. Incidentally the management of the meeting by the then captain, Sir John Simon, was one of the most masterly things of the kind I have ever seen. Hitler was said to be disappointed after Munich because there was to be no war, and perhaps some at that meeting, finding the ground cut from under their feet with supreme tact, were disappointed because they could not make their angry speeches. The main point was that something was done. A clean sweep was made of the old selectors, one of whom at least was thankful. This was I am sure entirely right and the only hopeful way of beginning afresh. A new committee was chosen from a rather wider area than ever before. Tolley, John Morrison, Thirsk, W. B. Torrance, from the East of Scotland, and Dickson from the West—those are the names that deserve to be "surrounded with a rich halo of enthusiastic cheering". They had many meetings and they decided on a trial match to be played at St. Andrews about the time of the R. and A. Spring Meeting. They chose John Beck as captain with a free hand to play himself if he wanted to, and they could not have chosen a shrewder or more cheering one.

The trial match did one particularly good thing; it gave all the possible members of the side, who came from different parts of the country and from different walks of life not always easily fused, a chance of getting to know one another under pleasant and friendly circumstances. They all stayed together and appeared to be from the first, in that hackneyed but sometimes valuable phrase, "a very happy family". The match was played in the rather curious form of a series of three-ball matches which I should have thought, if I had been personally involved, a peculiarly hateful one, not at all calculated to make men show themselves at their best. I should have been quite wrong, for the play was of a remarkably high standard. Everybody or nearly everybody played well and—here was a truly fortunate circumstance—those played best who were wanted to play best. There were no great disappointments, no sudden brilliancy on the part of anyone that should force him into the side against the selectors' predilections. When the match was over, all who had seen it felt really hopeful and the team the selectors chose was that which nearly everyone else would have chosen too.

I have left to the last one thing which contributed most definitely to the general hopefulness, and this was the magnificent and consistently magnificent golf played by Bruen. This young gentleman from Ireland regularly, whether in practice or in the trial match, went round the Old Course in about 69 or 70 and made it look quite an easy thing to do. Here it seemed was a real pillar of strength, a real No. 1. Bruen's fine golf sent all the other players' spirits up and set them a standard encouragingly high. In the match itself, when it came, he played well but not so well as he had done in the trial; but the best of his work had been done before, that of cheering everyone up. Let the Americans be who they might, they could not play better than *that*; such was the general impression, and starting with Bruen it gradually extended to the whole side.

The side ultimately chosen was, as they played in the foursomes, Bruen and Bentley, Thomson and Peters, Stowe and Alex Kyle, Crawley and Pennink. Ewing played in the singles. The American side had our old and true friend Francis Ouimet as captain; he might have played but he did not, and from our point of view I have sometimes thought it a good thing he was so modest. The American side was unquestionably strong; Goodman's previous achievements spoke for themselves; so did Fischer's. Yates had given his evidence before the match, if any were needed, by winning the Amateur Championship at Troon. Ward a year afterwards proceeded to win the American Amateur Championship in a most striking way. Kocsis had a beautiful swing and had beaten Goodman at Troon. Yet I do not think that as a whole they were quite so strong as some of their predecessors. I may well be wrong; it is a natural weakness to admire most those whom one knows best and with whom one has played. I may be wrong about practical results, but I am not wrong about one thing; these players, with one or two notable exceptions, had not got the lovely, flowing swings of the earlier ones. They were described by someone in America as "a bunch of hookers", and a rather forcing, hooky swing was characteristic of many of them. I cannot help thinking it a pity that the old smooth-swinging, essentially swinging, tradition has been forsaken by these young Americans, and I doubt if they will produce so many Evanses and Ouimets, to say nothing of Joneses, till it is restored. This may be an antiquated and mistaken view, but it is one to which I am entirely wedded.

When we know the issue of an event it is hard to remember exactly what we thought and expected beforehand or what other people thought. My chief recollection is one of intense anxiety as to a good, steady-going start. It had happened so often that our men had begun nervously and badly and so by lunch-time on the first day irreparable mischief had been done. If that preliminary catastrophe could be avoided then we had a real chance and might very well win. And there was no catastrophe; the start was reasonably and temperately encouraging, better perhaps than one too brilliant. Bruen was not in his all-conquering mood; it was almost too much to expect that he should be; but he was playing pretty well and he had an admirable helper in Bentley, who was through-out the day pre-eminently the glue of the partnership. They were against a strong pair, Fischer and the new player Kocsis. On the whole it was the American pair that looked the more likely to win, but there was really nothing in it, neither side was going away. One of our couples, of great possibilities and some uncertainties, Stowe and Kyle, were making rather heavy weather of it and must almost be written off. On the other hand Hector Thomson and Peters were beating Goodman and his partner (not quite the Goodman of old I thought) and were going along with victorious confidence; Crawley and Pennink although less decidedly, looked better than their adversaries and ought to win.

All these three forecasts turned out sound enough. It seemed that the worst we could do would be all square and if we could halve the first match we should have a small lead but an invaluable one, alike from the point of view of *moral* or mere arithmetic, against the singles. The first match still hung in the balance and I had to leave it, with the Americans a little ahead, to perch myself in Forgan's shop in order to broadcast. There came a glorious rumour that Harry Bentley had holed a long putt at the seventeenth and squared the match. Could it be really so? Yes, for there came another and more authoritative statement; they were all square and now here were the balls on the home green, the Americans' a good way off and ours fairly close. An American putted first and lay more or less dead. Bruen was going up to our ball. Then, thank heaven, we had only played two (there would come the awful thought that we had perhaps played three), and that meant that we were sure of a half at least. Bruen did not hole his putt for three; I believe he was half stymied, but nothing really mattered; we had got our one point's lead on the day.

John Beck showed himself a very good and decided captain before the singles. Who was to be left out? Bentley had done very well in the foursomes and Kyle not very well. Ewing the big Irishman was sure to come in, and in that case it was the general impression that Kyle would have to go. But the captain thought otherwise; Bentley had done his job and should rest on his laurels; Kyle had a great game in him and should have the chance of showing it. Beck was entirely confident in his own judgment and he was proved entirely right.

There were moments of anguish in the singles, as was inevitable. Pennink had soon to be written off as a total loss, for Ward played irresistibly, was round under 70 and leading by many holes. Bruen never looked as if he would quite beat Yates. On the other hand Thomson was going to beat Goodman; Peters was again in triumphant form; Kyle was justifying his captain; Crawley had played very well and had a valuable lead on Fischer. Lunch on the whole tasted very good. Nevertheless there were horrid set-backs in the afternoon; the horridest when we heard that Fischer had done six threes in a row and had beaten Crawley. That was a match that counted two on a division because we had relied on Crawley and had not expected that avalanche of threes. Stowe was hanging on grimly to Kocsis, but Kocsis was just keeping his nose in front and he was a very, very good player. There were times when a timid onlooker would almost have compromised with Providence for a halved match.

Then suddenly the atmosphere seemed to grow miraculously

clearer and brighter, and before we realised it the match was over and won. To me in my eyrie at Forgan's came almost simultaneously two great pieces of news; Stowe had beaten Kocsis by 2 and 1 and Kyle was dormy, it was said dormy five. If this last were true then the match was won, and, by Jove, it must be true for there, a sight for sore eyes, came a huge crowd, away from the fourteenth green and heading for the burn. Soon it had mingled with the other crowd coming with Ewing and Billows to the last green. One more flustered calculation; Thomson, Peters, Stowe and Kyle— yes, there was no doubt of it, four of our men had won. That was all we needed and now it was possible to watch Ewing with sympathy but without agony. He was dormy one, was he? well, so much the better, though it did not really matter. The next minute Ewing had laid a long approach putt beautifully dead; Billows had tried for his three and failed. We had won the Walker Cup by three whole points. *Nunc dimittis*.

Chapter 14

THE RYDER CUP

THE Walker Cup for amateurs has had its equivalent among professionals in the Ryder Cup, which was presented by the late Mr. Ryder of St. Albans in 1927. I do not know how much interest the matches for it which were played in the United States created in that country, but here, as it seems to me, they have been regarded with rather lack-lustre and defeatist eyes since they have in fact been regularly lost by considerable margins. In the matches in England on the other hand our players have done very well indeed, incomparably better than their amateur brethren, and there has been plenty of excitement, notably over the match at Southport in 1933, which our side won by a single putt. And yet I hesitate to set down these matches as an outstanding success and that for the obvious reason that they have consistently lacked a really worthy battlefield. This cannot be called anyone's fault. It is natural and reasonable that professionals should want to play on a course where they will be assured of a big gate, but the result is that the best players in the world have to be seen on courses that cannot by the wildest stretch of imagination be rated among the best or even the next best. I cannot rid myself of the feeling that the greatest matches should be played by the sea, and on some really classic course there, but this may be an antiquated prejudice and there are doubtless inland courses worthy of any match. When for instance Cotton and Densmore Shute played their 72-hole match at Walton Heath nobody could say that here was not a stern and worthy test, but the Ryder Cup matches have not been played and could not in the circumstances be played on that bleak and noble heath.

The first unofficial match between the British and American professionals, which was the begetter of the Ryder Cup, as the Amateur International at Hoylake in 1921 was of the Walker Cup, took place at Wentworth. The first Ryder Cup match proper played in this country was at Moortown near Leeds, and the next two were at Southport and Ainsdale,

which seems now to be regarded as the home of the match.
It has one or two good holes, it has a large and formidable
bunker which has received much publicity under its odd and
engaging name of "Gumbleys", and the Club spends itself
lavishly in staging and managing the show, but when all is
said this is not the best place in which to watch great golfers.
The crowd is enormous and it would be unmeaning flattery
to suggest that the majority know much about golf; their
emotions do not as a rule go beyond making pyrotechnic
noises over a big drive or frenzied clapping over a long putt.
The accompaniments of the match in the shape of booths and
side-shows and itinerant vendors are rather too much like
those of a Derby Day. The golf is too essentially "popular"
to give much pleasure in the watching. There may be crowds
as large at big events on Scottish courses, but there the people
understand what they are looking at. Though the individual
watcher may selfishly wish for his own sake that there were
fewer of them, he enjoys the communal excitement and
sympathises with Mr. Churchill's remarks approving of
"crowd and urgency" on a great occasion. It is otherwise
with a crowd, a large portion of which would be just as happy
at any other form of jollification. This is the price that
professional golf has to pay for popularity and, whether or not
these views are "undemocratic", I confess that this is one of
the few matches I do not dream of watching again with any
passionate enthusiasm.

It is rather a curious thing about the series of matches in
this country that they have sometimes proved most deceptive
pointers to the Open Championship which succeeded them.
When we have been uplifted over the result of the match the
Championship has provided an unpleasant douche of cold
water, and when we have been depressed over it the Championship has come to revive our drooping spirits. The first
unofficial match at Wentworth in 1926 was won against a
strong team of invaders with ridiculous ease and, coming as
it did after four of the last five Championships had gone to
America, the victory sent public spirits soaring; the tide had
surely turned and our players would do wonderful things at
St. Anne's. And what in fact happened at St. Anne's? The
first four players were Americans, two of them to be sure
amateurs, Bobby Jones and Von Elm, who had not played at

Wentworth; and then, after a small British sandwich of two, came three more from the United States and one from South America.

Three years later at Moortown much the same thing happened. We won the match and this was a much more serious match with the invaders out to do their best, though still, as I cannot help fancying, with a main eye on the more definite and glittering prize of the Championship. When the Championship arrived the first three were Hagen, Farrell and Diegel. Again at Southport in 1933 we won a truly desperate match and the Championship, at St. Andrews too, provided a cruel humiliation—two invaders in a tie for first place, followed by a solitary Englishman and then three more Americans. And now for the converse picture. At Southport in 1937 the United States put an extraordinarily formidable team into the field and won the match comfortably. Despite this I cannot say that we felt hopeless; we had great faith in one or two of our players, for by that time we had had evidence that they could win their own championship; but we realised to the full how good the invaders were, and when at Carnoustie they returned as a body astonishing scores in the qualifying rounds the future seemed black. Then that invading host "on the morrow lay withered and strown" and in horrible weather not only did Cotton win but British golf as a whole reasserted itself. Altogether the Ryder Cup match has given very unsound grounds for prophecy.

To take these matches briefly one by one, many words need not be spent on the first at Wentworth, because in looking back its result was too obviously fallacious, altogether too good to be true. Our men headed by Mitchell and Duncan played beyond doubt superb golf and perhaps they had "reached the peak" too early in the year. This their opponents clearly had not done nor had had any intention of doing. They had not very long landed, and they were meaning to settle down and be at their best for the Championship at St. Anne's some time later. They took the match, unless I misjudge them, with light hearts. The result was a sweeping victory for our side. They won every foursome, Duncan and Mitchell setting the pace beating Hagen and Barnes by 9 and 8; they won eight out of the ten singles, only Compston losing by a hole to Mehlhorn and Ernest Whitcombe halving with Emmett

French. It was magnificent but, as subsequent events proved, it was not war. Our men had the golf in them but somehow when it came to that Championship, they did not play it.

In 1927 the Cup matches proper were initiated and the first played at Worcester in Massachusetts. As I did not see it I will say merely from a book of reference that the U.S.A. won by 9 matches to 2 with one halved, and so back to this country and to Moortown near Leeds two years later. This match was an altogether different thing from that at Wentworth. It was official, the American team had been deliberately chosen for it with Hagen as captain and had come over in good time. This was the real thing and there was a mighty crowd to see it. If we have sometimes complained in international matches of not having the weather we wanted, we had it at Moortown. It was horribly, piercingly cold and the American players put on more and more jerseys and woolly waistcoats and yet looked and doubtless were frozen. I remember thinking that Joe Turnesa, a slightly-built player with a most beautiful swing, had the air of a poor little shivering Italian greyhound. Another memory is of our visitors warming themselves and "limbering up" by hitting an immense number of practice shots before starting, and of the crowd staring open-mouthed, half amused and half alarmed, at such tremendous preparations. The foursomes were a little disappointing to us, for at one time it looked as if we were going to win them and at the end of the day we were one down. Farrell saved the top foursome against Charles Whitcombe and Compston by a great recovering pitch to the home hole from behind masses of gorse to the left of the green, and generally speaking hopes were not quite realised.

The most alarming player on the American side, both that day and the next, was Leo Diegel. This was the first sight that most British spectators had had of him and he was in one of his inspired moods. His swing was not graceful but he was driving a long way and very straight, and his putting, in an attitude such as had never been seen before, was uniformly deadly. Within a week hundreds of British golfers were assiduously conjugating the verb "to diegel" and trying to attain what they believed to be his pose. His chin nearly touched the top of the putter shaft, his elbows were stuck out at the extreme angle physically possible, his wrists were stiff as pokers, and, apparently with his shoulders, he pushed the ball unerringly into the hole. He had, I think, got a new putter to reinforce this new style and was still trying experiments with it, in the form of having the shaft painted a new colour. At any rate I recollect seeing him practising gaily with it after he and Espinosa had handsomely won their foursome, as if he could not hole enough putts and could not be too happy.

Diegel was unquestionably the hero of that match for on the second day in the singles he murdered Abe Mitchell to the tune of 9 and 8, and that was a thing that it seemed impossible for anyone to do. He was playing with utter and victorious confidence, with none of that pacing up and down like a caged lion which sometimes beset him in tense moments. But most of the other heroics in the singles were on our side and our men as a whole wrought nobly. Duncan, in particularly fine form, 10 up and 8 against Hagen, C. A. Whitcombe 8 and 6 on Farrell, Compston 6 and 4 on Sarazen, here were three cheering wins and they were cheering from the very start. When we knew that Cotton had humanly speaking got Watrous beaten, we knew that the match was won. Cotton by the way had in the morning signalised his first appearance by disappearing into the gorse to the right of the eighteenth green and holing his pitch for a three. My recollection is that the fact that the last couple, Ernest Whitcombe and Espinosa, had halved only reached me when I was back in my hotel in Leeds. If this sounds like lazy watching, let anyone go to a Ryder Cup match and after struggling all day to see more than the " 'oofs of the horses" see whether he does not take any car he can get and long to be home again! The only other winner besides Diegel on the American side was Horton Smith who beat Robson by 4 and 2. There was great curiosity to see him play (he had been left out of the foursomes) as he had been winning all the tournaments and all the winter money in the South. Moreover he had sprung very suddenly into fame, having originally learnt his game, as one was told, on a rather primitive course at some unknown town in Missouri. Perhaps it was this that made one think his style just a little artificial and studied, but there could be no doubt about its practical merits, and his putting has always been, as I recall it, a joy to watch, easy, elegant and of a horrid certainty. The United States have sent us a number of great putters from whom to choose models, but I am disposed to doubt if they have sent a better than Horton Smith. Like his namesake Macdonald Smith he has won almost everything in his own country but never the Open Championship.

In 1931 the match was played in blazing weather at Columbus and the home side again won comfortably enough by 9 matches to 3, Mitchell and Robson, who had won together at Moortown, being the only pair to win their foursome, W. H. Davies and Havers winning their singles. Then came the first match at Southport, which provided perhaps the most exciting finish ever seen in a team match, if only one could have seen it properly, as I did not. I only heard it in excited whispers and at last in frantic cheers through a solid wall of humanity. Crowds can be so large as to be frightening, and some time before the end one thing became apparent to any prudent man, namely that if he did not get back to his base at the clubhouse betimes he might never get back at all.

The public excitement over the match was very great and had been stimulated by much preliminary writing. For the first time the British team had a non-playing captain and a Tartar at that, though a very friendly Tartar, whose every wave of his umbrella has encouragement in it, J. H. Taylor. He had a free hand to dispose of the men chosen as he thought best and he took to himself an ally in the shape of Alex Stark, Andrew Kirkaldy's son-in-law, a physical instructor at St. Andrews University. There were many stories of the ferocious training that the team was supposed to be undergoing, but I take from Taylor's book, *Golf: My Life's Work*, an account of what they actually did. They were called, he says, at 6.30, went out for a run on the sands before breakfast and were then rubbed down by the expert hands of Mr. Stark. The proof of the pudding is that they won the match and, though no one can say how much this course of training had to do with it, it is tolerably certain that everything, even matutinal suffering, which contributes to a communal existence is good for a team. Another small piece of inner history I borrow from J. H.'s book. He had an engagement with Hagen, the opposing captain, to exchange lists of the couples set out in their order for the foursomes but Hagen with his incorrigible casualness did not keep it, and again at a second appointed time was not ready with his list. A third hour was named and this time J. H. delivered an ultimatum that if the list were not handed over at the right hour he would declare the match off and the world should know the reason why. The lists were thereupon exchanged and all was well.

Duncan disappeared from the British side and Cotton had lately gone to Brussels. The players were in their foursome order Alliss and Charles Whitcombe, Mitchell and Havers, Davies and a new-comer Easterbrook, Padgham and Perry; Lacey took Perry's place in the singles. The Americans had several players new to us: Olin Dutra from California, destined to win the American Open in the following year, a big, strong man with a drowsily easy swing; Densmore Shute, of Westward Ho! ancestry, who was going to win our Championship in that very year; and Craig Wood, a dashing and attractive player who was to tie with him; Dudley, from Bobby Jones's Atlanta and with something the same grace of swing; Paul Runyan, a small man with a great reputation as a pitcher and putter, dowered with accuracy rather than power, a most successful tournament player in his own country, but not seen to very great advantage here; Billy Burke, sound rather than exciting but, like all Americans, a good putter and a good enough golfer at any rate to be their Open Champion in 1931.

The interesting thing about the American pairings was that Hagen and Sarazen played together as first couple. There was a vague general notion that they did not agree very well and this was supposed to be a gesture to disprove it. I have not the least idea whether this was true; very likely not. At any rate they seemed to get on perfectly well together without either being perhaps quite at his best. Alliss and Charles Whitcombe, who has had a very good record in these matches just as Padgham has had a surprisingly unfortunate one, halved with this top pair, so formidable on paper, and there could be no complaints, though of course there had been moments when we had hoped for more. Our next two pairs won their matches, and though Padgham and Perry lost, rather disappointingly, to Burke and Dudley, one up on the day was one up and of good augury.

I am bound to say that I remember more of the general

crowd and excitement than of the details of the play in the singles. Mitchell early looked like beating Dutra, as he did by many holes, but then Padgham was down to Sarazen, which was a set-off. Lacey for a while was keeping his nose in front of Hagen and if he could win that match surely all would be well; that point would be worth much fine gold, but somehow Hagen would probably just do it in the end, as he did after a hard fight. Alliss and Havers were keeping their leads but Whitcombe looked like losing to Horton Smith. Gradually the fate of empires seemed more and more to depend on Easterbook and Densmore Shute, the former the more dashing and attractive player of the two perhaps, but Shute a match player of great toughness who looked as unlikely as any man to miss a decisive putt. By the time these two were coming to the home hole all square, with the whole match all square, I had, as I have said, made a strategic movement to the safety of the clubhouse and all I know I heard from others in front of me who heard in turn from those who could see at least something. Both were on the green in two, and Easterbrook had putted and laid his ball more or less dead; a halved match, both individually and collectively, seemed the likeliest end. After an eternity, as it appeared, Shute had putted. What had happened? Clearly he had not holed and that was something. In fact he had gone rather boldly for the hole down a slope and on a slippery green. How far past he ended I do not know, not very far, but far enough to miss coming back. There was another eternity and then a yell: Easterbrook had made no mistake with his short one and the match was miraculously won.

In 1935 there came yet another American tragedy, at Ridgewood in New Jersey when our side was beaten by eight matches to two and thus back to the hurly-burly of Southport again and the last Ryder Cup match before the war. Again there were some new visitors on view. There was Guldahl, not an attractive player, unquestionably a powerful and resolute one, in whom the Americans themselves had a great belief, as one capable of tremendous things at a pinch. Byron Nelson was a very neat and engaging player who has done great things since. Manero, an Open Champion, also very neat and accurate, seemed a little lacking in power perhaps for the severest tests, and Picard was an interesting and

intelligent golfer, good at all points; Revolta, a deadly putter
having a curious stance, with his right foot almost behind the
ball, and a curious grip of his own. Above all, there was
Sam Snead, an eminently natural golfer with immense power
and a beautiful style, who looked as if he ought to be the best ·
that ever lived but has so far apparently lacked an essential
something, whether of thought or determination, to make him
so. These new-comers were reinforced by a solid body of
those whom we knew before, Sarazen, Shute and Dudley
(Hagen did not play), and the whole array was most menacing.
As far as I remember we were never wildly sanguine though
we too had some good new ones; Rees, a putter up to the best
American standards and a dauntless match player; Sam King,
as delightfully natural a golfer as Snead himself; Burton, not
yet quite come into his kingdom but of great possibilities.
Moreover we had got Cotton back, with all the prestige of
being the first man to throw off the foreign yoke.

In looking back it seems to me now that the British side
never recovered from the unexpected defeat of their first
couple, Padgham and Cotton. We had no right to be sure
they would win, for Nelson and Dudley were a fine couple,
good enough to beat anybody in reason; but still, with a
putting of two such eggs in one basket, I am afraid we were
sure, and the shock of losing was correspondingly great.
Padgham was that year suffering from an eminently pardonable reaction after his brilliant preceding one which had
culminated in the Championship at Hoylake. He was not
his best self at all and the defeat was not Cotton's fault, but
there it was. In fact it was the heaviest defeat of the day,
4 and 2, for the three other matches went either to the thirty-
fifth or thirty-sixth green. Whitcombe and Rees halved the
third match and Alliss and Burton won the fourth, but we were
one down, and everybody knew or ought to have known how
much that one point was worth.

Next day, a miserable, gloomy, wet day, had some bright
spots such as the indomitable little Rees's defeat of Nelson
and King's halved match with Shute; he holed a brave putt
to get his half. But again the luckless Padgham had given us
a bad start against Guldahl, and though Cotton duly beat
Manero, there was a feeling, perhaps unjustified, that he was
to some extent wasting his sweetness in that particular match.

There was a solid phalanx of four at the end of the American list, Sarazen, Snead, Dudley and Picard, who gave a collective sense of security to the side. Their opponents hung on nobly, they got back holes, but always the holes seemed slipping away again. That was the rather depressed way at any rate in which I saw the match, and in fact all those four Americans won, Snead very comfortably against Burton, the others only after struggles, but they all won. And so the visitors quite deservedly took away the Ryder Cup for the first time in this country. The next match which ought to have been in 1939 is due to be played in America, but some day, let us hope, it will be here again. If only it could be played, let us say, at Hoylake at full stretch, what fun it would be to look forward to!

Chapter 15

INTERNATIONALS AT HOME

A FEW years ago I met on a course in Wales a distinguished Irish golfer of my acquaintance. As I greeted him my eyes became riveted on his tie. Blue, with a line of red and yellow running diagonally across it, and some jolly, rampacious little red lions—yes, it was beyond question the Scottish international tie, and what was my Irishman doing with it round his neck? He explained with inimitable lightness that he and a Scotsman had exchanged ties after an international match, much, I suppose, as ladies and gentlemen exchange hats on a bank-holiday charabanc, and that he had worn it off and on ever since. This was a momentary shock to one brought up in too solemn a tradition of the sacredness of colours (I admit I should be terribly self-conscious in someone else's tie), but at the same time it was very agreeable, as evidence of the friendliness engendered by the international tournament between the teams of the four countries. This is at once a very serious and a very cheerful meeting and I think that the team spirit—an odious but useful expression— so notable in our victorious Walker Cup side, owed not a little to the acquaintance made at these yearly tournaments.

I am not going to attempt anything like a consecutive account of the international matches between wars, because it would be far too much like a catalogue and a dull one at that. But they deserve at least some mention because after 1932 they became not mere appendages of championships, but constituted a tournament on their own account, in which all four countries took part, played on their own course and at their own time, with no rival attraction to dim their brightness. I remember having originally some doubts as to whether such a plan would be a success. Perhaps these may have been generated by laziness and reluctance to watch yet another tournament. Whatever may have been my reasons I freely and gladly admit myself to have been wrong. These matches have not only been both interesting and exciting in themselves but have helped to bring to the front players who, from lack of opportunity or bad luck in championships, might otherwise have remained undiscovered. A man may be just knocked out in an early round of the Amateur Championship; he is forgotten in the crowd and no one is much the wiser; but if he plays for his country against the three others, two rounds a day, foursomes and singles, he gives his proofs one way or the other. Exactly how much general interest the tournament has created I do not know. In some ways it reminds me a little of Halford Hewitt Cup, as to which all at Deal, players and supporters alike, are wrought up to a high degree of excitement and the general public remains uncommonly placid. These international matches, though naturally possessing a wider public, are still a little in the same position; they have never wholly "caught on" save in the actual places where they are played. But they have produced lots of fine golf, plenty of excitement, plenty of friendliness, and have been extraordinarily well worth while.

A short dive back into past history may be allowed as showing how things have come about. In 1902 the Royal Liverpool Golf Club, that pioneer in the inauguration of golfing institutions, promoted the first match between the amateurs of England and Scotland, played at Hoylake by singles, the scoring being by the old ruthless method, for which incidentally there was plenty to be said, of holes. In the following year the match was officially adopted and the scoring changed to the more lenient method of matches. The match went on steadily for a number of years, but it was always overshadowed by the Amateur Championship which it immediately preceded. Some people thought that the strain of one more hard day's play was too much in addition to the Championship, and other people lost interest because the Scotsmen were too good and won too often. One way and another the fixture had not quite fulfilled the original high hopes. In 1912 at Westward Ho! an attempt at resuscitation was made by substituting foursomes for singles, but it seemed, sad to say, to have the opposite effect, and in 1913 the match was by common consent abandoned. Meanwhile Wales and Ireland had at times played matches against one another and at the Irish Open Amateur Championship meeting a scratch team collected from the English entrants had played Ireland, but

167

the general interest in these matches may be respectfully said to have been small and local.

After the war the England and Scotland match was revived at the time of the Prestwick Championship in 1922, and played by foursomes and singles, the two teams being chosen respectively by the English and Scottish members of the newly instituted Championship Committee. Then in 1924 there came what may be called a political upheaval of some importance. As to the Scottish side I cannot speak positively, but the English Union took over the choosing of our side in partnership with the Championship Committee. I remember the meeting of the selectors very well because there were so many of us and I was in the chair. I also recall the circumstance that for the last place on the side there was a spirited and entirely friendly contest; I and all my Championship Committee colleagues voted steadily for my exclusion, while the Union representatives were as firm for putting me in. They had a majority of one and so I played. Thank heaven I won my single and—this is purely egotistical—had the satisfactory swan-song of captaining a victorious England side against the ancient enemy at St. Andrews.

Clearly however there were too many cooks and this was not a good plan. After that the Unions took over the match altogether and it has been their concern ever since. Of the years from 1922 to 1932 it must be enough to say this: Scotland won the first two matches in their old style; then they decidedly fell off and England with some very good sides, for we had Wethered, Tolley and Holderness and more besides, had a long spell of success and of the next seven matches won five and halved two. In 1931 Scotland won again and then in 1932 the match was taken away from the Championship meeting and fused in the tournament between the four countries. Scotland was now breeding a new generation of very good young players and beat England six times running, until at Porthcawl in 1938, amid all the excursions and alarms that preceded Munich, England at last managed to win again.

When the tournament started there was a general opinion that Ireland and Wales could not hold their own with the other two countries, and I suppose generally speaking this has been borne out, but, even if they have as a rule lost, they have at the least made their conquerors go hard; all the matches have been full of interest and the Irishmen have twice beaten England and once beaten Scotland. It must be admitted that the score of the Welshmen is still blank, but to say only so much is to do them grave injustice. One victory, and that the most desired, was once by all accounts in the hollow of their hands. I was not at Portmarnock in 1937, when Wales and Scotland halved, but I am credibly informed that if one Welsh player, who shall be nameless, could in vulgar language have kicked his hat along at the home hole, Wales must have won. Alas! he did not accomplish the feat, which at that particular home hole is not so simple as it sounds, and so Scotland escaped; but even so it was a good match to halve. Apart from that the leaders of the Welsh side have done wonderfully well. At Troon in the first year of the tournament Henry Howell, an excellent golfer and a particularly fine putter something in the Ouimet manner, triumphed consistently in the singles, and towards the end of the period, when Howell was not quite so good as he had been, Wales produced four players at the top of the list, Duncan, Roberts, Lewis and de Lloyd, who at the least held their own with the corresponding players on the other sides. With so comparatively small a number of players to choose from Wales has never yet been able to produce a tail quite strong enough and the many glories won by the scarlet jerseys in another game are yet to come in golf; but if keenness can do it—and South Wales is frantically keen—come they will some day.

Some of the Irish teams have been so good that it is surprising that they have not won more matches than they have. They have had an inspiring captain in Dr. McCormack; to see him sweep off his cap with a gesture as he salutes a conqueror or a victim on the last green is one of the most picturesque sights that golf has to offer. They have had in John Burke and J. C. Brown two of the best natural golfers in the four countries; Brown in particular is capable of extraordinary brilliance on occasions but is perhaps almost too dashing and has been apt to disappoint, lacking the cool solidity of Burke. They have had dour fighters in the two McConnells and Flaherty, a glorious hitter of the ball in O'Sullivan; in the last two years before the war they had Ewing arriving at his best, and above all they had Bruen. Here really were the makings of a side to win the mythical "triple crown", and what they could do was shown at St. Anne's by their beating Scotland by 9 matches to 6 and at Porthcawl by a crushing defeat of England by 11 points to 2. Certainly that English side was far from being one of the selectors' best efforts, but that is a detail; they were thoroughly overwhelmed and the Irishmen played extraordinarily well. It is the highest compliment I can pay them to say that in my view they have not done themselves full justice. They seem to lack some of the solid, stolid staying power of the Scots, who have been the unquestioned heroes of the quadruple tournament and have run their flag to the top of the pole with remarkable regularity.

Those Scottish sides had a great asset for several years in two unquestioned leaders. Whether McLean played first and Hector Thomson second or vice versa the team possessed what is so valuable to any team, a recognised and reliable head. But they had also a very good tail, and except for the two I have named the team might often have been turned upside-down and no harm done. McRuvie, McKinlay, McLeod, Campbell, Dykes and, very particularly, Gordon Peters—here are only a few names that catch my eye as I read over the old lists. In *Rodney Stone* Jem Belcher is made to say that Bristol is as full of young fighting men as a bin is full of bottles, and this, in the thirties, has been true of Scotland and especially of the West of Scotland. They were all young and keen, knew each other well and had played with each other often. In short they were essentially a team.

This was not so and perhaps can never be entirely so with the English teams. The area is too large and the players cannot know each other in the same way. To refer to a perhaps delicate subject, the problem of selection was not always very happily tackled. In the old days it is, I think, certain, and I write as one too often chosen, that the players from London clubs had too much of a "pull". Then when the Unions took over the task the pendulum swung a little the other way and too much importance was perhaps attached to county matches which are unknown in the South, with the result that the London and University players were not always chosen when they ought to have been. With the best intentions—and nobody imputes any others—this sort of thing is bound to happen now and then, but the bad time passed and the English side which won in 1938 at Porthcawl, with Cyril Tolley brought back to reanimate it as captain, was as good as it was a representative, harmonious and enthusiastic one.

The memories of that last meeting, of pleasant Porthcawl with its waves breaking in foam on the rocks and its gathering-place for news near the end (is it by the sixteenth green?) and the thrills of the narrow second shot to the home hole, are all, as I have said, a little shadowed by thoughts of war, which then seemed so imminent and was in fact less than a year away. The players kept their eye on the ball and their mind on the game but they did it with difficulty, and far clearer than that of any stroke comes back the vision of a silent, crowded clubhouse listening to the wireless and seeming to hear the Germans on the march. It was an ominous ending.

Chapter 16

UNIVERSITY GOLF AND GOLFERS

UNIVERSITY golf has made great strides between wars alike in the quality of its players and the attention they excite. It may be that they attain a slightly disproportionate amount of public notice from the fact that their matches are played in the winter or early spring when there is a lack of golfing news. They certainly work very hard at their game. On Saturday after Saturday and very often on Sundays too, when they are thinly disguised as 'The Divots' or 'The Outlaws', they play a trial match against some club usually in the neighbourhood of London and have to make long journeys by road to get there. Oxford are perhaps slightly better off in this respect in not having quite so far to travel as have the men of Cambridge, who are often well on their way and breakfasting at the Peahen at St. Albans while their prospective adversaries are still snug in bed. Even allowing for the resilience of youth, it is truly remarkable how well they play after their hideously early starts on wintry mornings. In more easygoing days they had time to reach the course at a reasonable hour, play a few practice holes and tackle the match when restored by lunch. Now the matches are of two rounds, singles and foursomes and they must be up and away to serious business as soon as they arrive.

Not only have University golfers become much better known than of old to the general golfing public, but they are no longer without honour in their own countries. In the last year before this war Cambridge attained the honour of a full blue. Whether they had ever had a legal right to a half blue is doubtful, for long years ago, *Consule* Mr. W. T. Linskill, their claims having been contumaciously rejected by the Blues Committee, they had taken to themselves a little light-blue cap with silver crossed clubs. I have one in a drawer to witness if I lie. This is not the day of caps, but at least the Cambridge side can now wear full blue scarves and look even an oarsman squarely between the eyes. Oxford have still a half blue only. Some years before the war they were, I believe, offered a compromise in the shape of five full and five half blues for the team, but the then captain, R. H. Baugh, said in effect that it must be all or none and spurned the proposal.

The University Match is a very different matter from what it was in the times of those light-blue caps, which, incidentally, even in my remote days were never worn and only dangled from the corner of a photographic group. Then the match consisted of only one eighteen-hole round on Wimbledon Common, and even after the venue had been removed to Sandwich, only one round was played till 1898, the famous blizzard year, when thirty-six holes were first played. In the first match after the first war the old conditions were renewed, but in 1921 at Hoylake the match became one of two days and seventy-two holes, with foursomes on the first day and singles on the second. This was a change universally approved. How much greater is the general interest taken in the match I can best illustrate by telling how in my own years at Sandwich, the habitués there, such as Mr. 'Tommy' Mills, did us the honour to watch us hit our first tee shots and, as soon as we were out of the way, played their own daily matches with perfect placidity. There was not a soul on the crest of the Maiden to see us hit over or into it. Again, there were no parents or hardly any. I can only recall two; Sir George Newnes at Wimbledon, who broke his umbrella on seeing his nephew miss a short putt which would have given Cambridge the victory, and at Sandwich the beloved Mr. Walter de Zoete who came to support his son Herman. I still remember with gratitude his encouragement during my own match. How different it is today when there is hardly a single poor Tiger who has not got his Christian. Fathers and mothers and younger brothers and sisters are thick on the ground, pretending to look at other people while they peer cautiously from behind sandhills to see how their champions are faring. I still recall with some alarm a match at Burnham. Cambridge was clearly going to win the decisive single on the sixteenth green and I was getting ready to shout when I realised I was as hopelessly encircled as ever were the Germans at Stalingrad by fierce Oxford mothers. I had just time enough to take evasive action and wriggle out before giving vent to my feelings.

I fancy that a great many more schoolboys have lately given serious attention to golf than they did, let us say, at the end of the nineteenth century and the first few years of the twentieth. As a result a considerable number of decidedly competent players come up to the University every year. In my own day any freshman who had played seriously as a boy was likely to walk into the side. Of late years he has had to fight hard to get in even though he be a good golfer with a handicap in at least the neighbourhood of scratch. From the earliest times there have usually been one or two really good players at the head of one side or both, but towards the end of the list there came a serious falling-off. Today the teams play well down to the tenth man, and if, as sometimes happens, the whole fate of the day depends on the last couple, they will give a thoroughly good show such as their leaders would not disdain. With the older generation of University golfers it has always been an article of faith that there never was such a side as the Oxford one of 1900, which beat its luckless enemies by 69 holes to nothing. They were a very fine side all through, with such golfers as J. A. T. Bramston and H. W. Beveridge playing last but two and last but one respectively. I am not going to give up my belief in them at this time of day but they were in their own time a wholly exceptional side, whereas now, year after year would produce one team and sometimes two, fit to hold up their heads in their distinguished company. Beyond that remark I will not be tempted into comparisons.

University golf got a great fillip on starting again after the war through Roger Wethered and Cyril Tolley (they may have Mr.'s in other chapters but not in this youthful one) going up to Oxford together, and they have had plenty of distinguished successors. Of those who have played between wars four have won the Amateur Championship, Tolley (twice), Wethered, Robert Sweeney and Martin Smith; three the English Championship, Pennink (twice), Crawley and Bourn; one the Welsh, Duncan. I have laboriously—no, for it was a labour of browsing love—searched the list of international players to find that eight have played for Britain in the Walker Cup, and twenty have represented their respective countries in domestic internationals. Oxford have a little the best of the record, and ever since I can remember University golf, indeed long before I can remember it, in the earliest times of Horace Hutchinson and Alexander Stuart, it seems to be a rule of nature that Oxford produces the greater individual players but not necessarily the better team, as witness the fact that in 1939 Cambridge led by five over the whole series of matches, and in the matches between wars they lead by as much as eight.

Outstanding players cannot make a team but they can contribute something more to it than the winning of their individual matches. It is a great thing for a side to have an unquestioned leader, to whom all the rest of the side look up and on whom they rely for a good start. His play is an inspiration and a begetter of confidence. At the same time his influence may be exaggerated by the unthinking, for whatever he may do at other games he cannot carry a whole side on his back. A good illustration was seen in the first match after the war at Sunningdale. Tolley and Wethered were carrying death and devastation among the London ranks in trial matches. They were very fine players and all England rang with them. The general run of golfers made up their minds accordingly that Cambridge had no chance. But two men, however good, cannot do the work of ten, not even when they are backed up by one very little inferior to them, John Beck. Cambridge had one very good player, W. L. Hope, who beat Beck after a fierce struggle; the two great Oxonians duly murdered their men but the Cambridge tail wagged gallantly. Oxford had some very vulnerable spots and Cambridge won by a match, the cheers proclaiming one victory at the thirty-seventh hole coinciding almost to a minute with those for another on the thirty-sixth.

Next year the foursomes were instituted and these have made still more valuable the possession by a side of some really outstanding figure. It is more than twice blessed, for he can generally help some rather lame dog in the foursome besides winning his single. In 1921 at Hoylake Oxford made no mistake about it, for they won by nine matches. Beck had gone down but Wethered and Tolley were this time backed up by a thoroughly sound side, including that rare phenomenon a really good left-hander, Ivor Thomas, who in later years became the mainstay of the Lerpoolians at Deal, and H. S. Malik who had all the litheness and traditional grace of

Indian ball-game players. Again the big men did all that could be asked of them, Tolley slaughtering a capital golfer in G. N. P. Humphreys and Wethered winning as good and exciting a match as any in the whole series against Jos Walker at the last hole. Walker was not an elegant player but he was a very strong and resolute one and a good putter, as he has shown since both in championships and for the Wykeham-ists at Deal. Wethered played his game but he could never get away and showed his fine match-playing qualities, as he so often has since, by refusing to be worried by a pertinacious adversary whom he was quite wrongly supposed to have at his mercy. Nobody is less self-conscious in these matters; he takes his adversary as he finds him and beats him if he can. It is a great quality and by no means a common one. Long after the issue of the whole match was decided the last two men, Cochran and Longbourn, came to the last hole locked in a deadly grapple. The two teams thereupon linked arms and went out in a spirit of what I can only term bank-holiday ghoulishness to watch them play the extra holes. The two poor wretches gave them plenty of fun for their money, for they went on till Cochran won at the thirty-ninth.

1922, when the match was played at Prince's, Sandwich saw Tolley still up at Oxford, though already enjoying the dignity of an ex-Champion. Cambridge were strengthened by a good soldier golfer, W. H. H. Aitken, R.E., who was doing a one year's course at the University. Tolley had a remarkable single against C. H. Prowse, which he began by losing four out of the first five holes. I doubt if the most enthusiastic supporter of Cambridge had even at that terrific moment any real hopes; it was too good to be true, and though Prowse hung on as well as he could he lost by 3 and 2. Stout-hearted golf by the tail end of the Cambridge side ultimately won the match by a margin of one, without any exciting finishes. One of the last four on the winning side was a not very large person, with a Jesus tie and a fox's head tie-pin in it, a very long swing and a putting stance of apparently agonising discomfort in which he holed out with deadly precision. This was one of the outstanding University golfers between wars, E. F. Storey, always called Eustace, presumably because his name is Edward. He did not then hit the ball very far though in the next year or two his length vastly increased, but

James Braid with A. Herd, J. H. Taylor and E. Ray

Roger Wethered

his putting and his resolute and sanguine temperament made him already a valuable player. Storey has always confounded the critics who adhere too closely to their own rules of orthodoxy and style and do not think enough of results. When he first played for Cambridge they were apt to say he would not "be any real good" because he swung the club too far. Yet by next year he was the leader of the side. A little later they said that as soon as he went down and did not get constant practice the long swing would find him out. He promptly reached the final of the Amateur Championship. Since then the critics have kept silence and he has remained year in and year out one of the best amateur golfers in the country.

Nevertheless in 1923 at Rye Storey had a set-back, when he was fairly and squarely beaten by Athole Murray. Murray played admirably, and looking at the various leading singles between wars I esteem his victory, by 4 and 3 and no half measures, perhaps the most meritorious in the whole list. Oxford that year had the aid of that universal game-playing genius R. H. Bettington, who has since won the Australian Championship. At this time he could hit the ball a very long distance rather than in any precise direction. On the Cambridge side Dale Bourn occupied a comparatively humble place for Cambridge and won both his matches. Rye had generally been regarded as a good course for Oxford, though the legend has since been dissipated, and they won very creditably by 9 to 6.

Cambridge won at Hoylake next year, an ally from America though a British citizen, Pulling, doing a fabulous number of threes, and Storey just and only just beating a good and graceful player in Mackintosh who, as far as public golf was concerned, vanished from that day forth. Much the same may be said of the man who unquestionably played the best golf at Hunstanton in 1925, T. H. Osgood. He beat Alan Cave unmercifully and I rank him very high among University golfers. So did the Scottish Selection Committee for they chose him to play for his country. After that work claimed him, to the decided loss, I fancy, of amateur golf. That year at Hunstanton, when the pendulum swung once more in Oxford's favour, saw the first appearance of three noteworthy players, Rex Hartley, who was already well known before he went up, L. G. Crawley and R. H. Oppenheimer. Crawley was then a butterfly scarcely emerged from the cricketer chrysalis, though he had already a fine style and much power. His single appearance in University golf did no sort of justice to his potentialities and after having a good lead at lunch he lost to Field, who added insult to injury by taking an iron club from the tee. Oppenheimer won both his matches and was clearly going to be valuable to Oxford for three years to come and to the Harrovians at Deal for much longer than that. Indeed he seems to me to have kept his best golf for Harrow and never to have done himself full justice elsewhere as an individual player. If I am wrong this is at any rate the highest compliment I can pay him. Since those days he has become the annual friend and supporter of the Oxford side at every University match and is at least equal to me on the other side in a fine, vindictive partisanship. For two days a year he and I are like the Yorkshire and Lancashire cricketers who say "Good morning" before the match and after that say nothing but "How's that?"

Next in 1926 to Burnham, which saw the first of four successive Cambridge victories, in weather so bitter that almost my chief recollection is of trying to keep warm in bed in a garret and failing miserably. Hartley won both his matches, his single only at the last hole against a good and successful Oxford golfer, A. R. Nall Cain, now Lord Brocket, and Maughan did very well to beat an all-round game player, J. S. Stephenson, at a blood-curdling thirty-seventh. J. H. Taylor, Junior, made a first and successful appearance under his illustrious father's eye, and two unfortunates, one on each side, competed for the honour of being beaten by more holes than had ever been lost before. Their names, as far as I am concerned, shall be lost too. Enough that Fell for Cambridge won by 14 and 13 and Maxwell of Oxford just wiped his eye with 15 and 14.

Hoylake, which saw the first appearance of Stuart Bradshaw for Oxford and Geoffrey Illingworth for Cambridge, was windy even by Hoylake standards. The match led to one reform which is heartily to be approved. Oppenheimer and Grimwade went to the forty-first hole before Grimwade won, and this seemed, especially in such a hurricane, "rayther too rich". Extra holes are necessary evils in a tournament, but in a team game they are superfluous cruelty since what better end can be there than a half whether to a single match or the whole match? Since then the horrid practice has been abandoned.

The next year, 1928, at Prince's saw Oxford two up in the foursomes only to be beaten by a strong counter-attack in the singles. They had five very good players in Oppenheimer, Taylor, Bradshaw, D. H. R. Martin and an American, Baugh, and as I look at the list I do not quite know why they did not win. What I thought at the time I scarcely remember, but I do remember a fine, fierce piece of fighting by Evelyn-Jones who beat Bradshaw and a most resolute display by the last two men on each side, Clayton and Rawlins. The whole issue of the day depended on them and they bore themselves like men and heroes. There was a great gathering of fathers at the dinner afterwards, and "J. H." made a speech, which for its sincere and touching quality will never be forgotten by those who heard it. At Rye in 1929 the top foursome was halved between Bradshaw and Baugh, Illingworth and Crouch, a fine match, and I come with a sensible relief, since I know I am suspected of partiality, to an Oxford win at Hoylake in 1930. They had three American allies, Baugh, Charles Sweeney and Scheftel, and they made the saddest mess of their enemies, by 12 matches to 3, almost the only ray of comfort on the other side being provided by Eric Martin Smith, destined not long afterwards to be Amateur Champion. The match will be chiefly remembered by a daring and as most people thought an ill-considered decision by the two captains. Hoylake was suffering from the effects of a very wet winter and most of the bunkers were full of water. There would inevitably be a prodigious amount of lifting and dropping, and to obviate this it was decided to allow a player who put his ball into a water-logged bunker to have a *locus poenitentiae* in the form of another shot. Rules are rules and it is better to stick to them, however tiresome they may be.

And now it is becoming painfully apparent to me that this chapter is degenerating into a catalogue and that I must put a little steam on. The more recent past needs, I may hope, the less recalling. Briefly Oxford won for the next two years; then Cambridge won at Prince's, then Oxford again at Formby, and after that Cambridge ran out with a break of five unfinished. During those nine years there have been a number of really good players on either side of whom John Rowell and John Lyon, both of Cambridge, and Kenneth Scott of Oxford have already fallen in the war. Some who were very good when they were up have for one reason or another disappeared from the ken of golfers afterwards, while others, such as Sweeney and Duncan, have gone on to do great deeds in championships, deeds which will be found duly referred to in other chapters. Among the best players of quite recent years, at the time they were undergraduates, whose names occur to me more or less in order of date, are for Oxford—Robert Sweeney, Middleton, Morrice, Pennink, Scott, Mitchell-Innes, Duncan: for Cambridge—P. H. F. White, Kenneth Thomson, Wallace, Lyon, Watermeyer, Lucas, Langley, Whitelaw. Of these three who must certainly rank high as undergraduate players may not even after a few years be as well remembered as they deserve. Watermeyer who played with extraordinary brilliance in one University match went back to his native South Africa; I do not know where Kenneth Thomson is but I am sure he was and must be still a beautiful player; Wallace seemed to fade away a little once he had gone down but he was undoubtedly formidable when he was up, being very strong (I think he put the weight in spare moments) and of a fine pugnacious temperament. Pennink is emphatically one of those who have come on and attained much higher fame after going down. With a very sound and leisurely style (I suppose his right elbow is not strictly orthodox but people do not make so much fuss about right elbows as they did) and a great capacity for pegging away, he gave his proofs once and for all by winning the English Championship two years running. By contrast the left-hander, P. B. Lucas, who beat him handsomely in their match at Burnham, has proved a little disappointing. A natural born golfer if ever there was one, he developed an apparently incurable tendency to wildness from the tee, which no pains could eradicate. Perhaps when he comes back from the war, with his flying honours thick upon him, he may have sloughed his crookedness and be once more the golfer that he has it in him to be. His true quality he showed in his freshman's year when at Muirfield his first three rounds in the Open Championship were 74, 73, 72. He lapsed a little in the last round but those three had been eloquent of the golf that was in him. He holds moreover one record in University golf that can hardly be beaten: in each of his three years he played first on his side and beat his man; and they were all three good ones, Pennink, Duncan and Mitchell-Innes. The last of those three by the way would, I think, have been as good as any if his putting had been in the same class or anywhere near the same class as the rest of his game, but on the green he seemed altogether too heavy-handed.

Cambridge were very lucky in getting such a golfer as Langley to take Lucas's place as leader of the side, and ought to be grateful to Stowe for this pair of golfers. In fact they overlapped for one year, but Langley was already a destined No. 1, since he came up from a school as a Walker Cup player, a distinction likely to remain unique. Once he was at Cambridge cricket kept him from the links in summer-time and he had few chances of showing his quality except for the University, but to the Cambridge side he was a prop and stay, not only a fine player but from the start a wonderfully calm, mature and grown-up one. His great rival on the Oxford side was Kenneth Scott, with whom he had the better, but only just the better, of their exchanges. To see those two playing one another was an aesthetic joy; it was University golf at its best.

Finally let me pay my tribute to the best combined golf that I have ever seen in a University match. I have no doubt about it at all. It was played by those two redoubtable Carthusians, White of Cambridge and Middleton of Oxford, at Prince's, Sandwich, in 1933. At the last two holes they faltered a little but up to that point they had played so well, with one brilliant thrust after another being met by an equally brilliant riposte, that they really seemed to have bewitched one another. They halved the match. The Cambridge man had, as I remember, a putt to win. He missed it, and I was glad of it. If I could say more I would.

Chapter 17

THE PRESIDENT'S PUTTER

No account of University golf and golfers between wars would be complete without a supplement; some word at least there must be of the tournament for the President's Putter which is played annually at Rye by the members of the Oxford and Cambridge Golfing Society. This wooden putter, originally Hugh Kirkaldy's, was presented to the Society by its captain for so many years, John Low, and there are now hanging to it twenty balls representing those who have won it from the first tournament in 1920 to 1939. Though the field is of necessity comparatively small it is always a very strong one. On the medal given to the winner are inscribed the words "Primus inter pares". They were translated by Arthur Croome "He was rather lucky to win", and in fact it takes a great deal of winning. No undergraduate has yet succeeded in doing so, but in the last few years before the war they came in much larger numbers to try, and made a very welcome blending of the present with the past. At Christmas 1939 I received a Christmas card from a friend in the Forces, now a Major, bearing after the conventional greetings, the words "And may we only miss one Putter". Already as I write we have missed five, but that wish of his represents, I know, the feelings of every single golfer who has ever braved the wintry winds of January at Rye or thawed himself at the Dormy House fire afterwards. To all who play in it this tournament is one of the few really sacred festivals of golf.

Those who first conceived the notion of playing it in January were unquestionably brave men, but the date has certain great advantages and the only time a change was tried to a more clement season the entry was poor and the tournament comparatively a failure. The overriding advantage is that there are no rival fixtures of any kind at the time of year and no one is prevented from playing for any golfing reason. And the bravery of playing then has been wonderfully rewarded by Providence. Only in two years out of the twenty has the ground been frosty, though the snow clouds

182

have lowered ominously. In one year the snow melted, as if by a miracle, on the very day before play began and it still lay deep in some of the bunkers, but there has never been as much as a single hole of play postponed. Cold and blustery and wet it has been, so that the early starters on a bitter, early morning or the late finishers in the freezing dusk have heartily wished themselves indoors. Golf on a big seaside course, in the weather we have sometimes had, is of an eminently testing quality, trying alike the heart and the skill, favouring those built to stand four-square to all the winds that blow; but we would never exchange it and the traditions that have grown up round it for any more balmy and enervating game. There is something about the conditions which I can best describe by the word 'Pickwickian', something to which only the author of that immortal work could do justice. Think of Tom Smart driving across the Marlborough Downs in the wind and rain and coming to the little roadside inn with the "strong cheerful light in the bar window" and the "matter-of-fact roaring fire piled halfway up the chimney"; think of the arrival of the Pickwickians at Dingley Dell in the frosty slate-coloured twilight; think of the "substantial lunch with the agreeable items of strong-beer and cherry brandy" which preceded the skating. Then you may faintly understand how pleasant it is after the day's work on the links to drive home across the marsh, seeing Rye perched above like a fairy citadel, and to subside into one of the seats by the big open fireplace, where the sparks fly up the cavernous chimney, and listen sleepily to the click of the pool balls.

On this subject my pen is always liable to run away with me, and it must not be thought that the weather has always been on so terrific a scale. On the contrary we have had many quiet and lovely winter days, with a blue heaven and just a freshening touch of wet upon the turf, days "sent from beyond the skies", when golf is a far better game than it can ever be in a baking summer, when there is no distracting traffic along the road to Camber and the course lies beautifully solitary, our own private and beloved playground. Fair or foul, we have had a very great deal to be thankful.

From this ecstasy of sentimental memories let me get down to the play. The records of the Putter are dominated by two names, those of Ernest Holderness and Roger Wethered.

Between them they have won ten times, five apiece, and of
the other ten victors no one has won more than a single time.
Till 1938 there was a gap in the list since Cyril Tolley had
never won, though he had fought three finals against Holderness. Then at last he did it and something like a reproach
was removed from the tournament, a reproach that was also
a compliment to the rest of the field as showing its aggregate
strength. The most famous of all the finals was that in 1926
between Wethered and Storey. The short winter day was
already most palpably drawing in as they halved their match
on the eighteenth green and set out again. They halved and
they halved and they kept on halving. The light grew ever
worse but there was no referee to say the word and the players
were so intent on their match that they seemed unaware of
the fact that they could scarcely see the ball to hit it. At last
in default of another, I pointed out to them that it was rather
dark and suggested that they should stop. It struck them as a
novel and luminous notion, but they decided to play one
more hole, the twenty-fourth. Mercifully they halved that
too and we then groped our way home from the coast-guard
cottages towards the clubhouse lights. It was later decided
that there should be no anticlimax in the way of a play-off
and so for that year two balls hang from the Putter's sacred
shaft.

What are the shots and matches that come back particularly
out of a welter of memories? There is a feeling of magnificence about the Holderness and Tolley final in 1923, which
Holderness won by two holes, but it is general rather than
particular. There is the superhumanly skilful pitch by Harold
Gillies off hard frozen ground played from behind the
eighteenth green in the semi-final against Tolley in 1925.
How he made it stop I did not know then and I do not know
now; it was in the nature of magic. It won the match for
him, and then after twenty minutes for lunch he went out
again and beat Holderness in the final by 4 and 3. There
was another shot of pure witchcraft in one other semi-final
played by Wethered against Maughan, when with his ball
lying in a rut in the sandy road he hooked it a quite incredibly
long way out and onto the green. There is the horrid little
shallow drain, which engulfed poor John Evans's ball at the
twenty-first hole in another final finished in the dark against

Leonard Crawley. There is the general splendour of Martin's hitting on a blustery day by which he crushed the life out of poor Rex Hartley, and a great brassey shot of John Beck's at the home hole against Martin whereby he saved his neck, to go on and win at the nineteenth.

When peace comes we shall begin again, I trust, with a new series of great matches and great shots which will become, in a comparatively small circle, historic. In the last two years before the war youth was beginning to come into its kingdom. In 1938 Kenneth Scott took Tolley to the last hole in the final and in the next year John Greenly, also not long down from Oxford, went surprisingly from strength to strength to win, and win handsomely, in the final. It is to be hoped that these young players will come in ever greater numbers, but now as I look back on these twenty years at Rye I may be forgiven if it is chiefly the older figures that I see. There is Arthur Croome playing the game of curling on the billiard table with a solemnity that is a reproach to the more light-hearted, calling to order those who throw their ball—or stone—in any but the orthodox attitude. There is Parson Tindall chuckling happily in a corner; Reymond de Montmorency a little worried before taking the chair at a too frivolous general meeting or palpably relieved and happy when it is all over; Humphrey Ellis and Ernest Smith as the stars of the billiard table; Cyril Tolley with unexampled dignity filling the clock with the pool balls and Harold Gillies impishly devising pyrotechnic displays under the billiard-room seats. And above all I see the figure of our secretary, now our captain, G. L. Mellin, unselfishly busying himself in half a hundred ways for the benefit of the rest of us who sit placidly by and let him do the work. I have written quite frankly to please myself, and the uninitiated will have skipped long ago if indeed they have not thrown away the book in a fury. I can only hope that a few may quote Dr. Watts (as did John Nyren of the Hambledon Club) and say—

> *I have been there, and still would go;*
> *'Twas like a little Heaven below!*

Chapter 18

OLD BOYS AT DEAL

IN 1924 Mr. Halford Hewitt became the founder of a great golfing feast when he gave the cup which bears his name for a tournament to be played by foursomes between teams of old public school boys. In that year it was played round by round on different courses on different dates, a rather tedious and exacting method, but in 1925 it was played off at a heat on three successive days at Deal. The three days later became the four, but Deal has remained the venue and has become, as it were the Lord's of the competition, round which there cluster the traditions of great matches already growing legendary. The tournament is eagerly looked forward to by all who take part in it, and the yearly arrival of that invading horde of golfers to take possession of their own particular hotels, hallowed by long use and wont, sees the narrow streets of Deal not only mataphorically but actually beflagged.

'Hordes' is the only word. Since considerably more than thirty schools enter (I am writing inevitably in the present tense) and each side consists of ten players, the tournament is, in an arithmetical sense, the greatest in the country. It is a standing miracle of organisation not only that they get their matches played, beginning at early dawn and finishing in the dusk, but that they have enough caddies to carry their clubs and always find a good lunch waiting for them in the club-house at all sorts of unseasonable and unreasonable hours. The names of Mr. Bernard Drew, the Secretary of the Royal Cinque Ports Club, and all the others who work so hard deserve to be "surrounded with a rich halo of enthusiastic cheering".

This tournament has never greatly attracted the general golfing public, not even perhaps the public school public. For those who are not actually present its very magnitude detracts from the interest; they grow weary of reading so many names and the results of so many ties. But among those at Deal there surges an intense and increasing excitement. It is often said with some justification that golf is a selfish and not a team game and that a team match is no more than an aggregation of single combats. As far as that reproach, if it be a reproach, can be removed, the thing has been done by this tournament. In the first place it is played entirely by foursomes. In the second the team spirit—a tiresome expression but a good thing—reigns supreme. No one cares about his own match except in so far as it brings victory or defeat to his side. Everybody having finished his own match rushes to encourage his comrades who are still struggling, with voice and gesture. There is a real passion of school patriotism.

That the teams are as large as ten aside is all in favour of the big battalions. It is difficult for the smaller schools, especially those whose old boys live mainly in the North, to put such a side in the field. This is on all hands admitted, but I think it is likewise admitted that if each school were represented only by one or two couples, the tournament would be by comparison a mere gladiatorial show and the element of comradeship, now so notable, would be sadly decreased. It is not perhaps remarkable that the few teams that have a chance of winning should be so enthusiastic as they are. What is remarkable is that every year there come teams whose highest hope of success is the getting through a single round. Without their support the tournament would be nothing, and the fact that they are so faithful to it and so unselfishly keen shows what a hold it has on the affections of its votaries. Whether after the war so many schools will be able to raise sides and so many players have the time and the money to come, no one can yet say: but if ever the sides have to be reduced it will be I will not say a death-blow to the competition but a very severe one.

At other games and sports the victories and the triumphant epochs of the old boys of particular schools are generally attributable to some advantages that they had when at school. The most obvious example is the good river which naturally makes a good rowing school, while famous coaches have provided famous eights or elevens or fifteens. But golf is not a school game and it appears to be a matter of pure chance that the old boys of one school are at any particular time better golfers than those of another. A year or two

before this war Stowe produced a sudden crop of good young
golfers, several of whom played for Oxford or Cambridge at
much the same time, but this cannot be attributed to the fact,
as I believe it to be, that the school has a couple of muddy
fields over which some boys casually and occasionally knock
a ball about. It is natural that the Scottish schools should
have a good choice of players, but that is only because golf is
so universal a game in Scotland. The same may be said of
the Lerpoolians, who so gallantly reached the final in one
year. Liverpool is ringed about with fine golf courses and a
Liverpool boy has every chance of a good golfing education.
Generally speaking, however, it is impossible to give any
reason why Charterhouse should have dominated the competition as it has lately done and have not only ten very good
golfers but a wealth of reserves. Before the first war it may
truthfully be said that Eton would year after year have carried
off the cup, had it then existed, with the greatest ease. In
1909 for instance it could have put a wholly international side
into the field, containing the two finalists and three out of the
last four in that year's Championship. This had nothing
discoverable to do with Eton, nor has the fact that the Etonians
won the Cup for four out of the first five years it was played
for and since then have not been in the hunt. These are
simply curious facts for which no reason can be given, unless
indeed—and I think it far-fetched—the exploits of their old
boys inspires in present-day schoolboys an enthusiasm for
golf.

A very large number of very good golfers has taken part in
the tournament, but it has always seemed to me one of its
interesting features that it makes reputations independent of
the greater world of golf outside. There are some fine players
who have not done so well at Deal as elsewhere, possibly
because their talents do not lie in the direction of foursome
play; there are others who regularly shine more brightly at
Deal than on any other course. The names of certain couples
have become Deal legends. What an invaluable and formidable last pair for Charterhouse have been Morrison and
Longhurst, the one now a Group Captain and the other an
M.P., as good as a point to their side before the match
started. While their companions were still struggling ahead
of them they were usually consuming a well-earned glass of

beer at the Chequers Inn, having duly and conveniently won by 5 and 4. A side that could afford to give them the last place was rich indeed. I may claim for my own side of Eton one very particular Deal reputation. Major Jack Hughes and Captain Dan Peplow were both good golfers but they were scarcely so good anywhere else as when they played together and at Deal. To these two was always given the responsible duty of bringing up the rear, and they did it nobly. It was not for nothing that they gained, and that not only among their own companions, the honourable sobriquet of Dumkins and Podder. In retrospect it seems to me that in some crucial match the score constantly stood at two matches all when this trusty couple would appear cresting the hill of the seventeenth green and waving to signify that all was well.

There have been so many of these fine combinations that I can only set down a few at random. Murray and Brock of the Watsonians swept so regularly to victory that when at last a dreadful rumour spread across the links that they had been beaten it was scarcely believed. Weare and Prain for Charterhouse had a long and eminently successful career. Graham and Boulton did great things for Marlborough, particularly in 1938 when the Marlburians gave general pleasure by winning the cup. Henriquez and Zair of Harrow, Darsie Watson and Cave of Rugby, Lister Hartley and Chapman of Westminster—these and many other names have a stirring and familiar ring. There is much good captaincy in the choosing of those who will run comfortably together in double harness, and also in parting those who will not. One of the most distinguished golfers who took part in the tournament, having seen his prospective partner play a few shots, damped his captain's enthusiasm by saying, "You don't expect me to win a match I suppose." That partnership was then and there dissolved and such exigent players are not very easy to match to the best advantage. As there is skill in mating players so there is in knowing the right moment for making a change. It sometimes happens that the longer and more uninterrupted has been a pair's victorious career the greater the loss of mutual confidence when once, as must happen at long last, they have been beaten. Then is clearly the moment to rearrange the side. It was to my mind the great strength of the Charterhouse stalwarts, their essentially team quality, that they did not worry overmuch about these things, since each man of the ten was ready at a moment's notice to fit in cheerfully with any other. On the other hand I can think of one side the members of which palpably worried too much, so that it was said of them that scarcely had they lost in one year before they had begun painfully redistributing their forces against the next. Happy indeed is the captain whose jigsaw puzzle contains no pieces of uncomfortable shapes.

As I said before, the size of the teams is in favour of the large schools and the number of winning schools has therefore been comparatively small. Charterhouse have won in all seven times between 1930 and 1939, truly a proud record. Eton won four times in the first five years and never again; Harrow won three times and have in addition lost four times in the final. Rugby and Marlborough have won once each. The Watsonians have ostensibly vast resources on which to draw but Scotland is a long way off; they have probably never had their best possible side, and though they have reached the final, they have never quite done it. Neither have the Wykehamists though they have three times been in the final and ought surely to have won once at least; yet there has always been an unlucky something when it came to the point. Uppingham, Shrewsbury and Liverpool have each reached the final once, to find the cheerful and indomitable Carthusians barring the way. Those big battalions have certainly had the best of it.

I find it hard to disentangle all the finals in my composite memory, and if I could I should be exceedingly tiresome to all but a devoted few. A few scenes come back clearly to my memory. Two are from the early Eton wins. The first is of the Harrow putt that came creeping straight for the middle of the nineteenth hole in 1925 to be diverted by the hand of Providence. It is followed even more vividly by the vision of Major Hughes, after a prolonged, ornate and agonising waggle, hitting the finest of all wooden club shots in the teeth of the wind right to the back of the twentieth green for victory. There is also a certain topped pitch that leaped lightly over the brook at the nineteenth hole against Charterhouse and a Westminster shot that did not jump over the ditch at the eighteenth, but this is to be brutal.

Of all the wins I think that of Marlborough, with a comparatively young and unknown side, was perhaps the most meritorious, but beyond a general impression of the exciting match in which Graham and Boulton hung on nobly to beat the formidable Crawley and Walker, no particular crisis or stroke survives. That which does clearly survive is Rugby's win, also against Harrow, in 1933 and the unfading glory of Martin and Gow. We may hope that the shade of Dr. Arnold rejoiced and owned that golf and moral earnestness are not incompatible. All depended on their match and the Harrow pair, Leonard Crawley and that toughest of warriors, now Lord Brabazon of Tara, were two up and three to play. There was seldom a spurt yet, however heroic, that did not get a little aid from the other side, and the Harrovians did help. A little pitch from the left to the sixteenth plateau went astray and that was down to one. At the seventeenth Crawley, who is so strong that he does not always know his own strength, pitched clean over the green, and with a model four the Rugbeians squared. Then at the last hole Gow played a lovely spoon shot to the green and Martin ran his long putt up stock stone-dead to win in a four, and, as the mad gentleman remarked to Mrs. Nickleby, "all was gas and gaiters".

One more finish I must briefly recall, not from a final, in a match between Charterhouse and Winchester in 1939. That was the last tournament before the war, and alas! the war has taken two out of the four players in the match, Dale Bourn and Kenneth Scott. The Charterhouse pair were Bourn and Middleton, the Wykehamists Scott and Micklem. At one time the whole match had looked certainly Winchester's, and even as these four set out to the nineteenth hole it seemed a work of supererogation. But no, after the first two holes had been halved there came the news that Charterhouse had miraculously recovered and all depended on this match. The Wykehamists played the long third hole with absolute correctness, two good shots and a pitch which ended a few yards straight behind the hole. Not so their adversaries, for Bourn's second went floating away to the right into the country of shingle and the best that Middleton could do was to dislodge it into the valley short of the green. Bourn did the right thing, he bumped the ball up out of the valley with some straight-faced iron and let it run to the hole. I see him now racing up to the hill-top and watching the ball pursue its relentless course to end stone-dead. If ever there was a brand snatched from the burning that was it, and somehow after that the end seemed predestined. True, Bourn, who had holed many nasty putts, had one to win at the Sandy Parlour and missed it, but Charterhouse, of which Dale was the spirit incarnate, won at the twenty-third and won the final afterwards. It was very, very hard on Winchester, but they had to yield to the devil that was that day in Dale's jerkin.

Five years, with goodness knows how many more to play, is a long time, and when, as is profoundly to be hoped, this tournament is set on its legs again, there will be gaps in the ranks, and new players, who were schoolboys in 1939, will have taken the places of some of the veterans. Yet it is pleasant to dream that some day we shall see again the pious founder sitting pale and agitated in the big plate-glass window waiting for news of "his boys", while John Morrison from below shouts up to him false and calamitous intelligence.

E. F. Storey

Robert Sweeney with Lionel Munn

A. H. Padgham

Chapter 19

ARCHITECTURE

THIS chapter will not be a discourse on golfing architecture in general, even if I were qualified to write one, because its coming into being as a distinct and recognised art belongs to a period before, though not so very long before, the first war. It was then that its principles were formed and began to take visible shape on many fine inland courses. At the same time those principles have enjoyed a peculiar continuity because the distinguished artists who gradually evolved them all remained after the war. John Low was still there as a preacher to uphold his favourite doctrine that golf should be "a contest of risks", and Messrs. Colt, Fowler, Simpson and Abercromby, to name four leading professors, were all more or less busily at work and built for themselves enduring monuments, alike in the designing of new courses and the "reconstructing" of old ones.

Is it possible to state their principles in a few words? It is extremely difficult and the result may be a fizzle, but I should say this; that they devoted themselves to the study of some of the holes, especially on old courses hallowed by tradition, which, having stood the test of time, are generally acknowledged by most good judges to be worthy of the epithet 'great'; holes which have shown themselves to be flexible and to possess the quality called by John Low 'indestructibility', so that though the change in clubs and balls may have changed the length of them, sometimes almost out of knowledge, they have kept their testing and interesting quality. Who laid out those holes is now unknown and indeed they were probably in many cases the result of happy chance. A bunker came into being perhaps quite fortuitously, as did the now defunct 'Tam's Coo' at St. Andrews because one Thomas or Tam tethered his cow there. Nevertheless such an accidental bunker was often found in practice to be, as it is now called, a dominating one, directing the whole course of play to a hole and giving it a perennial interest. It has been one of the virtues of the golfing architects that they sought to discover what it was exactly that made a hole or a bunker or a slope in the ground at once so defiant and so fascinating. Having made their discovery they acted on it, not by building up mere slavish imitations, which is seldom successful, but by applying their knowledge as far as possible to the nature of their material.

They have, I think, generally speaking eschewed the mere punishing of a bad shot directly and for its own sake and have rather tried to contrive that it shall ultimately bring its punishment in the subsequent play to the hole. They have not come down like a hundred of bricks on the bad player, who will always have plenty of trouble of his own, but have insisted as far as may be that the strong player shall be set problems. They have held out baits, tempting him with great advantages if he will make a particularly bold and accurate shot and trapping him if it is not quite accurate enough. They have tried more and more to match their wits against the player. They have demanded that he shall do more than hit what he calls a good shot, just because it is hard and clean, and that he shall hit it to a particular place. In their own language they have discarded the penal for the strategic. Many examples might be given from many courses which have been made or greatly altered between wars, but if I had to choose one as embodying the spirit of modern architecture I think it should be the eighth on the New Course at Addington laid out by Mr. Abercromby. The hole, as many people know, is but the length of a drive and a pitch; it is 350 yards or so and the drive runs rather downhill. There is apparently most ample room into which to drive from the tee. The green is narrow, guarded in front by a pond and having one bunker eating its way into the right-hand side of the green and another guarding the left flank. The whole point of the hole is in the angle at which the green is placed. Only the player who holds his tee shot well to the left-hand side, almost skirting the rough, is ideally placed for his second, having the length of the green in which to pitch. He who goes straight down the middle or drives to the right is faced with a shot which it is intensely difficult to keep on the green. An apparently simple hole is in fact extremely subtle.

That the architects have been highly ingenious nobody will

194

deny. If they have not wholly succeeded in their endeavours it is because such success is unattainable except perhaps on a course on which the general run of golfers will sturdily and even offensively decline to play. A long, strong hitter, who is likewise dexterous with his mashie niblick, will crash his way through many promising subtleties, and that statement leads up to a difficulty which has particularly confronted the architects between wars. The modern ball has taken to going so far, as hit by the strong man, that courses have generally grown too short, in the sense that they do not demand from the best players the fullest exposition of their quality. If those courses were only to be played on in championships much could be done by pure brute force of lengthening. When for instance I watched the last Open Championship at Hoylake, which had been stretched for the purpose, and saw some golfers still good but past the flush of youth, struggling with it, I realised what could be done by stretching. The carries alone were truly terrifying, much as were those in old gutty days from the St. George's tees, as they used to be called, at Sandwich. But such an expedient can only be an *ad hoc* one, because champions make an inconsiderable fraction of the population and all classes of players must disport themselves on the course. That is a difficulty peculiar to golf and to some extent it must be insuperable.

How if at all can it be got over? Not by a mere multiplication of bunkers surely, for the architect will then be lynched by the general run and will not have done much harm to those whom he would like to tease. Indeed Mr. Simpson calls many bunkers "light-houses" because he holds that they help the strong player to gauge the distance of his approach shot more accurately. The modern tendency is rather to economise in bunkers and to get the player in two minds by means of an apparently open green having no "light-house" in front, and an indeterminate background, perhaps running slightly away from the player. Everybody knows certain holes with which he may be perfectly familiar, at which nevertheless he is often a little puzzled as to what club to take. By reproducing this state of things in different ways the architect does his best. He employs that of which the Germans so constantly boast, a system of elastic defence. But the attackers are generally getting the best of it when the Germans use the phrase, and the golfer's attack, helped as it is by modern equipment, is hard to stop.

There is another difficulty in the way of the architects. The attitude of the general body of golfers towards them sometimes strikes me as like that of the public towards the police. Men know that they cannot get on without police and are in theory full of gratitude and admiration for them, but at the same time they are always on the watch to catch them out, and become on very slight provocation decidedly hostile. So the golfers are always ready to catch the architect tripping. They will not stand at his hands ingenuity that goes beyond a certain point. If he designs a hole with, as they think, too small a margin of safety; if the hole has too indistinct and baffling a skyline; if it calls for too exact an achievement; if it debars them from doing what they want to do and makes them do something that they don't want, they shout in chorus "Away with it", and that hole, sometimes rightly no doubt but sometimes wrongly, has to go. The average golfer does not appreciate subtlety and if he thinks he is being "got at" he raises the flag of revolution.

I recall one hole which I saw essayed by the players of all four countries in international matches. The architect meant them to play it one way and they were resolved to play it another. This was a one-shot hole across something of a dip, of the length, for such good players, of a full spoon shot. The green was small; it was guarded in front, and behind it was a wilderness of really appalling trouble. To stop a full bang on that green was very nearly impossible and its creator did not intend it to be possible. He had carefully designed a little place of safety, short and rather to the right, and he meant people to play an iron shot to this plateau and thence a run-up to the green, with a more or less certain four and the hope of a three. Would these lusty young internationals stoop to such a method? They would not. I only saw one man regularly play the hole as the architect had intended. The others crashed straight for the green and crashed straight over it into the horrors beyond. To the best of my belief I only saw one, a very strong man, stop a big high spoon shot on that green. The rest were like the little man in *Pickwick* who killed himself in defence of his great principle that crumpets were wholesome. They killed themselves to prove that a hole which is within their reach must be reached in one shot. It may be that the hole was not entirely satisfactory and I am not saying whether those young gentlemen were right or wrong, intelligent or rather stupid. They were at least quite determined to revolt; they sacrificed themselves for a cause and I believe the hole has since been altered.

One other revolution I must mention because it was against no subtlety but against sheer length. This was on a course of which I have known every blade of grass for over fifty years, a very engaging seaside course, not very long but certainly not very short considering the slowness of the turf. A national championship was to be played on it and some well-meaning but, as I think, misguided people, the ringleader being a great friend of mine, determined to make it worthy of the occasion. They called in an eminent professional and told him what they wanted and he delivered the required goods; he stretched it to its utmost and it *was* long. It was also to my thinking dull and much of the old charm had gone, but this is hardly a subject on which one who is rapidly getting older and shorter can express an impartial view. Then a strange and blessed thing happened. An appeal was addressed to the committee by a revolutionary party, and who were the leaders of that party? Why, the best players and longest drivers among the young members. Many years before Mr. Edward Blackwell had said that the carries at Sandwich were too long, and now these lusty young drivers said our course was too long. Naturally all the weaker brethren joined in the chorus, declaring that they had always thought so; a considerable number of superfluous yards was lopped off and the course was restored to its original state, to the general content. I am very far off urging revolutions against architects in a general way, but there are exceptions to every rule and here, in the words of the President of the United States to George Washington, was "a lesson useful to those who inflict and those who feel oppression".

And now to the courses that have either been made or considerably reconstructed between wars. Some of the best of them I am afraid I have not seen and so must speak of them from hearsay. To take, as is so justly their due, the seaside ones first, a quite new seaside course is now a rarity and I can only think of one worthy of mention: the new or second course at Saunton, laid out as was the original course, by the late Mr. Herbert Fowler. I have only played over it when it was still a little rough and I am afraid the war must have been bad for it. It did not seem to me quite so good as the first course, but it had much of the same bigness and quality. There is scarcely a piece of ground anywhere more "obviously designed by Providence for a golf course" than is Saunton. I always remember with joy a sentence in an old book describing how the wind "doth play the tyrant in this tract". In the course of its tyranny it covered up, I believe, an entire church and it certainly made noble hills and valleys. There is one hole on this new course where the player is bidden to drive at the last remnant of a submerged civilisation, an ancient fragment of a tree, I think a sycamore, still keeping its head above a mighty sea of sand. There seemed to me one or two holes which then, owing to their newness, were a little featureless, but there were some very fine ones too and the whole course, judged not merely by promise, was beyond doubt the real thing.

What degree of alteration constitutes a reconstructed course? Hoylake for instance has been considerably altered but it has hardly been reconstructed. Yet any material changes on such a course must be named. They are naturally regarded with a jealous eye by lovers of the old, but nobody, I imagine, will deny to Mr. Harry Colt unstinted praise for his eleventh and seventeenth holes, the new Alps and the new Royal. These are changes that count two on the division, for the old holes were poor and the new ones are admirable. The Alps consisted of an entirely blind one-shot hole and had little but its romantic name to recommend it. In its place is another one-shotter from an exhilarating tee to a narrowing green closely beset on one side by the shore and having perfect visibility. But this is a comparatively small improvement compared with that at the Royal. Today with its narrow green between devil of the road on one side and the deep sea of a horrid bunker on the other it is as fine and frightening a seventeenth as anyone can desire, and I imagine that many a reasonably stout heart with a good medal score will be tempted to play it by instalments. It has already been the scene of one classic shot, Walter Hagen's second when he wanted two fours for the Championship. It is worthy to be compared with another seventeenth in which a road plays its part.

The other three changes, namely the new greens at the Far or eighth hole, and the twelfth or Hilbre and the wholly new thirteenth, which has inherited the old name of the Rushes, are more open to criticism; not on the ground of any lack of ingenuity on the architect's part, but because, fine holes though they are, they are comparatively like many other fine holes to be found elsewhere, whereas those they have superseded were unique; they were essentially Hoylake. This conservatism can be pushed too far; I am ready to give up the old Hilbre, despite the fascination of that open simple approach made frightening by the pond behind the green; but I must shed a tear over the old Far green with its engaging run-in from the right. I cannot quite weep over the old Rushes, but I always remember what John Ball, to be sure an immovable Tory, said about it; that at the old hole the player had to do for himself the work of getting the ball into the air and stopping it on the green, whereas at the new one the high tee did it for him.

I do not criticise the disappearance of the old cross-bunker at the Dun because that had been made inevitable by the modern ball and modern driving. It was sad to see it go if only because the soberest might fall into it after dinner—I have seen them do it—in finding their way home across the darkling links; but it had to go and the present Dun is a fine long hole. Trying not to be Blimpish and die-hard and to look at the course with eyes unblurred by sentiment, I solemnly and sincerely declare that Mr. Colt made a great job of it. When I last watched a Championship there I might sorrow a little that the course and the greens in particular had taken on something of an inlandish perfection and lacked the old hard and ruthless quality that fought ever against the player, but in point of design Hoylake seemed to me as fine a test of the best modern golfers as was to be seen anywhere in the world.

A seaside course that has been wholly reconstructed is Hayling Island near Havant, where sailors used to play much of their peace-time golf. Here Mr. Simpson had a task after his own heart and one in which he could not but be successful. He was in the fortunate position of a new head master who takes over a school of fine material and traditions, too long allowed to stagnate under a predecessor grown too lazy and set in his ancient ways. Hayling had always possessed true seaside material of a quality second to none, but it had been laid out in the days when there was a confusion of thought between golf and steeplechasing. Even as Mr. Wemmick said, "Hullo, here's a church. Let's have a wedding," so the early fathers of architecture said, "Hullo, here's a sandhill. Let's have a drive over it." There were far too many such shots on the original Hayling, with the result that ideal valleys, or rather narrow ways between hills, were not used to the best advantage. The new broom had to do a great deal of sweeping-away and did it thoroughly. The result is a links that can hold up its head in the best company and yet has lost nothing of its ancient charm.

The same architect, with a lady to help him in Miss Molly Gourlay (thus as Sherlock Holmes would say "breaking fresh ground"), has done two other pieces of reconstruction work at the seaside. These are both in Ireland at Ballybunnion, which is in County Kerry, and at Baltray (County Louth); but alas! I have seen neither. I can therefore only say that in Ireland—and nowhere is a more critical and intelligent interest taken in such matters—they are both reckoned high in the first class.

To return to England again, one more piece of seaside reconstruction must be mentioned, namely that at Birkdale, which from having been a thoroughly pleasant course with something of the hills and valleys and general qualities of Formby on a minor scale, has been made far fiercer and longer than before and has leaped into a much wider fame. The English Amateur Championship was played there just before this war and the popular professional tournament called the Dunlop-Southport has taken place there several times. J. H. Taylor was the architect and he has unquestionably made of Birkdale a 'big' course on which it is good fun to see the big men stretch themselves. There seemed to me rather too many holes of one type, with greens running up to a point at the base of a hill (very convenient for the sedentary spectator) and having heathery banks on either hand. They have grown a little intermingled in my head which may be my head's fault, but so it is. However that may be, no bad player is going to win over Birkdale, and yet it is no slogger's paradise, for in the English Championship the final was fought between Arnold Bentley and W. Sutton, who are neither of them particularly long drivers.

When we turn inland we find several truly excellent English courses which belong wholly to the period between wars. I have already mentioned the new course at Addington, which is the one I know most familiarly, and it will long remain a witness to Mr. Abercromby's skill. He had admirable material, the country of sand and heather and birch trees, and with what an artistic eye he used it! How imposing is the old yew tree, once a monarch of the surrounding forest and now standing in lonely grandeur, as a sentinel over the ninth green. How slender and pretty is the row of birches which divide the tenth fairway from the eleventh green! There are certain holes where with unenvious eyes I like to see the long drivers hit their way home in two, the fourth for instance up the slope with the big cross-bunker and the way of safety round by the right for those less gifted; the round-the-corner sixteenth. Here too is a seventeenth, not perhaps quite in accordance with classical tradition since it is a one-shotter, but a hole to strike awe and terror, with its narrow green wholly beset with sand and heather. A penal hole rather than a strategic? Perhaps so, for the penalties for error are abounding and severe ; but it takes a man and a golfer to play it at a crisis, and that is no bad test of a hole.

I rate this second Addington as high as any of its contemporaries, but as regards pure affection, perhaps slightly unreasoning affection, I incline to put two before it, Liphook in Hampshire and Pulborough in Sussex. Both have a peaceful and unsophisticated charm and Liphook suggests in some indefinable way golf on a common, with cold beef or sandwiches for lunch, such as we used once to play in less elaborate days. Liphook is interesting as being the single masterpiece of one who never laid out another course, Arthur Croome. He did it wonderfully well, all the better perhaps because he had not much money to do it with and must rely as far as possible on kindly Nature. There are not many bunkers, there are certainly no superfluous "light-houses"; there is an agreeable sensation of plenty of room, but the golf is far from easy. For sheer beauty I think I like best the second hole, a short one with its knowing little bunkers waiting by the fringe of the green and its clump of dark trees keeping watch and ward behind. The fifth too is picturesque with its big golden bunker and its stream. That which for pure golfing quality I am told by Mr. Simpson that I ought to like best is the fourteenth, and it is unquestionably a fine two-shotter, dog-legged and deceitful since the longest way round is the shortest way home.

The day on which to see Pulborough, if not to play our best on it, is one when the wind is blowing hard, for the sand is wafted in great puffs, like white clouds across the course, so that we can scarcely believe that the sea is not round the corner. Pulborough was discovered by the late Commander G. W. Hillyard and that in so strange and romantic a manner as to suggest the prospectors of Poker Flat or Roaring Camp. He was selling his house in Leicestershire; the buyer mentioned that he had a house in Sussex and Commander Hillyard thought that something might be done by way of exchange. He saw the Sussex house, liked it and took it accordingly, with no thought of golf. Only when he had settled in there did he discover near by a pocket of priceless sandy ground. There was enough of it and no more to make a golf course; it was a little sandy jewel set in the Sussex clay. This treasure trove was bought and the course laid out by the late Major Cecil Hutchison and Sir Guy Campbell, who made of it an extraordinarily good job, while ever afterward Commander Hillyard hovered lovingly over it, his mind seething with notions for possible improvements. It is the sandiest of the sandy, it has heather and fir trees, a noble stretch of distant view and a most restful sense of peace and solitude. It is not too fiercely long but full of interesting shots and gives players of all classes a chance. What more can anyone desire?

I am told on good authority and fully believe that I ought to bracket with Liphook and Pulborough another course, a creation of Mr. Colt's, at Blackmoor, not far from Bordon, in Hampshire, but here is one of the sad gaps in my education. I have always been going to see Blackmoor but never have. So I can only say that everyone who knows it says that it is, like the heroine of a novel, as good as it is pretty.

There is yet another course or rather two in the heathery country not to be omitted; the two courses of the Berkshire

Club, in the neighbourhood of Ascot. Both are in a high if not quite perhaps the highest class among inland courses; one, called the Red Course (on the analogy of conflicting armies in military manœuvres), which is the full-dress course for major competitions; the other, the Blue, which some people prefer, a little less 'big', but by no means a secondary course. The country is essentially undulating and interesting and full of natural beauty. These two courses were laid out by Mr. Herbert Fowler, who had as an architect an "eye for country" second to none. He made up his mind very quickly, for even as he looked at it a waste of trees and heather seemed to arrange itself in a pattern of holes and his original scheme, to the ordinary eye miraculously arrived at, wanted very little revision. The Berkshire courses have more of charm perhaps and less of austere grandeur than Walton Heath. Walton and Saunton are the two best memorials to Herbert Fowler, but the Berkshire makes a worthy supplement to them.

One more club, among many, must be named; Wentworth. Here is a whole group of courses, a really huge enterprise, the work of Mr. Colt and his partners Mr. Hugh Alison and Mr. John Morrison. There is the East Course on which several important matches and competitions have been played; the Centre Course which is good fun but shorter and more easy-going for the less strenuous; and finally, made at a later date, there is the West or as it is sometimes called the Tiger Course, which is intended to test that rampacious animal to the full. It is a little hard to assign the Wentworth country as a whole to any precise class. There is heather and there are trees and yet it is not quite of the same nature as its near neighbour, Sunningdale. It is set in park-like surroundings, and yet it is certainly not what is usually called a park course. It is a cross between the two, though the Tiger Course has about it least of the park and most of the heathery character. In short this congeries of courses is in a little class of its own, not quite the highest but a thoroughly good and attractive one.

I seem to have treated Scotland very scurvily in this chapter, since I cannot think of any course there that comes strictly under the 'between wars' limits. Certainly however a word of particular praise should be given to Major Hutchison's reconstruction of the Old Course at Turnberry; he left it as pretty and charming as he found it, but in a different class as a test of golf. There is Gleneagles too. To be sure Braid and Major Hutchison had been hard at work at it before the first war, but as regards play it may be called a post-war course. The beauty of the place is beyond all question; the exact merits of the course perhaps more difficult to decide. When I first saw it with the ground very slow it was unquestionably terrific. I recall Taylor and Sandy Herd shrugging their shoulders and saying it was too long for them. What it was for lesser mortals may be faintly imagined. Then the ground hardened miraculously under the constant tread of the human foot and instead of being almost too fierce it went, from the good player's point of view, a little too far in the other direction, and scores became astonishingly low. Perhaps for the general run this is as it should be; that which was once a tail-twisting test for tigers has turned into very good and jolly holiday golf for those who do not mind a little hill-climbing. It has names for its holes of such desperate Scotticism that they remind me a little of those of the various competitions at a Chicago Competition called the 'Twa Days' at which I was once present, when pipers conscientiously paraded the course. American golfers always deem it a paradise and if I do not quite share that view I readily admit that, in mild and prosaic language, it is a very pleasant place to play golf.

Chapter 20

CLUBS, BALLS AND CHANGES

As was said in the first chapter there has been in these twenty years no upheaval comparable to that produced by the appearance of the Haskell ball, but there have been changes of an important if of a much less revolutionary character. Chief among these has been the introduction of steel shafts. These did not burst suddenly upon us as the rubber-cored ball had done. They had been heard of for a considerable time. Indeed I recollect that a golfer at Aberdovey, who was killed in the first war, had got hold of one or two from America before 1914 and used to play with them. They can then hardly have got past the experimental stage and there is a long interval between 1914 and 1929 when they were finally made lawful. Before that historic year they had percolated here in considerable quantities and a great many people had tried them and held various opinions on the subject. Everybody must have his individual memories of what he now rather dimly believes to have been his sensations. My own for what they are worth are that somebody gave me two steel-shafted drivers, that one had a prohibitively bad head and was discarded, but that with the other I used to hit secret shots in my field and that I seemed to get rather farther than with my ordinary clubs, but did not fully realise how these shafts would a little later take the world by storm. Other people were more enthusiastic and told stories of immense shots that they or others had hit. There was, I should say, a fairly general desire to try the experiment and a fairly general belief that the Rules of Golf Committee, always credited in certain quarters with stick-in-the-mud qualities, would die in the last ditch rather than sanction it.

These prophecies were shattered when in November 1929 the Rules of Golf Committee announced that they regarded steel shafts as not offending against the rule about the form and make of golf-clubs. And so in a twinkling of an eye in the simplest manner and with no laborious legislation the thing was done. Then there was a great rushing to the shops to buy a club or two with steel shafts, at first almost entirely wooden clubs. Here again everyone must have his own particular memories, even as he has, if he be old enough, of the first shot he ever hit with a Haskell ball. My own centre round a spoon which I bought at Woking and, taking it for my tee shot to the second hole, sent the ball flying across the green into the gorse beyond it, a wholly delightful catastrophe. Rosy visions of driving vast distances for ever more filled my brain, visions unmarred by the reflection that everybody else would do likewise. In fact such heavenly dreams were for a little while almost universal, and then we came down to earth again and took stock more calmly of the situation.

The general impression was that the new clubs helped the weak player to get perceptibly farther, but had little if any effect on the hitting of the big men. Such an impression would clearly make for the popularity of steel shafts among the rank and file, and in looking back I think it was a tolerably sound one. The big hitters certainly did not show the same enthusiasm as the short ones and some of them did not adopt steel for some time; Bobby Jones for instance won his four Championships in 1930 with wooden-shafted clubs. It was the hope of length that made steel popular, for men will do anything in reason to add a cubit to their stature as drivers. But there was something else as well; the new clubs were easier to hit straight with, though each of us probably attributed any improvement in that respect to some new virtue in himself. Especially did they make smooth the path of the slicer. The days of slicing on a really grand scale had long since departed with the gutty. Never again would anybody be able to write, as did a facetious friend of mine to the maker of a patent club, "It has added fifty yards to my slice". Still slicing remained, as it always will, a common failing and it was easier to avoid with a steel shaft. I will attempt no scientific explanations as to "torsion". The head came through more "all-of-a-piece"; it was not so easy to leave it behind or turned out to the right.

The man in the street was at once convinced that he liked a steel shaft in his wooden clubs; he was not so quickly converted in the matter of irons, and most good players remained for some time strongly in favour of wooden-shafted irons. They said, and I think they were right, that in playing the shorter iron shots there was a quiver in the steel shaft. However their wooden shafts gradually wore out and there were very seductive "matched sets" of steel shafts on the market and so gradually they fell away from their old allegiance. By the time the second war began it is a fair generalisation that, except for putter shafts, steel reigned supreme.

The precise effect on the club-making industry I am not qualified to discuss. Only this is certain, that the season of the great individual clubmaker, the man from whom a special club could only be wheedled as a special favour and who would fashion it with the loving and lingering care of a true artist, has to a great extent departed. Long gone are the days when a particular driver, once the property of Tom Kidd, could be recognised years afterwards by Tom Morris, as soon as he saw it in the hands of a new owner on the first tee. This is a perpetual if gentle sadness to those who had an eye for a fine club, whose bags were the envy of all their acquaintance; but for the general run the more or less mass production of steel-shafted clubs has brought unquestioned benefit. It is comparatively difficult nowadays to find a really bad shaft. You may pick a club at random out of the bag of the least skilful player, having no pretensions to taste, and the chances are that it has a shaft that a connoisseur would not wholly disdain. Club society has attained to a state of equality in which there are few aristocrats or plebeians, and in these days of democracy that is a state of things over which all good citizens should rejoice. But it is rather dull.

There has been another innovation in club-making which in its original form was altogether outside the range of the law-makers, though in the end it led indirectly to their taking action. This was the coming of the "matched set" in which each club was known by a soulless number so that the old individual names became atrophied. The system is one often believed to have originated in the United States, and it first there attained general popularity, but its invention may be claimed for a good Scottish golfer, Mr. John Low. It was he who in his engaging little book *Concerning Golf* first suggested the plan of taking to a forger of iron heads your favourite iron and getting him to make several others on the same model but having different degrees of loft. That this was a wise principle no one can doubt and as cultivated by skilful clubmakers it can produce a set of irons so admirably matched and balanced that the owner hardly knows which he has in his hand without scrutinising the head. It ought to make iron play easier and more consistent, and no doubt it does. Here again it may be urged that the change makes for dullness, and that not merely because more or less the same swing can be used for a larger number of shots. Once upon a time a collection of good irons was the work of a lifetime; each had its separate history and origin; some might even have pedigrees extending through several distinguished owners in the past. Today by comparison we buy "the game of golf complete in a box". Again the matched set has tended to make us extravagant. Once if we wanted a mid-iron we bought one. Now the lure of a peculiarly dazzling No. 4 may lead us on to buying all the other numbers as well. The vendors moreover acted on this little weakness with great ingenuity, in bringing out sets modelled on those of some famous player. To buy a Bobby Jones driver, for the principle soon extended to wooden clubs, was to be tempted to buy the brassey and the spoon as well, since a single newcomer might not agree with the older denizens of the bag. However whether we wax virtuous over such recklessness or sentimental over the past is of little moment, because the numbered sets have come to stay. They are beyond question beautiful clubs and pleasant to play with and a deliberately retrograde movement is in this respect unthinkable.

Nevertheless the making of matched sets, being like many other originally good things most monstrously overdone, did lead in the end to the law stepping in. It did so not long before the second war and limited these clanging armaments by the decree that no man should go forth to war for any particular round with more than fourteen clubs in his bag. I have been looking again at a horribly seductive advertisement of a set that was published in an American golfing journal. There were, the writer admitted, a good many in the set and they cost a good many dollars—"But, man—oh, man," he exclaimed, "what a difference in your game!" There certainly were a good many. To begin with there were four wooden clubs, including a No. 2 spoon, but it was among the irons that the numbers had to be duplicated. There was a No. 7, a mashie niblick with a flat sole for hard ground, and a No. 77 with a round sole for ground that was soft and wet. More infamous still there were two niblicks, No. 8, an ordinary workaday one, and No. 88, "laid way back for the trick trap shots the experts get through deliberately regulating the angle of the face". In all there were sixteen clubs in the set, and if the owner carried a second driver in case of accidents and a second putter, lest the first should not be happily inspired, he would approach twenty, which is absurd.

The advertiser suggested that with these clubs the purchaser would "give the boys a surprise". To one boy at least, his caddie, he would have given a very unpleasant surprise, and had there been a caddies' trade union it would surely have taken action against these outrageous burdens. As it was authority interfered not merely on the ground of cruelty to animals, but because these farcically swollen bags were making a fool of the game. Years ago when golf was comparatively new onlookers would wonder in audible tones what the golfer wanted "with all those sticks". He had perhaps seven or eight in his bag and now one player in an Open Championship at St. Andrews had more than twenty. The limitation to fourteen did not please everyone. It naturally did not please the trade; it offended at once the fanatical lovers of liberty and those who desired a much more austere measure of reform and deemed half a dozen the maximum. It was, as are many reforms, a compromise but it was at least a step in the right direction. A man who seriously asserts that he needs more than fourteen clubs may be a successful hitter of a ball but he is not a golfer.

There were two other pieces of legislation about clubs. One, already referred to apropos of Jock Hutchison's Championship, was the forbidding of club faces excessively "corrugated, ribbed or slotted". The other dealt with those having faces much more pronouncedly concave than formerly, notably that known in the United States as the sand-wedge. Both there and here there was a feeling that such clubs were not in the best interests of the game and they were barred accordingly. People sometimes talk rather too airily of "buying a shot in the shop"; there always remains the fact that "the ball maun be hit". Both the slotted face and the sand-wedge were however reasonably open to this imputation, and their disappearance is now as little lamented as it is remembered.

One modern fashion in clubs deserves perhaps a word, namely that of having shafts so springy that they almost wriggle out of the player's hands like so many live eels when he waggles them. The sensation of hitting a ball with a limber-shafted club, when it *was* hit, was decidedly pleasant and gave a sense of majesty, and of added length, this last not always borne out by the cold arbitrament of the yard measure. That some people played well with them is not to be disputed, and curiously enough it was not always, as might have been expected, those having slow swings, for some rapid swingers mastered the art of timing. Yet I think it is no injustice to these spring-heeled Jacks to say that a great many of them were relegated to the cupboard after a few experiments, since their owners could not gain consistency of striking. Few things are wholly new and these abnormal shafts are certainly not. In 1857 the author of *The Golfers' Manual* (he called himself 'A keen hand' and he was a writer of plays, H. B. Farnie by name) remarked on the tastes of certain 'non-agile' golfers. "Their play clubs in general", he said, "are remarkable for very long shafts either very stiff or—no *juste milieu*—very supple. In fact, as the golfing Vulgate hath it, perfect tangles." It was ever thus; about 1903 and 1904 all the world was trying to play with very long-shafted clubs called "Dreadnoughts", and that fashion has long gone with the rest. It is to be noted that the professional who has his living to make by hitting the ball straight, seldom indulges in these eccentricities. He may pander in the way of business to the amateur's fads, as is only right and proper, but for himself he sticks to the *juste milieu*.

A far thornier and more complex problem than any concerning clubs and one less successfully tackled has been that of the ball. In the little that I shall say about it, I shall assume it as axiomatic that the modern ball goes too far for the good of the game, the more so as there is some devil within it which disproportionately favours the very strong, hard hitter. This last remark may be the complaint of those who in the natural course of events are themselves growing weaker and shorter; we are all inclined to look at these questions too much from our own point of view. This much is certain however, that courses have had to be stretched and stretched again, if really strong players are to play anything but a series of drive-and-pitch holes. This had made the best golf a comparatively monotonous affair and reduced to a minimum many beautiful strokes. Much more important to the general run of golfers, it has called for more land and so more money, an objection which may be far more serious after the war than it has ever been before.

There have been all manner of proposals for limiting the flight of the ball, but the reformers have been hampered by their inability to agree amongst themselves as to what they want. Some thought no reform worth while less than a return to the gutty. They, I take leave to say, were tilting against windmills; their proposals were wholly impracticable. Others wanted a middle course, something in the nature of a floater. Others wanted—I am really not sure what they wanted, but half of them held that the golf ball should be hit high in the air and half thought exactly the opposite. Again there was the question of a "Championship ball" for big men and big competitions, while the smaller fry amused themselves with what balls best pleased them.

That is but the briefest summary of the various suggestions for reform. They were all alike in one respect, that the average golfer took a strictly modified interest in them; but in so far as he was interested he was decidedly hostile. He regarded them all as being directed against him personally, with a view to spoiling his pleasure and putting up his handi-cap. With the floater he would have nothing to do, holding exaggerated notions of the difficulty of controlling it in the wind and seeing himself in imagination wandering for ever in the rough. The fact that he would find it far easier to pick up with a wooden club through the green he did not appreciate. It was the same with any other proposal to limit the distance the ball would travel. He found the courses quite long enough as they were, and what would become of him if his drives were not quite so long? The thought that a less far-flying ball might lead to shorter courses and so spare his legs did not apparently occur to him. He had moreover a rooted and instinctive objection to his best drives being docked of even a few yards, not understanding that the pleasure consists in hitting the ball as hard and clean as possible and that it is not diminished by the fact that a rather less resilient ball does not go so far; that there was just the same satisfaction in hitting a gutty 180 yards as there is in hitting a rubber-core 250; that in short such pleasure is relative and not positive. In all these notions he was encouraged by that kind of writer who, whatever the game, always abuses the authorities and finds a tirade against them for interfering with the liberties of the subject the cheapest and easiest form of writing.

In the face of these difficulties something was done, but it cannot be said to have been much or to have had any great effect. I am not good at "those damned dots" and so will merely state, from a book of reference, that the Rules of Golf Committee decided that the weight of the ball should not be greater than 1·62 ounces avoidupois and the size not less than 1·62 inches in diameter. The United States Golf Association adopted a slightly different specification and the ball legal in America is a little larger than that elsewhere, but not, I imagine, with any marked result on the game. It is of course likely enough that had no restrictions been made the ball would by this time have gone much further still; so there is something to be thankful for. In the earlier part of this last war, before it had come to the United States and put an end to serious golf there as it had here, we read of further experiments being made and especially of something like a solid ball, which had about 80 per cent of the efficiency of the rubber-core and was to cost, in the words of Mr. Montague Tigg, "the ridiculous amount of eighteen pence". All such news has, as I write, long since vanished from the newspapers; golf balls of any kind grow ever more rare and precious and what will happen after the war and what will be the amount of rubber available for ball-making I, for one, have no notion. The only prophecy in which it is the least safe to indulge is that there will be less money to spend, that courses may therefore grow contracted and that people will be glad to play with cheaper balls if they can get them. That state of things may lead to some change of the law, or again, as a Greek Chorus would observe, it may not.

Chapter 21

SOCIAL AND POLITICAL

IT was not long after the first war that I was at Gleneagles watching a tournament. Among the spectators was a gentleman from Falkirk who was heard to say in a dejected tone: "I have not had a good cheer all day nor a chance to shout 'Well played!' " He was presumably a supporter of that distinguished football club, Falkirk Tryst, and found the proceedings at a golf match altogether too slow and decorous for him. He was one of the forerunners of a large new class of spectators who have taken an interest in golf between wars. I am not thinking so much of Scotland, where golf has always been a game of the people, though even there it has enormously widened the bounds of its empire. To be in a Glasgow railway station on a Saturday and watch the number of travellers carrying golf-clubs is highly instructive. I am thinking rather of England and of English spectators. There are to be seen masses of them who before the first war would barely have known of the existence of golf, save perhaps as a subject for humour. Now they know at least enough about it to like watching it. Occasionally, as at Southport on a Ryder Cup day, they like to watch without knowing anything about it at all, merely enjoying the scrambling up and down sandhills and the contiguity of a large number of their fellow creatures in a jolly bank - holiday atmosphere. Old Mr. Sutherland would doubtless have remarked, as he did one day long ago at St. Andrews, "It is disgraceful of the railway people bringing a parcel of uneducated brutes down here when they knew a real match was going on." By "uneducated" the old gentlemen meant not knowing golf. Today there has arisen in his sense of the word a large body of partially educated onlookers and as far as one can tell they have come to stay.

They watch primarily the professionals and that not merely because they are the best worth watching, but because there are so many big professional tournaments in different parts of the country for which the promoters want all the notice and all the spectators they can get. There used perhaps to be more exhibition matches in the early days of the triumvirate, but now (apart from this last war-time in which exhibitions have raised large sums for good causes) the tournaments have ousted them and give much more watching for the money. Thus the names of the leading professionals are far more widely known than ever before. At the end of the nineteenth century Vardon was so all-conquering that he was famous among non-golfers, but he was an exception, and even so I doubt if a reference to him then would have been understood and appreciated as a reference to Cotton would be today. How much the general public knows of great players, whatever the game, may be gauged by the titbits of personal information about them, their wives and their homes and their private affairs which the press now provides as it never did before. Once upon a time the leading golfers were heroes only to a body, a large and ever-growing body to be sure, of initiates. Today the powerful goddess, Publicity, has taken them under her sometimes rather shoddy wing. She has, as she would doubtless describe it, built them up into national figures. It may be snobbish or old-fashioned or whatever else you please to repine over this phenomenon, but it is an interesting one which it is futile to deny, and no doubt all is for the best in the best of all possible worlds.

Perhaps I have only been laboriously saying that golf has become "democratised", as it certainly has. There is at least one respect in which the most obdurate die-hard cannot be anything but pleased with this process, namely in the great increase in public courses and also in "Artisan" Clubs, the members of which are allowed for some very small subscription to play over private courses. In Scotland, as I said before, golf has always been popular in the more literal sense of the word, and there have always been courses where anybody and everybody could play; but in England the public course movement is a comparatively new one and owes a great deal to J. H. Taylor-amongst other of its champions. Nearly all big towns have courses where a man can pay his money and play his round, and the movement is one which, as far as one can penetrate the future, is bound to grow.

I am afraid I have not much personal knowledge of these

public courses, but I have had some small experience of the working men's clubs that play on private courses, and have the honour of being president of one of them, though the course has alas! for the moment returned to Nature after a severe 'blitz'. Such clubs are not new in England. There were several places where the inhabitants had certain rights over the course and had their own clubs. The first of them was, I believe, the Northam Working Men's Club, which had among its members J. H. Taylor and the other fine professional players who learnt their game at Westward Ho! The Villagers' Club at Hoylake, the Artisan Club at Bulwell, the Cantelupe Club at Ashdown Forest, bristling with serried ranks of Mitchells—these are other obvious instances; but there were not many such clubs, and there were few cases of what may be called the parent club deliberately throwing open its course to its less well-to-do neighbours. Now this gesture, at once sensible and graceful, has become common and, as far as I know, has been invariably successful. Very often the Artisan Club, to give it its usual name, has a nucleus of keen and good players who have learnt the game as boys in that best of schools the caddies' shed, and want to continue it as grown men. But in the case which I happen to know best there was no such nucleus, for the parent club itself was new; there had been no golf in the immediate neighbourhood and the artisan players had to start, not in the technical golfing sense, from scratch. Nevertheless, there was the greatest keenness to join the club, and in a year or two considerable patriotic fervour was aroused over the matches played by the team in a small local league of some half-dozen such clubs. It was delightful to walk up to the course after tea and watch for the coming of the visiting side in its lorry; it was a lesson in the enthusiastic use of limited time to see them tumble straight out of it and start there and then from the first tee.

Very pleasant too can be an annual match between the parent club and its offspring. I once or twice had the pleasure of playing for Woking against the Hook Heath Artisans, many of them old friends, whether as greenkeepers or caddies. The driving up to the course, when the cabman looked at one with an eye of amicable hostility and asked if one was going to play against "our chaps"; the large tea, a little like a school treat, during which shyness thawed gradually into cheerful conversation; the foursome match itself with so many couples a-side that they had to start from various tees; the jovial supper afterwards from which the parental side gradually and discreetly withdrew—these things made up as good and friendly an evening's golf as anyone could desire. It is much to be hoped that with other good golfing things such matches will come back after the war.

There is another point in this "democratising" of the game which is, I think, both noteworthy and interesting. That is the shifting of the balance of power; not legislative, though no doubt the Unions have in some degree affected this, but playing power. I may take as an example the Scottish side in the first Amateur International match in 1902. That side consisted of five players who were members of the Royal and Ancient or the Honourable Company or both; two exiled Scots from the Royal Liverpool and one from London, and those two fine golfers, James Robb and Fred Mackenzie, members of that great artisan body, the St. Andrews Club. In short the team, which was a very good one and the best that could be produced, was drawn from a very small number of clubs, and, if it may be said without offence, to the extent of four-fifths from one definite class of the community and one-fifth from another. Now if one looks at the names of the at least equally fine sides which played for Scotland in the last few years before this war, one finds a considerable change. There are still some artisan players in the side, but there is no single member of the Honourable Company or the Royal and Ancient, for the members of the Royal and Ancient who have played in international matches, either domestic ones or against America, have been Englishmen. The balance of playing power has shifted from the East to the West of Scotland and particularly to what may be called the young business men of Glasgow. It is altogether a more popular and, for want of a better word, more democratic side than it used to be.

Something of the same sort, but not, I think, to the same extent has happened in England in regard to the international sides. Once upon a time there can be little doubt that London and the South had rather too many players. This was no sinister portent; it was merely because the selectors knew the Southern players best and were guided by what they knew. So the Midlands, only just beginning to produce some excellent golfers, and the North had not quite a fair deal. Leaving of course such giants as Mr. Ball and Mr. Hilton out of the reckoning, the Southern players were the stronger, but not so much the stronger. In course of time the choosing of the team was handed over to the English Union and there came a swing of the pendulum. Perhaps it swung a little too far, but if so there was again nothing sinister about it; people attached importance to that which they knew best and the knowledge of some of them was uncommonly narrow. It was only an inevitable phase, and it duly passed away, but it was an interesting and instructive one.

May I add this? The finally victorious Walker Cup team was chosen from all sections of the golfing community and gave universal satisfaction. This showed what could be done by a well-chosen, open-minded Committee, each knowing well some part of the country, who took a very great deal of pains over their task. It is not always possible to get such a Committee, but at least the members of this one deserved all the good things said of them. With that respectful compliment to them I may end a branch of my subject which is rather embarrassing but yet cannot honestly be left out of a review of the period.

I said just now that the balance of legislative power had not shifted, and this is true; St. Andrews still holds supreme power, freely granted to it by free subjects. Any question of the rules of the game, though chiefly in the hands of the Rules of Golf Committee, is ultimately in the hands of the Royal and Ancient Club. It may be something of an anomaly that the rules should be made by a miscellaneous body, the members of one particular club, some of whom may have no great interest in or knowledge of the subject, but if so it is one that has worked well in practice, even as has another such anomaly, the dominion of the M.C.C. in cricket. That dominion is administered in no 'totalitarian' spirit, but in consultation with other bodies both at home and overseas. It gives far more general satisfaction today than in older days, when questions were answered perhaps a little brusquely and without sufficient consideration of the conditions, widely differing from those at St. Andrews, under which they arose. It is probably quite untrue that the Rules Committee ever replied that they had no cognisance of trees on golf courses, but there was at one time an impression that this imaginary answer represented a real state of mind. That is certainly so no longer and the atmosphere is, I venture to say, generally pleasant and unclouded.

One illustration of this generally co-operative spirit was the new edition of the rules of the game adopted in 1934. Probably only those who were on the Rules of Golf Committee (I was not then myself a member) can appreciate how much work was done in preliminary consultations with the ruling bodies in the United States and in the Overseas Dominions before that code was made ready. When it was ultimately completed it did represent, as far as possible, the considered opinion of the golfing world. Into the niceties of its changes I do not propose to go. The most obvious and important change was the equalisation of penalties for a lost ball, a ball out of bounds and an unplayable ball. This was not received with unanimous satisfaction, and I have a vivid recollection, since I had to occupy the chair at the meeting of the Royal and Ancient, of the late Sir Ernley Blackwell bringing his heaviest guns to bear against it. The particular offence complained of was the liberty given to the player to deem his ball unplayable at his own discretion. Admittedly there is something that goes against the grain in a player deeming a ball unplayable when it is palpably nothing of the sort, because he finds it more profitable or less costly to do so. However the meeting decided, and I think the golfing world in general agreed, that the greater simplicity was worth attaining, even though tradition was to some extent flouted. At any rate a tranquillity bordering on indifference has reigned on the subject ever since.

In one respect, that of the management of the Open and Amateur Championships, the power has in a sense been more narrowly rather than more widely exercised. Soon after the first war, at the end of 1919, the clubs that had jointly controlled the Championships invited the Royal and Ancient to take over the entire control. This was done and a Championship Committee appointed, of which most but not all of the members were also members of the Royal and Ancient. This Committee was made as far as possible representative of golf in general, but its headquarters were at St. Andrews and it was called "The Royal and Ancient Championship Committee". Its Chairman from its inception and till the time of his death was Mr. Norman Boase and no mention of the Committee, however brief, must be allowed to lack a tribute to all his hard and unselfish work. An ordinary member of the Committee, such as I was for a number of years, might preen himself in a blue rosette at times of Championships, and attend meetings, sometimes very long meetings, with a certain not wholly justified sense of virtue: but Norman together with the late Henry Gullen, than whom there never was a better Secretary, was at it all the time. For him there was no surcease. True, he liked, and was interested in the work, which many people would have found irksome, but that does not diminish the credit due to him. I can think of no one who has so wholeheartedly given so much time and trouble to the necessary but less attractive tasks of golf as did Norman Boase and I hope his devotion will never be forgotten.

Thus in two very important respects the only change has been in a greater concentration of power, but there are other respects in which the power and the work have been delegated by mutual consent. The four Unions have naturally charge of their own championships, and those championships have been very successful and popular. They have organised and taken over the management of the annual international tournament between the teams of the four countries, which have now assumed the place of the original match between England and Scotland played immediately before the Amateur Championship, and of the rather more casual matches in which Ireland and Wales had been used to take part. Likewise the British Golf Unions' Joint Advisory Council have been responsible for the system of standard scratch scores and handicapping, approved by the Royal and Ancient, and for the setting-up of the Board of Greenkeeping Research, by means of which greenkeeping problems are scientifically studied near Bingley.

Similarly in the domain of purely professional golf the P.G.A. entirely control their own tournaments and international matches. The Ladies' Golf Union are likewise, of course, mistresses in their own house. In short the growth and spread of golf have led naturally to the existence of something like a commonwealth of golfing authorities, each doing its own work and managing its own affairs, while freely paying allegiance to one supreme authority. In graver matters there are some who prefer the term 'Commonwealth' and others who cling affectionately to 'Empire'. In golf at least there is no necessity to quarrel over exact terms in describing a complex, and perhaps in some ways anomalous system, which like Topsy "grow'd", and now achieves its main purpose with a minimum of friction and very considerable success.

It may well be that in this brief sketch, despite my best endeavours, there has peeped out something too much of conservatism and of a lazy liking for things as they were when the golfing world was smaller and more casually managed. "The atrocious crime of being a young man," said Mr. Pitt, "I shall neither attempt to palliate nor deny," and I shall not deny the converse accusation. An imperviousness to new ideas and a lack of enthusiasm for brave new worlds are doubtless the penalty to be paid for having played golf for sixty years. But having said so much in timid, and I fear egotistical propitiation, let me add that I look forward to golf after this second war not merely with gratitude for the past, but with confidence in the future. At least for other people, and that is the main point, it will be as good as ever it was. So let me end with the words of one of the earliest as he was one of the most attractive of golfing writers: "We cannot refrain for the life of us from closing our remarks on golfing with some expression of our intense attachment to it. . . . Golf, thou art a gentle sprite; we owe thee much!"

OPEN CHAMPIONSHIP

Year	Winner	Course	Score
1920	G. Duncan	Deal	303
1921	J. Hutchison	St. Andrews	296
	(after a tie with R. H. Wethered)		
1922	W. Hagen	Sandwich	300
1923	A. G. Havers	Troon	295
1924	W. Hagen	Hoylake	301
1925	J. Barnes	Prestwick	300
1926	R. T. Jones	St. Anne's	291
1927	R. T. Jones	St. Andrews	285
1928	W. Hagen	Sandwich	292
1929	W. Hagen	Muirfield	292
1930	R. T. Jones	Hoylake	291
1931	T. D. Armour	Carnoustie	296
1932	G. Sarazen	Prince's, Sandwich	283
1933	D. Shute	St. Andrews	292
	(after a tie with C. Wood)		
1934	H. Cotton	Sandwich	283
1935	A. Perry	Muirfield	283
1936	A. H. Padgham	Hoylake	287
1937	H. Cotton	Carnoustie	290
1938	R. A. Whitcombe	Sandwich	295
1939	R. Burton	St. Andrews	290

AMATEUR CHAMPIONSHIP

Year	Winner	Runner-up	Course
1920	C. J. H. Tolley	R. A. Gardner	Muirfield
1921	W. I. Hunter	A. J. Graham	Hoylake
1922	E. W. E. Holderness	J. Caven	Prestwick
1923	R. H. Wethered	R. Harris	Deal
1924	E. W. E. Holderness	E. F. Storey	St. Andrews
1925	R. Harris	K. F. Fradgley	Westward Ho!
1926	J. Sweetser	A. F. Simpson	Muirfield
1927	W. Tweddell	D. E. Landale	Hoylake
1928	T. P. Perkins	R. H. Wethered	Prestwick
1929	C. J. H. Tolley	J. N. Smith	Sandwich
1930	R. T. Jones	R. H. Wethered	St. Andrews
1931	E. Martin Smith	J. de Forest	Westward Ho!
1932	J. de Forest	E. Fiddian	Muirfield
1933	Hon. M. Scott	T. A. Bourn	Hoylake
1934	W. Lawson Little	J. Wallace	Prestwick
1935	W. Lawson Little	W. Tweddell	St. Anne's
1936	H. Thomson	J. Ferrier	St. Andrews
1937	R. Sweeney	L. O. Munn	Sandwich
1938	C. Yates	C. Ewing	Troon
1939	A. Kyle	A. A. Duncan	Hoylake

LADIES' CHAMPIONSHIP

Year	Winner	Runner-up	Course
1920	Miss C. Leitch	Miss M. Griffiths	Newcastle, Co. Down
1921	Miss C. Leitch	Miss J. Wethered	Turnberry
1922	Miss J. Wethered	Miss C. Leitch	Prince's, Sandwich
1923	Miss D. Chambers	Mrs. Macbeth	Burnham
1924	Miss J. Wethered	Mrs. Cautley	Portrush
1925	Miss J. Wethered	Miss C. Leitch	Troon
1926	Miss C. Leitch	Mrs. Garon	Harlech
1927	Mdlle de la Chaume	Miss D. Pearson	Newcastle, Co. Down
1928	Mdlle Le Blan	Miss S. Marshall	Hunstanton
1929	Miss J. Wethered	Miss G. Collett	St. Andrews
1930	Miss D. Fishwick	Miss G. Collett	Formby
1931	Miss E. Wilson	Miss W. Morgan	Portmarnock
1932	Miss E. Wilson	Miss C. P. R. Montgomery	Saunton
1933	Miss E. Wilson	Miss D. Plumpton	Gleneagles
1934	Mrs. Holm	Miss P. Barton	Porthcawl
1935	Miss W. Morgan	Miss P. Barton	Newcastle, Co. Down
1936	Miss P. Barton	Miss B. Newell	Southport and Ainsdale
1937	Miss J. Anderson	Miss D. Park	Turnberry
1938	Mrs. Holm	Miss E. Corlett	Burnham
1939	Miss P. Barton	Mrs. T. Marks	Portrush

INDEX

INDEX

225

Afterword
by Ben Crenshaw

When my golfing life began around the age of eight, I was preoccupied by any number of boyish pursuits, namely football and baseball, and, rather curiously, through a friend of mine, I started a study of birds, of all things. My friend and I would study and note different species, with which the state of Texas is well-endowed, and draw and color them to our hearts content. I have retained this fascination with birds and, through the years, I have kept a somewhat amateurish record of certain species encountered in my travels. I tell you these ponderous things because my first encounter with the Darwin family came through Charles Darwin, the famed evolutionist, along with my love of birds. In my studies, I found his travels fascinating, voyaging on the H.M.S. "Beagle" and doing a major part of his field work on the then unknown Galapagos Islands among different creatures such as giant tortoises, marine iguanas, hawks, and finches on these islands where time seemingly stood still. Out of this incredible field study Charles Darwin wrote "On the Origin of Species" and changed the world.

The first golf book I ever read was Charles Price's "The World of Golf", a happy and extremely fortunate choice indeed. In the first few pages there appeared a photograph of none other than "Bernard Darwin, grandson of the famed evolutionist". I was quite astonished to know this fact, and I rather think this had a lot to do with my golf history research in the incubation stages. I began to read and research these two geniuses with more gusto.

Bernard Darwin could simply write about any subject whether it was children's books or sporting books or any subject that appeared in his many wonderful publications. He was the first golf writer to transcribe facts and figures into real journalism. He was unashamedly a lover of sports and games in general, and could never hide his deep affection for golf. To me he appealed to the reader on the most individualistic terms. He TALKED to us, apologized to us, cried to us, bared his temper to us, and made us laugh with him, all in an attempt to reveal his deep, deep love for golf to us. The world has been made better for it. His writings have an incredible timeless quality about them, which is the hallmark, of course, of any great writer. I think I am inclined to say at this point, that we sometimes forget that the game is still the same after some four hundred glorious years, whether we are swinging with hickory or graphite at a feathery or a balata. We all suffer the same eternal indignities. Lastly, Bernard Darwin has helped us educate ourselves in the English language and also about life in general.

"Golf Between Two Wars" was the wonderful result of Darwin being persuaded ingeniously by a few friends to write the book. At first he thought that there was not enough material to warrant the book, but then he thought that nearly "everything" had happened between the two great wars. No doubt his reluctance to write about the period in question was influenced by the passing of the Great Triumvirate (Harry Vardon, J.H. Taylor, and James Braid), who had placed the British Isles on the top of the golfing world. For another thing, there had been a dramatic change in equipment, first with the Haskell ball around the turn of the century, and later on by the coming of the steel shaft. These improvements brought about lower scoring and, more importantly, influenced the direction of golf course architecture in the ensuing years. Such a transformation of equipment and courses certainly shook the world of golf as at no other time in its life, and this led to much heated controversy.

At this time amateur golf was also experiencing a transformation as fresh younger players were taking over. The amateurs of the period before the First World War were so great and so tall that the world knew it would be a long while to find golfers to measure up to their standard of play. The truly great Mr. John Ball, Mr. Horace Hutchinson, Mr. John Ernest Laidlay, Mr. Leslie Balfour-Melville, Mr. S. Mure Fergusson, Mr. Alexander Stuart, and the younger giants-to-be, Mr. Harold Hilton and the tragic Mr. Freddie Tait—these golfers comprised a generation that reigned supreme from the 1880s to the First World War. Such a cast of fine players left a gap in the ranks that wasn't filled until the arrival of Mr. Cyril Tolley, Mr. Ernest Holderness, and Mr. Roger Wethered (brother of the greatest woman player in the eyes of many, Joyce Wethered, later Lady Heathcoat-Amory). At the same time, there came an onslaught that Darwin called "The American Invasion", which was led by Walter Hagen, Gene Sarazen, and the greatest of all, Mr. Bobby Jones.

A never-changing aspect of golf was that it was a game not only for the well-to-do but for amateurs from all classes who continued to be the backbone of the game, and still are, really. For a long while the amateurs were referred to with a "Mr." in front of their name, and the professionals were not. Amateur golf became still healthier with the inception of the Walker Cup Matches in 1922 at the National Golf Links of America. And, incidentally, when a member of the British team became ill, Mr. Darwin substituted for him and won his singles match. As for university golf, briefly, the two great universities, Oxford and Cambridge (Darwin's beloved Cambridge Blue), waged battle each year in the University Match. Golfers who had played for either Oxford or Cambridge instituted after the First World War Darwin's favorite tournament, the President's Putter, which is held annually at Rye in winter. Darwin's feeling for this tournament is delightfully cozy as he describes the atmosphere around the huge fireplace at the Dormy House where the golfers gathered after completing their rounds in the Jan-

uary winter blasts. Another tournament Darwin loved, which revealed the sentimental side of his nature, was the Worplesdon Mixed Foursomes, a wonderful and engaging format indeed. Darwin apologized to the reader for "having entertained himself" by writing about these tournaments, but it always made for first-class reading.

The ladies are described with much affection by Mr. Darwin, especially Miss Joyce Wethered, who won four Amateur Championships. Darwin always said that one of the greatest matches he ever witnessed was the final between Miss Wethered and Miss Glenna Collett at St. Andrews in 1929. There were other top lady golfers. For instance, Miss Cecil Leitch won three British Ladies' Championships as did Miss Enid Wilson.

My favorite chapter in the book is "The Immortal Bobby" which Darwin starts with a certain finality: "Still sticking to the amateurs I come now with faltering pen to the greatest of them all." Could we really ever describe how great this gentleman was? In my own mind, Mr. Darwin came the closest to really describing this man and his heroic deeds, for he was loved on "the other side of the Atlantic" as much as on his own shores. Sample, if you will, this line when Jones won the 1927 Open Championship at St. Andrews: "He holed his short one (at the Home Hole), and the next instant there was no green visible, only a dark seething mass, in the midst of which was Bobby hoisted on fervent shoulders and holding his putter, Calamity Jane, at arms length over his head lest she be crushed to death". I need not apologize for having my mouth wide open on reading that sentence, and neither should you. The whole chapter lifts you. Darwin paints a beautiful portrait of Bobby Jones, whose fine human qualities and impeccable manners touched us all.

Turning to professional golf in the period between the wars, two players, a Scot named George Duncan and an Englishman named Abe Mitchell did much to resurrect British hopes for keeping the Open Championship and other leading tournaments in British hands. It was Duncan's year in 1920 at Deal, and Darwin came very close in his description of this great golfer by comparing his ball-striking ability to that of the legendary Vardon. Duncan could, as they say, get "white-hot" on occasions and leave players far, far behind him. Abe Mitchell, on the other hand, was a terribly tough match player, but Darwin described him as being "fond of golf, but not fond of big golf." He challenged again and again in the Open Championship but, alas, like Macdonald Smith, that great transplanted Scot, he never won the Open, which is sad. Duncan and Mitchell fought gallantly, but at the time America was "coming". In 1921, another transplanted Scot, Jock Hutchinson, won at St. Andrews, technically the first American to carry the Open trophy back to the United States. Only Arthur Havers' victory at Troon in 1923 prevented the Americans from taking the Open trophy back thirteen straight years. Then Britain struck back, starting with Henry Cotton in 1934 and continuing until the outbreak of war.

Let us return to the 1920s when the United States became a world power in golf. Leading the American troops was the one and only Walter Hagen, who Darwin described like this: "There have been, I think, more skillful and certainly more mechanical and faultless players than Hagen, but none with greater sticking power or a temperament more ideally suited to the game". His flamboyant and dashing style did much to elevate the professionals in the eyes of the golfing world, and he backed it up by winning four British Opens. His air of nonchalance fascinated the conservatively oriented British no end, and year after year he was a most welcome visitor.

All professionals must pause to pay tribute to another man named Gene Sarazen who Darwin said was one of his favorites, partly because Sarazen's game resembled the style of British players. This exuberant, tough little fighter with his charming grin endeared himself to British galleries. He won the British Open in 1932, his golden year, when he also won the U.S. Open. (He is the player I love to watch hit those spanking firm pitch shots.) Along with these two giant

American professionals was Tommy Armour, who in 1931 won at Carnoustie back in his homeland. Having won the U.S. Open in 1927 at Oakmont, his victory at Carnoustie was the climax of his career. He later, of course, became one of the finest teachers the game has ever known.

The Ryder Cup was started in 1927, five years after its amateur counterpart, the Walker Cup. I think these two competitions have created incalculable good will throughout the golfing world. These biennial events continue to thrive and, to my mind, the spirit of the game is re-revealed whenever they are held.

In closing, I can only say that Darwin's writings have given me as much pleasure and as sound an education as anything in my golfing life. His words express closely what we feel about the game, if we have taken this game to our heart, as he did.